TELLING STORIES

TELLING STORIES

The Use of Personal Narratives in
the Social Sciences and History

**Mary Jo Maynes,
Jennifer L. Pierce, and
Barbara Laslett**

CORNELL UNIVERSITY PRESS   **ITHACA AND LONDON**

First published 2008 by Cornell University Press
First printing, Cornell Paperbacks, 2008

Printed in the United States of America

Library of Congress Cataloging-in-Publication Data

Maynes, Mary Jo.
    Telling stories : the use of personal narratives in the social sciences and history / Mary Jo Maynes, Jennifer L. Pierce, and Barbara Laslett.
        p. cm.
    Includes bibliographical references and index.
    ISBN 978-0-8014-4617-7 (cloth : alk. paper)—ISBN 978-0-8014-7392-0 (pbk. : alk. paper)
    1. Social sciences—Biographical methods.   2. Oral history—Methodology.   3. Oral biography.   4. Autobiography.   I. Pierce, Jennifer L., 1958–   II. Laslett, Barbara.   III. Title.

    H61.29.M39 2008
    300.72—dc22   2008002910

Cornell University Press strives to use environmentally responsible suppliers and materials to the fullest extent possible in the publishing of its books. Such materials include vegetable-based, low-VOC inks and acid-free papers that are recycled, totally chlorine-free, or partly composed of nonwood fibers. For further information, visit our website at www.cornellpress.cornell.edu.

Cloth printing   10 9 8 7 6 5 4 3 2 1
Paperback printing   10 9 8 7 6 5 4 3 2 1

Contents

Preface

Telling Stories is written in a consciously interdisciplinary way by three University of Minnesota scholars—one historian, Mary Jo Maynes, and two sociologists, Jennifer L. Pierce and Barbara Laslett. The conscious choice to adopt an interdisciplinary perspective reflects interests we share with each other and with many scholars across the disciplines; it also reflects the influence of the feminist scholarly communities in which each of us has participated, separately and together. A language of interdisciplinarity and cross-disciplinary reading and conversation has been essential to the genesis and writing of this book.

Although we share an interest in personal narratives, the three of us have worked with different kinds of personal narrative evidence and analyses in our own research. M. J. began research on European working-class autobiographies in the 1980s. Her interest in personal narrative sources led her to join the interdisciplinary feminist research collaborative, the Personal Narratives Group, at the University of Minnesota; work with that group, which collectively wrote *Interpreting Women's Lives* (Bloomington: Indiana University Press, 1989), brought her into conversation with literary scholars working on personal narratives as well as with historians and social scientists. Her autobiography project culminated in *Taking the Hard Road: Life Course in French and German Workers' Autobiographies in the Era of Industrialization* (Chapel Hill: University of North Carolina Press, 1995). Jennifer combined ethnographic fieldwork and career life stories with paralegals and lawyers for her first book, *Gender Trials: Emotional Lives in Contemporary Law Firms* (Berkeley: University of California Press, 1996). She has also collected life stories from feminist academics for her co-edited volume,

Feminist Waves, Feminist Generations: Life Stories from the Academy (Minneapolis: University of Minnesota Press, 2007) and she is currently working with the Twin Cities Gay, Lesbian, Bisexual, and Transgender Oral History Project. Barbara has published a series of articles based on her biographical research on the influential early twentieth-century American sociologist William Fielding Ogburn. With Barrie Thorne, she also commissioned and co-edited a collection of life stories from feminist sociologists: *Feminist Sociology: Life Histories of a Movement* (New Brunswick, NJ: Rutgers University Press, 1997).

Our theoretical concerns began with questions about individual human agency; interest in how this might be explored empirically was at the center of our early reading of analyses of personal narratives. We had grappled with questions about human agency in our own work; we knew that historians and social scientists from a variety of disciplines were increasingly using personal narrative evidence in their research, and that they were finding interesting new approaches to working with such forms of evidence. Since working with personal narratives was less common in the social sciences than in history, we also realized that there were many epistemological, theoretical, and methodological questions that we needed to address if we were to discuss how personal narrative analysis "works" for an interdisciplinary audience. We thus began a program of common reading and discussion of scholarship in history and the social sciences that uses personal narratives as their primary source of empirical data. We didn't choose the works we discuss in *Telling Stories* by following a particular system. Instead, we started from key works in our areas of research that we knew provided food for thought and would be the basis for productive interdisciplinary conversation. Since personal narrative research was particularly prominent in oral history and in interdisciplinary feminist scholarship, we drew heavily on publications in relevant publishers' catalogues and journals in these areas. We read widely, but our reading has always aimed to be exemplary rather than exhaustive.

We were also influenced by our individual political experiences, values, and intellectual priorities. We are of different generations. Barbara was born during the Depression of the 1930s and had become involved in left-wing politics in the immediate post–World War II period; she began her career in sociology before second-wave feminism emerged and was one of its pioneers. M. J. was a student during the social movements of the late 1960s and 1970s; her graduate studies were shaped by both "history from below" focused on the experiences of ordinary people and emergent feminist revisionism. Jennifer was a post–second wave feminist who did graduate work in the 1980s and whose scholarship has been influenced by feminist theory, feminist methods, and ethnographic studies of work. The books that interest us the most tend to reflect these orientations as well as our academic areas; we thus draw heavily on studies using personal narratives to examine class relations, especially working-class history, trade union movements, and professionals; gender; race relations and the civil rights movement; social movements more generally; and global inequalities. We found, not surprisingly, that studies based on the stories of people who occupy subordinate social positions have played an especially prominent role in the emergence and development of personal narrative analysis.

Co-authorship presents its own rewards and challenges. We faced the dilemma of how to write in one collective voice even while at times drawing on our individual research findings. We decided to use the first person plural when writing as a collective author: the *we* in this book is neither royal nor editorial—it's the three of us speaking. When we discuss the work of any one of us, however, we treat it the same way as we treat work by the many other scholars on whose research this book is based—we cite ourselves individually by last name in the usual third person form.

Over the years we have worked on this project, we have received inspiration and assistance in a variety of forms. We all participated in the stimulating intellectual community around *Signs: A Journal of Women in Culture and Society* when it was edited here at the Center for Advanced Feminist Studies at the University of Minnesota between 1990 and 1995. We are grateful to the Graduate School at the University of Minnesota, the Fund for the Advancement of the Discipline of the American Sociological Association/National Science Foundation, and the Life Course Center in the Minnesota Department of Sociology for financial support. Several graduate assistants provided help and insights—thanks to Martha Easton, Amy Kaler, and Deborah Smith, who were then graduate students in Minnesota's Department of Sociology. We are also appreciative of feedback on chapter drafts from the Minnesota Department of History's Comparative Women's History Workshop, and from panelists and audiences at the Social Science History Association and the American Sociological Association. We would also like to thank Kevin Murphy and Teresa Gowan for their close reading of the entire manuscript. And, finally, we are appreciative of the comments provided by the anonymous external reviewers for Cornell University Press, of the encouragement of our editor, Peter Wissoker, and of the adept support throughout the editorial process provided by Ange Romeo-Hall and Cathi Reinfelder.

Minneapolis, Saint Paul, and Seattle
August 2007

TELLING STORIES

THE USE OF PERSONAL NARRATIVES IN THE SOCIAL SCIENCES AND HISTORY

The relationship between the individual and the social has been a problem of perennial concern to social scientists and humanists alike. In the second half of the twentieth century, theorists from various disciplines and often competing tendencies—ranging from structuralist sociologists to feminist theorists, and from the "new social historians" to their Foucauldian critics—converged around theories that undermined classical understandings of the individual as a purposive social actor. The critiques went to the core of much modern Western social, political, and historical analysis; more deeply, they raised new questions about selfhood as it is understood, articulated, and practiced by individuals.[1]

Beginning around the same time, ironically, there has been an outpouring of scholarly work based on personal narrative evidence—that is on retrospective first-person accounts of individual lives. The impulses behind the increased interest in individuals' personal narratives are multiple, as we discuss more fully below. One primary motivation is the desire to examine varieties of individual selfhood and agency "from below" and in practice, as constructed in people's articulated self-understandings. More specifically, analyses of personal narratives have served to introduce marginalized voices (e.g., those of women or globally subaltern people) and they also have provided counternarratives that dispute misleading generalizations or refute universal claims. For some researchers, the goal of personal narrative analysis has simply been to work from an empirical base that is more inclusive. However, the grounding for many studies based on

1

personal narratives is in critical traditions (such as Marxism, feminism, subaltern theory, or queer theory) that question the epistemological foundations of positivist social science, recognize the historical and social specificity of all viewpoints and subjectivities, and emphasize the perspectivity intrinsic to knowledge production.

Telling Stories enters into these discussions through a cross-disciplinary examination of analyses of personal narratives. We have been able to write this book at this juncture precisely because of the continuing groundswell of new and creative approaches to personal narrative analysis across disciplines. *Telling Stories* argues that analyses of personal narratives, beyond the contributions they make to specific areas of empirical research, can also serve to reorient theories about the relationship between the individual and the social by calling attention to the social and cultural dynamics through which individuals construct themselves as social actors. In so doing, they have the potential constructively to intervene in the theoretical impasse resulting from the collision between skepticism of hegemonic individualism, on the one hand, and the persistent, even increasingly urgent interest in understanding selfhood and human agency, on the other.

Personal narrative analysis, we argue, demonstrates that human agency and individual social action is best understood in connection with the construction of selfhood in and through historically specific social relationships and institutions. Second, these analyses emphasize the narrative dimensions of selfhood; that is, well-crafted personal narrative analyses not only reveal the dynamics of agency in practice but also can document its construction through culturally embedded narrative forms that, over an individual's life, impose their own logics and thus also shape both life stories and lives. Finally, *Telling Stories* calls attention to the subjective and intersubjective character of the analysis of personal narratives. In contrast with many other approaches to social-scientific and historical analysis, many of the insights that personal narrative analyses provide flow from tapping into subjective takes on the world (those of narrators, analysts, and readers). Moreover, the attempt to generate intersubjective understandings—between narrator and analyst and between analyst and audience—are a distinctive feature of this approach and of the knowledge it produces.

The connections among individual agency, historically and socially embedded processes of self-construction, and the culturally specific narrative forms in which individuals construct their life stories and subjectivities are interwoven throughout *Telling Stories*. These connections drive its arguments about theorizing the relationship between the individual and the social and also its arguments about methodologies for effective personal narrative analysis.

Personal Narratives: Connecting the Individual and the Social

For scholars who analyze personal narratives, it is important to recognize that stories that people tell about their lives are never simply individual, but are told in historically specific times and settings and draw on the rules and models in circulation that govern how story elements link together in narrative logics. *Telling Stories* thus necessarily draws on wide ranging understandings of and approaches to life stories and their analysis—historical, social-scientific, and literary. What people do and their understandings of why they do what they do are typically at the center of their stories about their lives. Empirically, they provide access to individuals' claims about how their motivations, emotions, imaginations—in other words, about the subjective dimensions of social action—have been shaped by cumulative life experience. Although life stories vary greatly in the detail they include, partly because of the variance in individual lives and personalities and partly because differing norms of storytelling shape life story plots, we argue that it is inappropriate to regard life stories primarily as idiosyncratic. Individual life stories are very much embedded in social relationships and structures and they are expressed in culturally specific forms; read carefully, they provide unique insights into the connections between individual life trajectories and collective forces and institutions beyond the individual. They thus offer a methodologically privileged location from which to comprehend human agency.

Personal narrative sources, moreover, are infused with notions of temporal causality that link an individual life with stories about the collective destiny. In analyses of life histories, two salient temporalities continually interact. Historical time contextualizes a life course, even while the narrator's moment in the life course affects how he or she experiences, remembers, and interprets historical events. Both temporalities, then, inform life histories: any methodologically sound employment of such stories for the purposes of social-scientific analysis needs to keep both temporalities in mind. In other words, when events happen within the individual life course and when they happen with reference to historical temporalities are, we suggest, analytical keys to understanding people's lives and the stories they tell about them.

Finally, personal narrative analysis pushes the investigator to move beyond the distinction between what sociologists call the macro and micro levels of analysis (or, put differently, between the social and the individual realms of experience) and instead to focus on the connections linking them. Once the individual life is explored in its subjective detail and temporal depth, the line between individual and social tends to dissolve. We are not arguing, of course, that the strong sense of self as distinct from a collectivity that marks personal narrative claims about agency, especially in Western cultures, is merely delusional. On the contrary, the problem of this relationship is precisely the focus of our book; it is our contention that personal narrative analysis that keeps an eye open toward the interconnectedness of the individual and the social provides a basis for a new understanding, even recovery of, the individual as a focus of social-scientific and historical inquiry.

Personal Narratives as Documents of Social Action and Self-Construction

Telling Stories emphasizes the *storied* quality of personal narratives, which rely simultaneously on literary and historical logics. Stories that people tell about their lives deploy individual "plots" in a way that resembles the construction of literary narratives; they also embed their subjects in larger narrative frames with historical plots and temporalities. *Telling Stories* thus draws on a wide range of approaches to narrative—historical, social-scientific, and literary. These stories, we argue, are individual creations but are never simply individual creations; they are told in historically specific times and places and draw on the rules and models and other narratives in circulation that govern how story elements link together in a temporal logic.[2]

Narrative analysis is not as common or well-established across the social sciences as other forms of analysis, but scholars from a variety of disciplines now increasingly employ it in their research and also have generated an ongoing discussion of relevant epistemological and methodological issues.[3] The aims and techniques of narrative analysis are diverse. Our focus in *Telling Stories* is quite specific and differs in aim and focus from much of the narrative analysis now common in fields such as medical and legal sociology, social psychology, and social work. Our interest centers on a specific subset of narrative analyses; namely, on research employing the analysis of personal narratives. A *personal narrative* (we also sometimes use the more common term *life story*) in our usage is a retrospective first-person account of the evolution of an individual life over time and in social context. Specifically, we are primarily interested in social-scientific and historical analyses based on such forms of personal narrative as oral histories, autobiographies, in-depth interviews, diaries, journals, and letters.

Personal narratives according to our definition contrast in key ways with other types of narratives often used in social-scientific research such as narratives of illness that focus on one specific dimension of experience, or conversational transcripts that capture a self-presentation in a particular setting and moment in time. There are points where the issues we discuss here have a lot in common with narrative analysis in this broader sense. Temporality, for example, is an important dimension of most types of narrative analysis. However, it plays a different role in different types of narrative analysis. Close attention to sequencing or pauses in people's accounts may be a crucial aspect of temporality in conversational analysis or in the analysis of a narrative of illness, for example, whereas in personal narrative analysis of the sort that we discuss in *Telling Stories,* the temporality of the life course and its intersection with historical temporality are of the essence. And just to be clear, while narrative researchers employ the term "personal narratives" to describe a wide range of sources, we are defining the term more specifically and narrowly in this book. We focus on analyses of particular types of personal narratives as we pursue our general arguments about the relationship between the individual and the social. Despite this focus, we are concerned with many of the same theoretical and methodological questions that all narrative researchers confront.[4]

Subjectivity and Social Science: The Epistemology of Personal Narrative Analysis

Scholars in the social sciences have often regarded life histories with unease and suspicion. Many sociologists and political scientists dismiss analyses that focus on individual actions as guilty of the logical errors of methodological individualism or volunteerism. Within positivist strains of social science, life stories are reduced to the status of the anecdotal, adding color or personal interest but unreliable as a basis for generalization. In the 1960s and 1970s, social historians also contributed to this skepticism by criticizing the "great man" approach to history and emphasizing instead the relatively unforgiving structures and mentalities that change only slowly and constrain individual choices.

Life histories, and the individual subjectivities they presume, have also been subject to challenges from scholars operating within post-positivist epistemological frameworks and theoretical traditions. Poststructuralists, particularly those influenced by the work of Michel Foucault, regard individuals and the stories they tell about their experiences as primarily constituted through discourse. Similarly, in the 1980s, the narrative turn in anthropology undermined the transparency of the life history and ethnographic descriptions that had been a mainstay of the anthropological method by attending to the generic forms, rhetorical conventions, and authorial and institutional power relations that produce them. Importantly, feminist theorists in many disciplines have deconstructed the quintessential Western concept of the autonomous individual, a conception of the self that often masks the dependencies and inequalities on which its "autonomy"—and the basis it postulates for individual agency—rests.

Despite these forms of skepticism we argue that *it is precisely their subjective character* that has made personal narratives increasingly interesting to social scientists and historians aiming to open up space for new understandings of the relationship between the individual and the social. Within this broad theoretical and empirical agenda, personal narrative analyses address a range of specific aims. Some explore in depth a particular *social, categorical, or positional location* and thus address critical dimensions of social action that are otherwise opaque. Often the very titles or subtitles of personal narrative analyses of social-structural categories reveal such aims; for example, *Academics from the Working Class, The Polish Peasant in Europe and America,* "Life Stories in the Bakers' Trade," *Life Course in French and German Workers' Autobiographies in the Era of Industrialization, Auf dem Weg ins Bürgerleben* (on the path to a bourgeois life), *Stories of a Lesbian Generation, An Intimate History of American Girls,* or *Family Firms in Italy.*[5] In these analyses, individual stories are treated as interesting in and of themselves, but their analytic value rests on their ability to reveal something new about a social position defined by and of interest to the analyst but more legible through an insider's view. Thus, for example, sociologists Daniel Bertaux and Isabelle Bertaux-Wiame started with the puzzle of how to account for the survival of artisanal baking in Paris. Their answers came from the life histories of male bakers, and their wives, that when analyzed together revealed the gender and generational dynamics of bakery succession.[6] Particular characteristics of personal narrative evidence—for example, its documentation of the lifelong consequences of transformative experiences, or the operation of temporal logics that data from one point in time cannot capture, or its revelation of details of everyday life that prove only in retrospect to have been salient—make it especially useful for capturing certain types of social-structural dynamics.

A large number of personal narrative analyses have been designed pointedly *to introduce marginalized voices into the record.* Feminist uses of personal narrative analysis provide a good illustration. While some feminist research has sought mainly to bring women's voices and perspectives to light, others focus on the analysis of gender as an organizing principle of social life. Personal narrative analyses have played a major role in both types of feminist projects; conversely, many scholars who use personal narrative analysis make claims based on feminist epistemological grounds. Initially echoing the political techniques of consciousness raising that emerged in second-wave feminist groups and organizations in the United States in the late 1960s, at the core of feminist epistemology is the claim that new insights about gender relations and power emerge from women telling stories about themselves and their lives and that the process of telling reveals past oppressions that had been suppressed or unrecognized. As the editors of *Interpreting Women's Lives: Feminist Theory and Personal Narratives* wrote in 1989, "For a woman, claiming the truth of her life despite awareness of other versions of reality that contest this truth often produces both a heightened criticism of officially condoned untruths and a heightened sense of injustice."[7] This insight was extended to the more general claim that just as social relations are embedded in a nexus of hierarchical gender relations, so too is knowledge production itself.[8]

In a similar vein, explorations of alternative sexualities have relied heavily on personal narrative analysis. Like consciousness raising, "coming-out stories" were a mainstay of gay and lesbian personal politics in the era of emergence of gay rights movements. Telling counternarratives moved readily from emancipatory politics to gay-lesbian-bisexual-transgender (GLBT) scholarship, often designed to reveal the damage inflicted by blatant homophobia suffered by homosexuals, or the more veiled dynamics of heteronormativity. Since the introduction of queer theory and feminist critiques of essentialism, personal narrative analysis more frequently has been used to document the construction and reconstruction of sexual identities understood to be unstable, rooted in particular practices, and mutable.[9] Personal narrative analysis can capture this dynamic construction process, even as the stories themselves document historic shifts and variations in the experience of particular sexual identities.

Beyond the women's and GLBT movements, an outpouring of oral histories from the late 1960s onward also drew political insights from the U.S. Civil Rights movement, peace movements, trade union movements, antipoverty movements, and Third World liberation struggles and applied them to critical scholarship in history and the social sciences. Not surprisingly, then, many of the best examples of personal narrative analysis have emerged in the areas of African American studies and ethnic studies more generally, labor and working-class history, Latin American studies, and African studies. Like feminist claims, the power of the analyses results from bringing new voices and previously untold stories into conversations on topics about which these voices provide invaluable witness, critique, and alternative narratives. In the arena of African American studies, the long tradition of testimony going back to slave narratives has offered a distinctive basis for knowledge about black history and culture.[10] Among historians, probably no field has been more creative in its use of personal narratives than African history. Prior to the 1960s, much African history was written from the perspective of colonial or former colonial powers and was based on their archival records. In the anticolonial movements and in postcolonial Africa, many historians of Africa (among them Africans, Europeans, and North Americans) sought out African perspectives, African voices, and African narrative traditions for their studies of the past and their revisions of history. Not surprisingly, oral histories and life stories featured prominently.[11]

Class analysis has also relied on personal narrative research. Labor and working-class history have almost always been written from a subaltern location within the discipline of history. Marxist epistemologies have at times explicitly informed these histories, especially when they emerged from socialist intellectual milieus; in some settings, such as the German Socialist Party of the late nineteenth and early twentieth centuries, workers were encouraged to tell their stories for the edification of fellow workers and for the betterment of social research. Their personal narratives were meant as substantiations of the class coming to consciousness. The energy with which labor history was infused beginning in the 1960s as a result of the developments of new social history and "history from below" led to a renewed interest in the stories of workers and labor organizers.[12]

Within this enormous body of literature that rests on critical epistemologies and centers on marginalized voices, some studies deliberately use personal narratives as *sources of counternarratives to undermine misleading generalizations, correct commonly misused analytic categories, or refute historical claims based on other types of evidence or other modes of inquiry.* For example, historian Wally Seccombe turned to letters from working-class wives in early twentieth-century England to cast doubt on demographic generalizations about fertility control based on the common presumption among demographers that choices about fertility were made by married couples.[13] Seccombe's interpretation of the letters revealed how the category of "couple" disguised how men's and women's stakes in fertility decisions could differ and hid the power dynamics that affected whose desires prevailed in the outcome. He pointed to the significance of factors that cannot be captured by usual statistical correlations focused on family size, occupation, income, and education. Instead Seccombe argues that in accounting for European fertility decline, relationships between husbands and wives, and historical factors such as medical arguments in favor of contraception that could be used with authority by wives and then enforced through moral suasion, play a role even before male cooperation could be counted on as a "rational" response to changing economic conditions. The logic of his argument, then, is to point to truths found in personal narratives that lie beyond the reach of more commonly used techniques.

Closely related are personal narrative analyses that *reveal "hidden histories" or revisionist understandings* of a phenomenon or event because they bring to light not merely new or untapped perspectives but also suppressed or deliberately hidden histories. These kinds of analyses, whether based on life stories gathered by the researcher or on extant sources such as memoirs or letters, open possibilities for revealing "private" or "privileged" information that is relevant to our understanding of a historical or social phenomenon, but is normally beyond the reach of all except insiders. The claim here, then, is that personal narrative sources can reveal a social or historical dynamic that has been deliberately silenced or distorted by interested parties. For example, Mary Jo Maynes's analysis of the autobiographies published in the context of the German socialist movement emphasizes that movement's determination to present workers as competent historical subjects, and to counter the dominant culture's attempts to pathologize the working-class family. Still, as Maynes suggests and as some subaltern and feminist theorists have argued, there is never an "authentic" identity transparently revealed in personal narratives or any other sources.[14] The circulation and preservation of politicized identities are always matters of contest; personal narratives can be valuable documents of such contestation.

Some personal narrative analyses *provide entrées into the black box of subjectivity* by exploring its psychological as well as its social dimensions. Their knowledge claims rest on insights about deep motivations, irrationalities as well as rationalities, and their connections to actions—connections that are not transparent but emerge only when the narrator's psychological history is revealed. Relatively few in number since this sort of analysis is beyond the reach of most personal narrative evidence, these studies can nonetheless succeed as rich social-scientific accounts under the right circumstances. Historians and sociologists have ventured onto this terrain with personal narrative analyses that, while rooted in social relations nevertheless see the psychological and the social as intertwined. Letters, diaries, and other personal writings become keys to making sense of, not just an individual's motivations, but more generally the psychological construction of social action and the social construction of the psyche in a particular context. To offer one example, Barbara Laslett uses the personal writings and public papers of the prominent early twentieth-century American sociologist William Fielding Ogburn to suggest the interconnections between private aspects of his life story and the development of his ideas about how scientific sociology should be defined and practiced.[15]

Finally, some analyses of personal narratives result in forms of knowledge that are *accessible only through intersubjective or dialogic processes.* Sometimes this knowledge emerges only because of the emotional responses triggered by the interview situation itself. Obviously, these sorts of encounters become ethically difficult when narrators tell analysts something that might strike them as morally objectionable or personally offensive. One striking example is Helena Pohlandt-McCormick's reaction to a life history narrator who told her of having been involved in a killing during the Soweto uprising.[16] (We will address her analysis more fully in chapter 4.) Paying close attention to such moments can be fruitful, for it is precisely the emotional intensity of the interview encounter that signals that revelations of an uncommon sort are occurring. Perceived silences can also be an indicator of boundary crossing, marking the distinction between publicly

acceptable forms of discourse and private thoughts and feelings. Though analysts may not be able to get beyond a narrator's silence, discomfort, or reluctance, they can nevertheless read them productively for insights into norms
about taboo topics, emotions, or opinions within different narratives and in
different contexts.

Because personal narrative analysis is based on distinct epistemological and
methodological presumptions, it produces a different type of knowledge than
do many other types of social-scientific and historical analysis. It contrasts with
much of the research in the social sciences—especially common in the disciplines of sociology, political science, and economics—that focuses on the statistical analysis of aggregate data about entire populations or large samples. In these
types of analysis, the overarching purpose is to establish correlations between
variables or to predict general patterns and trends.[17] Personal narrative analysis,
by contrast, builds from the individual and the personal. It gleans insight not
only from subjective perceptions about social phenomena and events as revealed
through participants' stories, but more particularly through narrative forms of
experiencing, recalling, and making sense of social action. Subjectivity and narrativity are at the core of the alternative epistemological presumptions associated
with personal narrative analysis.

Personal narratives can offer interpretations about many aspects of social life,
but given their epistemological and methodological assumptions, historical and
social-scientific analysis of them can support corresponding types of knowledge
claims. In contrast to demographic studies and survey research, which often
reduce individuals to a cluster of variables such as race, ethnicity, gender, or
political affiliation, effective personal narrative analysis provides evidence about
individuals as whole persons. By offering insights from the point of view of narrators who see themselves as persons in context, and whose stories reflect their
lived experiences over time and in particular social and historical settings, personal narrative analyses proceed from a logic that is quite different from other
types of social-scientific analysis. (We will discuss all of these claims more fully
in chapters 1 and 5.) The interest in *whole persons* is key to the distinctiveness of
personal narrative approaches when compared with the types of social-scientific
epistemology and practice that came to prevail in the United States in the course
of the twentieth century. To consider whole persons involves understanding
multiple aspects of an individual's life and experiences over the life course and in
historical time. Studying whole persons involves an epistemological strategy that
sees individuals *both* as unique *and* as connected to social and cultural worlds
and relationships that affect their life choices and life stories. Learning about
and interpreting these relationships, we are arguing, entails soliciting stories
that individuals tell about their lives and in their own terms, rather than simply

categorizing them in analytic terms that research questions impose on them. Personal narrative analyses are certainly appropriately informed by theories and conceptualizations derived from the analyst's interests and categories. But the analytic categories must also be responsive to the terms in which narrators make sense of their world.

It is worth elaborating this epistemological point here through reference to the evolution of American sociology and its presumptions. Within sociology, change in the organization and nature of empirical research after World War II made it more difficult to study "whole persons" because the criteria for drawing professionally acceptable "scientific" conclusions from empirical research were changing. In his study of the five top-ranked U.S. sociology departments (Columbia University, the University of Chicago, the University of Michigan, the University of Wisconsin, and Harvard University), George Steinmetz argues that a tolerance for methodological and epistemological diversity that characterized these departments before World War II began to erode shortly after it. By 1950, the earlier "balanced or splintered epistemic condition had disappeared…Methodological positivism was becoming orthodox or even *doxic*, that is, its practices and proclamations were increasingly recognized even by its opponents as a form of scientific capital, however much they disliked it."[18] This did not mean, of course, that other methodologies ceased to exist. What it did mean is that the accumulation of rewards—professional status, respect, and recognition—supported methodological positivism and the accompanying use of quantitative methodologies. It therefore became less common to do the sort of in-depth research required for understanding the beliefs and actions of "whole persons"; favored methods tended to reduce and simplify the analytic categories that sociologists (and other social sciences) used; along with this limitation there evolved an overly simplified understanding of individuals and of human agency.

Writing up analyses based on personal narrative evidence also presents particular methodological and rhetorical challenges to social scientists and historians. The forms of evidence are distinctive, and logics of persuasion rest on epistemological grounds that are at odds with the assumptions embedded in much mainstream social science. What makes a personal analysis persuasive as argument? What kinds of truth claims can be made on the basis of individual life stories? What forms of generalization are appropriate in personal narrative analysis? Transparency and clarity about the processes that shape the production and analysis of the personal narratives, we argue, goes a long way toward making arguments persuasive. Furthermore, such transparency also serves to educate audiences who are perhaps more accustomed to other types of analysis about how to read and evaluate knowledge claims based on personal narrative evidence. In the end, we argue, the way of knowing that is characteristic of personal narrative analysis is necessarily distinctive from the knowledge claims of positivist social science.

Organization of the Book

In the chapters that follow, we draw from studies employing personal narrative analysis across several disciplines emphasizing but not limited to history, sociology, psychology, and anthropology to make our broader arguments.[19] We discuss scores of examples, but we return over five chapters to a several of the studies. Our logic for revisiting studies is twofold. First, we want readers to become familiar enough with these works and the life stories on which their analyses are based to fully understand our arguments. Indeed, one of our arguments about writing persuasive analyses based on personal narrative evidence is that analysts must retell enough of the life story or stories on which it is based for readers to make their own sense of them. Our elaboration of key examples helps to demonstrate this rhetorically and methodologically. Second, some exemplary works illustrate different specific arguments we make in various chapters. We may return to a study, for instance, that not only illuminates how an analysis effectively contextualizes the subjectivity of its narrator (in chapter 1) but also serves as a persuasive form of argument because it clarifies the analyst's process of interpretation (in chapter 5).

As a starting point, chapter 1 introduces a wide range of theoretical and methodological issues pertaining to the individual, social, and historical construction of subjectivity; these issues, we argue, are central to the interpretation of personal narrative evidence. First, we sketch out aspects of the evolution of ideas about the self and subjectivity as they have informed both social-scientific theories and everyday life practices involved in constructing and telling life stories. This historicization of the self, we argue, is a necessary component of the analysis of personal narratives. We then examine subjectivity and human agency as theorized in a range of different social-scientific traditions and suggest how personal narrative analysis can enrich these theories. We argue that personal narrative analysis, through its capacity to unpack and historicize subjectivity, can advance the understanding of the relationship between the individual and the social and of human agency.

Chapter 2 highlights the ways in which personal narratives are constructed with reference to historical contexts and to the intersection of varying personal and historical temporalities. Some of these are close to the narrator's life and its temporal rhythms and experiences, such as the histories of institutional or organizational settings through which the narrator navigates over the course of his or her life; others shape the life story at more of a distance, such as the histories of national events or large-scale processes such as postwar reconstructions or industrialization. Implicitly or explicitly, subjective accounts of social action over the life course theorize and document the interplay between individual and historical dynamics, in specific locations, over a single lifespan but also within historical time. We also examine the operation of historical narratives as devices that frame, and are challenged by, individual life stories.

In chapter 3, we turn to the influence of genre on personal narrative sources and their interpretation. Forms of telling a life story draw on culturally specific rules and expectations, conventions, rhetorical strategies, notions of what is interesting or important or significant, and previous models of life stories or other life accounts. Consequently, the specific shape and content of any life story are marked by the cultural norms and forms of personal narrative that prevail at the time and place of its emplotment. As this chapter demonstrates, each form of personal narrative evidence—oral histories and life history interviews elicited by researchers, autobiographies, letters, and diaries—raises somewhat different formal considerations. The particular forms that these different personal narrative sources take, the audience for whom narrators are writing (or speaking), and the conditions of their production inevitably shape the structure of an account, what is included in the text, and what is not. To analyze these sources effectively, we suggest, analysts must not only carefully consider these issues, but explicate as fully as necessary how they are reading their sources in light of them. The questions under consideration change somewhat as we examine hybrid forms of personal narrative analysis in the final section of the chapter. These kinds of analyses utilize considerable autobiographical material about the analyst. In contrast with other genres we discuss, these studies are at once a particular generic form and a method of analysis.

Just as personal narratives are mediated by culturally specific conventions that shape how any individual tells his or her "own" story, they are also created through interpersonal and intersubjective relationships. In many cases personal narratives come into being through a research process that involves two or more interested parties; where research involves in-depth interviews, these would include the life story narrator and the interviewer and/or analyst. But even where this is not the case, research using personal narratives involves an intersubjective understanding. In chapter 4, we argue that these interpersonal and intersubjective processes inevitably shape the content and form of personal narratives and thus require attention, acknowledgment, and critical examination. Some of the issues we consider include reflection about the positionalities of analyst and narrator (that is, how their different social, gender, or geopolitical positions shape their knowledge) and their respective agendas as well as the processes of transcription, editing, and publishing. In addition, we consider the intersubjective dimensions of analysis and interpretation. As we argue, effective analysis means not taking personal narrative evidence at face value, but rather providing context and even alternative evidence as needed for interpreting its meaning and significance. While the face-to-face interview situation may magnify many of these issues, as we show, attention to this intersubjective dimension is also relevant when the analyst is drawing on preexisting personal narrative texts such as autobiographies.

While chapter 4 underscores epistemological, methodological, and ethical considerations that stem from the interpersonal and intersubjective construction and interpretation of personal narrative evidence, chapter 5 addresses questions relating to rhetorical techniques involved in presenting arguments based on personal narrative evidence, the formulation of truth claims in analytic writing, and the relationships between the analyst and audiences. Writing analyses of personal narratives that are persuasive *as social science* profits from transparency about the processes, including the intersubjective processes, that research and interpretation involve as well as from acknowledgment of the contingent nature of life stories and of knowledge based on them.

AGENCY, SUBJECTIVITY, AND NARRATIVES OF THE SELF

The problem of understanding human agency as simultaneously individual and social has long been at the core of theoretical and methodological debates in Western social sciences. In *Telling Stories* we demonstrate how analyses of personal narratives enrich these discussions. In this chapter we begin by examining the relationship between the individual and the social by delving into the identity of the *narrator*—that is, the person through whose authorial voice and subject position a life story is told and whose life is at the same time the story's focus. Since narrators and analysts both draw on ideas about self and agency, we start out by historicizing the individual and selfhood as theoretical concepts and as everyday practices that develop over time and vary in different settings. We then review some of the major theoretical approaches to the historical and social-scientific study of individual agency and discuss the contributions to this field that analyses of personal narrative evidence can provide. We examine how their engagement with subjectivity distinguishes analyses of personal narratives from many other social-scientific approaches to human agency. By drawing on scholarship from a range of disciplines primarily within the social sciences and history, we develop a concept of the individual self that, while recognizing the social character of self construction, nevertheless does not reduce the individual to a mere constellation of social attributes such as race, class, or occupational status. We argue that the special importance of personal narratives in this regard lies in their ability to document the significance for social action of individual subjectivity as it is constructed and reconstructed over the lifetime. The chapter concludes with a discussion of memory—individual and historical—which serves as a bridge to chapter 2 on interpreting personal narratives in historical context.

Historicizing the Individual as Social Actor and as Life Story Narrator

The dominant theories and methods of the social sciences have tended to view individuals and their actions primarily through categories (e.g., race, gender, sexual orientation, social class or occupation, citizenship) that locate them in the "outside" or social world.[1] Motivations, predispositions, and actions are typically explained largely through reference to these categorical affiliations. Individuals are thus reduced to clusters of social variables that serve as proxies for persons. Consequently, within such frameworks, human agency is reduced to social position; understandings of the relationship between the individual and the social remain superficial. Social actors are treated as if they had little or no individual history, no feelings or ambivalences, no self-knowledge—in short, no individuality.

Personal narrative analyses, in contrast, offer insights from the point of view of narrators whose stories emerge from their lived experiences over time and in particular social, cultural, and historical settings. These analyses offer insights into human agency as seen from the inside out; as such they can bridge the analytic gap between outside positionalities and interior worlds, between the social and the individual. They allow scrutiny of key subjective dimensions of motivation—emotions, desires, accumulated wisdom, acquired associations and meanings, clouded judgments, and psychic makeup—all of which are the product of a lifetime of experiences. The evidence presented in personal narratives is unabashedly subjective, and its narrative logic presents a story of an individual subject developing and changing through time. Alessandro Portelli sums up well the distinctive advantage of personal narrative evidence in his discussion of the methods of oral history: "The fact that a culture is made up of individuals different from one another is one of the important things that social sciences sometimes forget, and of which oral history reminds us."[2]

Paradoxically, however, analyses of personal narratives are most effective when, rather than conceptualizing narrators as autonomous agents whose testimony offers transparent insights into human motivation, they explicitly recognize the complex social and historical processes involved in the construction of the individual self and, more deeply, of the ideas about selfhood and human agency that inform personal narrative accounts. Personal narrative analyses must draw on and can provide important insights into the history of the self and its variations at the same time that they have the potential to enrich theories of social action and human agency.

Conceptualizations of the self—of the knowing, feeling, acting subject—although of keen interest to philosophers, are rarely scrutinized explicitly in the realm of everyday life. Still, abstract notions about the self and subjectivity inform everyday practices. Awareness of the historicity of the self, of changing philosophical and practical postulations of the self, is important for thinking about personal narratives and about human agency. In *Telling Stories* we engage primarily with modern Western understandings, narratives, and theories of the self. However, it is important to keep in mind that notions and narratives of the self have altered through history and also have varied across the globe. We will on occasion draw on evidence about comparative notions of the self as a means of highlighting the potential for cultural variability. Moreover, as we discuss more fully later in this section and elsewhere, prevailing understandings of the self are never monolithic; they can vary according to such contours as gender, social hierarchy, race, religion, or region. For example, scholars of Native American culture argue that fluid and communalistic understandings of the relationship between the individual and society have typified some Native American cultures in contrast with a more sharply drawn self-society demarcation that came to predominate in hegemonic European cultures.[3]

Modern Western notions of subjectivity have been constructed in and through Enlightenment and post-Enlightenment intellectual discourse as well as in everyday activities such as seeking employment, writing letters, going to confession, shopping, parenting, or visiting the doctor's office.[4] Innovative presumptions about human agency and motivation contributed to the emergence of modern political theory and practices, economic institutions, social-scientific disciplines, and personal ambitions. Enlightenment thinkers imagined a sturdy and boldly universal human subject, one who was more self-assured and more capable of clear thought and autonomous action, whether in the realm of ethically correct choices or of market investments, than had previously been presumed. Enlightenment theorists did not speak with one voice, nor did they subscribe to a common epistemology. However, they shared an interest in and emphasis on the individual human's capacity to reason and subsequently to act accordingly. Kant's postulation of the possibility of ethical action, Rousseau's social contract, and Smith's *homo economicus,* for all of their differences, shared this commonalty. More subtly, modern notions of the human subject also informed a variety of genres of writing in addition to theoretical treatises; these include personal narrative genres such as letters and autobiography as well as the wildly popular fictional form—the novel. It is not a coincidence that Rousseau wrote in all of these genres in addition to writing political theory. (We will discuss various genres of personal narrative writing more fully in chapter 3.)

Central to the Enlightenment project was the search for universal truths discoverable by all reasoning persons. Not surprisingly, Enlightenment claims about human subjectivity also tended toward the universal. Historicizing these inherited notions of subjectivity and agency—that is, rethinking them in light of the historical moment and settings in which they were produced—has been an important component of critical traditions in Western philosophy and social science. This critical perspective has also been at the center of intellectual projects such as subaltern theory and other strains of postcolonial theory. Historicizing the subject is a necessary dimension of understanding and interpreting personal narratives.

Michel Foucault is certainly among the most prominent, controversial, and influential critics of Enlightenment thought and its understandings of the human subject. As Richard Wolin writes:

> Foucault...seeks to demonstrate the compromised origins of the modern "subject." In his view, the illusions of autonomy conceal a deeper bondage...From early childhood, the subject is exposed or "subjected" to what Foucault labels the "means of correct training": an all-pervasive expanse of finely honed behavioral-modification techniques that suffuse the institutional structure of civil society, schools, hospitals, the military, prisons, and so forth.[5]

According to Foucault, Enlightenment human sciences and modern institutional practices have disciplined modern subjects in an unprecedentedly intrusive fashion, even as subjects began to proclaim themselves to be free agents. Foucault's own historical investigations, and those of his followers, document the operation of this institutionalized disciplining of the self.

Feminist postmodernists have developed a related critique of Enlightenment ideas about human agency. Joan Scott argues in her book *Only Paradoxes to Offer* that French feminists who contributed to and employed Enlightenment language were inevitably drawn into untenable positions. In their efforts to grant women political status they ran aground on paradoxes which are inherent in the liberal concept of citizenship, and the concept of the individual that underlies it. For example, Olympe de Gouges' rewriting of "The Declaration of the Rights of Man" tacks back and forth between universality and particularity as she attempts to include women in the category "human."[6] The critique of the hegemonic Western self launched by Foucauldians and feminists is critical to our framework for discussing personal narrative analyses. We emphasize, however, that historicizing the self does not make individuals or their senses of self disappear. Historians and social scientists still need to grapple with questions of particular forms of agency and types of relationship between the individual and the social even after "the death of the subject."

But the theoretical terrain is quite complex. Ongoing and wide-ranging discussions in social theory, history, and political strategy point to the tension between projects aimed at criticizing Enlightenment understandings of the self (as coherent, autonomous, and stable) on the one hand, and others that call for a redefined selfhood or identity as a still necessary basis of political action, on the other.[7] The Enlightenment postulation of a universal human subject, critics agree, often disguised underlying presumptions that linked rationality and political selfhood to "independence" and hence excluded women, enserfed or enslaved people, and in some schemes even wage-earning men. Still, philosophical debates about the Enlightenment waiver between criticizing its particular ideas about human agency and capturing some version of that agency for subalterns. Within the strictures of Enlightenment discourses, women and other excluded groups did indeed use the universal language of human rights to claim political agency.[8]

Carla Hesse's biographical study *The Other Enlightenment: How French Women Became Modern* illustrates several important dimensions of the emergence of modern notions of the self; it also shows the links between gendered ideas about the self and forms of personal narrative. Hesse argues that the practices of the literary marketplace as it was legally reformed in the French Revolutionary era set up new possibilities for the articulation of female selfhood. Within clear institutional and legal limits, women writers "used the cultural resources of modern commercial society to ... [stake] a successful claim for themselves as modern individuals in the public world."[9] Hesse focuses on the life and work of Louise-Felicité Kéralio-Robert (1758–1822), a historian and novelist, and the novelist Isabelle de Charrière (1740–1805). She examines specific social practices rather than just prescriptions and theories. Women were not as "free" in practice as men because of legal constraints such as those limiting married women's ownership of intellectual property, and the requirement for married women writers to secure their husband's consent to publish. "During the French Revolution," Hesse argues, "the legal identity of married women writers ... was a dual identity, recognized as at once morally autonomous and juridically subordinate. Free to write, they were not free to make their writings public, or to create independent public identities."[10] This "doubled identity" made a woman writer a complex sort of an individual, located in a very specific and contradictory subject position. Pseudonyms (often male) disguised the not-fully-autonomous persons behind the seemingly morally and politically autonomous authorial personae. However, despite the ongoing constraints on female authors, there was an explosion of female writing and publication beginning with the Revolution. Women authors asserted their moral and intellectual agency through their writing, even if their works reflect the contradictions women authors faced as political and legal subordinates.[11]

Hesse's study reconstructs a historically specific selfhood. She also underscores the close link between modern claims to individual selfhood and the evolution of specific forms of writing, which in this era were primarily though never exclusively the domain of educated elites. We will take up the question of forms of writing and narratives of the self more fully in chapter 3, but for now it is important to point to the connections between the emergence of hegemonic modern Western notions of the self and the social and cultural history of reading and writing. European social and literary historians have noted and tracked connections between narrative forms such as autobiography and the novel and middle-class identity formation.[12] Autobiography in particular has been regarded as a literary expression of the individualism that was also a central tenet of emergent liberal economic and political philosophy. The connection between writing and defining the self marginalized not only most women but also lower-class men, people from oral cultures, and other subaltern voices. This observation cautions us about the historical limitations of personal narrative analysis: Where we rely primarily on written records, available narratives of self will perforce be skewed toward the elite perspectives these embody.

There have been historical forays into non-elite sites of personal narrative writing that can further nuance the history of the self and self narrative.[13] For example, in her study of French and German working-class autobiographies, Mary Jo Maynes points to specific connections between literary representations of the self and emergent working-class identities. According to Maynes, "the search for a sense of self is not restricted to a single class or gender."[14] Autobiographers who have emerged from popular or proletarian milieus do defy conventions of the genre, and in so doing also offer critical insights from the margins into the history of the self. For one thing, the model of a successful autobiography with the progressive unfolding of an individual personality (also the structure of the classic novel type, the bildungsroman) breaks down.[15] More deeply, in their formal structures, workers' autobiographies often resist the heroic self-presentation thought to characterize "Western" notions of the autobiographical self. They also often define the self in reference to political community. For example:

> working-class autobiographers often denied their individuality and emphasized how ordinary their life was. Like Ottilie Baader they claimed that their story was the story of "thousands of others." The collective identity that working-class authors often assumed in their texts was both a rhetorical device to establish links between author and audience and an effort to contradict the individualism presumed to be at the core of personality.[16]

These studies suggest techniques for analyzing personal narrative evidence with an alertness to the historically specific notions of the self that frame their authorial voices and narrative presumptions; they also show how personal narrative analysis enriches our ways of thinking about and historicizing the self and human agency and for exploring counternormative projects of defining the self.

Conceptualizing Subjectivity, Agency, and the Self in Social Theory

The modern social sciences originated in Enlightenment thought; it is not surprising, then, that their notions of human agency reflect their historical roots. Prominent traditions of Western social science have been based on concepts of human motivation that take for granted the coherent, autonomous, rational actor of Enlightenment discourse.[17] Margaret Somers and Gloria Gibson point this out in an essay on narrative and social identity:

> Agency and social action became theoretically embedded in the historical fiction of the individuating social actor…Marx's celebration of bourgeois society as a necessary societal stage in the progression of freedom, Weber's autonomous individual as the only valid subject of action, and the early Durkheim's moral individual freed by the overturning of *Gemeinschaft* all confirmed the sociological appropriation of this revolutionary idiom.[18]

Of course, views about agency in the social sciences are neither monolithic nor static; alternative theoretical tendencies have always existed in opposition to or as uneasy components of classical theory. In fact Marxist and Weberian theory paradoxically also offer suggestions about and space in which to explore the historical construction of the social actor. Post-Freudian psychoanalytic and psychological approaches to human behavior, moreover, have influenced subareas within nearly all of the social sciences. For example, in the first half of the twentieth century Maurice Halbwachs, French historical sociologist and associate of French sociologist Émile Durkheim, drew on psychoanalytic and linguistic theory to begin to develop a concept of the individual as constructed in and through interpersonal encounters and collective history.[19] From another direction, American pragmatists of the early twentieth century posited a less abstract and more socially grounded self that has been at the core of social-scientific inquiry in such subareas as social psychology and symbolic interactionism.[20] And, in alternative theoretical traditions rooted in the work of later twentieth-century European theorists such as Philip Abrams, Anthony Giddens, and Pierre Bourdieu, there are influential conceptualizations of the individual human actor as socially and historically constructed, as capable of development over time, and as complexly motivated.[21] We now turn to a closer examination of some of these various traditions of understanding agency in social theory to discuss how the conversation can be enriched through the perspectives that come to light through personal narrative analysis.

Agency

What are social scientists talking about when they theorize agency? A useful starting point is the approach of British sociologist Anthony Giddens. In his influential work *The Constitution of Society: Outline of the Theory of Structuration,* Giddens theorizes *agency* as a social actor's capacity to "have acted differently."[22] If a social actor cannot have acted differently in a given situation, he or she cannot be said to have agency. However, even so basic a definition as this one leads to many further questions. What has to be known to figure out what an actor otherwise might have done? What would have been required of the actor to recognize alternative courses of action and to have had the capacity and desire to act upon any particular choice?

For many social theorists, the answers to such questions have resided in the situation itself, in social structures and objectively defined positions or in categories that the actors inhabit, and in the resources they command. Assumptions about agency that link it to the set of possibilities for action inherent in a situation and in an actor's social positioning implicitly or explicitly inform the work of social theorists as diverse as the structural functionalist Talcott Parsons, the Marxist political theorist Nicos Poulantzas, and the feminist scholar Patricia Hill Collins.[23] Even more starkly, rational choice theorists conceptualize social actors as strategic individuals who seek to maximize self-interest; this "self-interest" is usually presumed to be transparent, inherent in any given situation.[24] For rational choice theorists, explicable human behavior results from a calculus of the costs and benefits of the possible choices available at a decision point.

Other structuralists take more nuanced approaches in grappling with the problem of agency. Theorists like Michael Burawoy, for example, theorize agency as a form of socially constructed consent; still others emphasize, not consent, but rather resistance to structurally determined oppressions.[25] Still, there is not a lot of attention to individual particularities. In reviewing these various efforts to conceptualize agency, sociologist Avery Gordon notes that, in many sociological studies of structure and agency, subjectivity is conceptualized in a limited fashion; it is mainly understood as an answer to the question of whether people are "victims" of social structure or "superhuman agents."[26]

These diverse structuralist approaches operate from a truncated concept of the individual actor. What is missing is an alertness to, or more than superficial interest in, key components of motivation: how individual actors come to understand their options, the varied meanings and orientations people take from their past experiences and bring into new situations, the components of their choices that are driven by emotions or dearly held values rather than by interests more narrowly or broadly conceived, and, at a deeper analytic level, how social actors understand their own capacity to act in a given setting. Since individuals evolve in and through particular social and temporal trajectories, the ensuing ambiguous, multiple, or fluid positionalities that inform their understandings are beyond the grasp of methods commonly employed in structuralist research.

Symbolic interactionists in sociology (like many cultural anthropologists), in contrast to most structuralists, begin with the assumption that social actors are meaning makers. From their perspective, every social interaction is imbued with meaning and, in the work of more recent sociologists and anthropologists, with emotion as well.[27] Their interpretations of action and agency emphasize cultural meanings and often intersubjective negotiations. The limitation typical of these approaches, we suggest, stems not from a disinterest in subjectivity so much as from the difficulty of capturing its temporal and social formulation that occurs through processes beyond the scope of usual methods of ethnographic observation.[28] The self conceptualized in symbolic interactionism is rarely historicized. For example, Everett Hughes, in his classic book, *Men at Work,* presents research about men in a variety of work contexts from garbage collectors and plumbers to lawyers and brain surgeons, and argues that they all share a common concern in searching for dignity in their work. However, in restricting himself to observing workplace practices, Hughes fails to locate the meaning men attribute to their work and the place of work in masculine subjectivity beyond these most immediate contexts. There is no attention to how work came to play the role it did for American men's self-understandings as these evolved within the larger political, cultural, and historical framework (the United States in the era of the Cold War) when his research was conducted. The theory became more nuanced in later work such as Howard Becker's exploration of the meaning and development of "careers" leading to marijuana use and other so-called deviant behavior. Still, despite Becker's emphasis on career as a process that extends over a person's lifetime, he did not consider how broader historical and cultural changes also play out in its meaning. The understanding of agency operative in Erving Goffman's dramaturgical approach to social life is similarly limited, and is in the end not all that different from the market individual presumed in the more structuralist accounts that we discussed above: Goffman assumes that actors are essentially blank slates who seek to maximize self-interest in a given setting by learning scripts and figuring out rules operating within a given context.[29]

Certainly Freudian and subsequent psychoanalytic theories challenge rationalist and structuralist ideas about motivation that presume that it can be read from the interests inherent in any given situation or social position. Psychoanalytic and psychological approaches, coexisting in uneasy tension with more dominant structuralist or rationalist models, provide a more complicated understanding of human subjectivity and motivation. However, psychoanalytic understandings of personality seldom look beyond the encounter between doctor and patient and rarely posit influences beyond the normatively defined individual family. Moreover, like most symbolic interactionist accounts, they are notoriously ahistorical.[30]

There are important and relevant exceptions that have informed our thinking, especially among feminist and narrativist psychological theorists. In her book *The Power of Feelings,* feminist sociologist and practicing psychoanalyst Nancy Chodorow argues that "childhood psychological experience and cultural determinism are filtered, and in a sense personally created, in and through psychological activity which is always contingent, historicized, individual, and biographically specific."[31] For Chodorow, psychoanalysis provides a theory of how people create personal meaning. In particular, she explores unconscious dimensions of motivation—psychic processes such as projection and fantasy—that unfold from birth on in interaction with others and enable people to create meaning throughout life.[32]

In contrast with many other theorists in the psychoanalytic tradition, Chodorow is interested in embedding subjects more fully in the social and historical context. Human development is in her view emphatically relational; "feelings are always located," Chodorow writes, "in a self-other field, even if this field is entirely intra psychic."[33] Moreover, her interpretation of the psychic processes moves beyond early childhood, conceptualizing a subject who is continuously developing over the life course. Fantasies and emotions are projected onto the social world, events, and relationships beyond the individual and, at the same time, shape the felt experiences that are fed back into that world. The social world, and the experiences and relationships that occur within it, are animated by feelings and meanings internalized within the individual. Processes of both projection and introjection involve, for Chodorow, psychological activity and individual agency. Still, for all of her accomplishments, Chodorow's theoretical and empirical work as a social scientist pays insufficient attention to the specific contexts that shape individuals or to the problem of historicizing psychodynamics and subjectivities.[34] Historicizing the self requires a more pointed examination of the intersection between internal psychodynamic processes and the external world of social relationships, organizations, cultures, and social structure. Ultimately such historicization would no doubt challenge basic models of psychoanalytic processes, still largely understood as universal.

Anthropologists Maureen Mahoney and Barbara Yngvesson move this discussion further in the direction of understanding subjectivity and agency in a manner that bridges the social and the psychological realms.[35] They call attention to the construction of desire as a social process. For them, "agency describes the subject's capacity to make meanings in her interaction with others, while desire describes the 'wants' that compel action."[36] Moreover, the subject constructs meanings "in and through these relations [with caretakers or others]...as an active participant in the construction of her own subjectivity."[37] Like Chodorow, Mahoney and Yngvesson envision the infant as already an agent in the construction of individual meanings rather than a blank slate who merely absorbs the lessons or examples of parents and other caretakers. Mahoney and Yngvesson see their overall account as having three components that differentiate it from other formulations of psychoanalytic theory:

> First, we see the infant as an active participant in the construction of her own subjectivity; second, we argue that desire and motivation are constructed in ongoing social relationships suffused by power relations (not just language); and third, the negotiation of meaning in these relationships allows the ground for creativity as well as conformity, for accepting the traditional and for breaking away from it.[38]

Conceptualizations like these drawn from psychological and psychoanalytic traditions can complement and enrich theories of motivation in other intellectual traditions and bring relevant dimensions of subjectivity such as affect into the conversation. Of course, this interest has always been present in areas such as social and political psychology. However, Mahoney and Yngvesson offer a particularly promising approach by emphasizing the social construction of the subject through time and in a social and relational context with implications that go well beyond the boundaries of these subdisciplines.

Like Chodorow and Mahoney and Yngvesson we regard as important the meanings, associations, and feelings that social actors create through and draw from their life experiences and the variety of motivations that inform their actions. Their conceptualization of human agency as formed in particular social contexts and motivated—unconsciously as well as consciously—by complex feelings, meanings, and psychological processes is a nuanced one. Such an understanding highlights what is lost in conventional social-scientific accounts of social action: the range of meanings that shape decisions, the feelings that animate them. This understanding makes it possible to posit individual motivations, feelings, and meanings as located within larger social and historical context and as developing in time and over the life course. For psychologists and psychoanalysts, agency primarily involves constructing individual meanings and making individual decisions. Our focus here is rather on the encounter between the individual and the social.[39] Still, we take from social psychologists the idea that human agency necessarily includes an appreciation of the operation of motivations constructed by the individual through a lifetime of relationships. Such an understanding highlights what is typically marginalized in conventional social-scientific accounts of human agency—the personally and temporally constructed subjectivity that is the locus of motivation and decision making. Personal narrative research, especially that based on in-depth life stories extending over a considerable period of the life course, is able to offer a far more complex view of the subject—a subject constructed through social relations, embodied in individuals with histories and psyches, living and changing through time.

Cases in Point: Two Different Stories from the Same Social Position

Sociologist Sara Lawrence-Lightfoot provides a helpful example of such research in her study of social stratification, racial hierarchy, career trajectories, and family relationships based on the collection and analysis of African American life histories.[40] Two of the life stories collected by Lawrence-Lightfoot, those of Charles Ogletree and David Wilkins, both African Americans, and both members of the Harvard University law faculty, reveal the subjective dimensions of motivations for social actions, even while embedding subjectivity in specific social and interpersonal contexts. The life stories suggest how relationships and emotional saliences dating back to childhood continue to operate in the formulation of identity and achievement in adulthood. Comparing the two stories demonstrates how different two people can be while occupying the same social-structural position.

The life story that Charles Ogletree told to Lawrence-Lightfoot sets its early chapters in Merced, a small agricultural town in California where he grew up in a family of migrant farm workers.[41] He recalled having great drive and energy as a child. Ogletree's success in the local public schools provided a route out of Merced—he received a scholarship to attend Stanford University. However, family and community emerged in Ogletree's life history as significant not just in his accounts of his early years but as persistent and long-standing influences in his later life.

For example, Ogletree specifically locates his interest in the legal profession in his early experiences. As a child, according to Lawrence-Lightfoot,

> he felt very vulnerable, like all of his south side neighbors, the boys and men especially. Several times he had witnessed the painful spectacle of his father being picked up by the police at their home after a domestic dispute between his parents. Charles would watch his father's desperate resignation, his head hung low, his body slumped, as the police led him away…His father would "look so defenseless. It was as if the man was no longer a man…It is horrible to see your father with handcuffs on him"…He does not condone his father's abusive acts, but he does understand his [father's] desperation and feeling of impotence, an impotence that made him unleash his rage on his wife…"If I could become a lawyer, I'd have the power to control the police."[42]

Ogletree's orientation toward the law was heightened by "the most powerful and tragic" event of his life, one that still "haunt[ed] him daily."[43] A close friend of his, Gene Allen, was sent to a youth camp for violent criminal behavior; after a race riot there, Gene was sent to San Quentin. Twenty years later, at the time Ogletree was telling his story, Allen was still in prison and Ogletree still working on the case on his behalf. These personal events of childhood resonated further when, as an undergraduate at Stanford, Ogletree worked with others in the defense of activist Angela Davis. "It was a consuming, energizing, 'mind-blowing' experience for the small-town boy from Merced…What was, perhaps, even more 'mind-blowing' was that Davis was found 'not guilty.'" As Ogletree recalled it, "I didn't trust the system to treat her fairly," and the success of the movement for her acquittal led him to conclude "that lawyers can play an important role…in the fight for social justice."[44]

Another important and lasting influence from Ogletree's early life was his grandfather, who taught him a lot of the skills he needed to be a successful public defender (his first job out of law school). He taught Charles the pleasures of fishing but also the virtue and necessity of patience, applicable not only in fishing, or in doing trial work, but also in just surviving. Lawrence-Lightfoot describes Ogletree's remembering in this way: "Charles sees the face of his family and his childhood friends when he teaches criminal defense to his law students at Harvard and challenges the biases and perspective that grow out of their privilege…Charles is both burdened *and* inspired by these ghosts from his past, which direct his present commitments and give them purpose and meaning."[45]

Ogletree came of age during the social movements of the 1960s and 1970s and was active in the causes associated with civil rights. His decision to go to

Harvard Law School was rooted in the search for the grounding necessary for using the law to fight for social justice. But the experience of attending Harvard was disappointing: "mostly he struggled against the legalistic perspective that insisted upon objectivity and neutrality... 'It went against every instinct in my body.' But, nevertheless there were things to be gained at Harvard: 'You see,' he said, 'I had to come up with an argument to articulate my resistance' and he found out that he didn't have to give up his values or his commitments."[46]

Lawrence-Lightfoot sees ongoing effects of Ogletree's past in his determination to insist on "a convergence of his academic and political work" in his career. His early political formation lives on in his style as a professor, in his joining of clinical and conceptual work, in his insistence on an open and dialogic pedagogy, and in his support for black students who still find Harvard an alien space.[47] Lawrence-Lightfoot continually draws connections between past and present in her analysis. According to Lawrence-Lightfoot, "For Charles, liberation arises from 'responsibility to roots.' He experiences freedom—to be himself, to do his work, to sustain meaningful relationships—to the extent that he remains true to his origins and responsible to his 'home folks.'"[48] Lawrence-Lightfoot demonstrates how Ogletree's decisions at key points in his career, his way of approaching his work, and his juggling of career and political activities have been shaped not just by opportunities and resources but also by the influences, feelings, and values accumulated over his lifetime and in a variety of specific social relationships and settings.

David Wilkins, also an African American professor of law at Harvard University, inhabits as an adult the same social location as Ogletree, but he has a very different story to tell about the trajectory that brought him there. The story that Wilkins tells emphasizes the weight of "a family legacy of male high achievers who were filled with self-doubt, who seemed sturdy and proud on the outside but also felt empty on the inside. His father, uncles, and grandfather were stunningly successful in their chosen fields; a success that brought acclaim but not necessarily peace of mind; a success that seemed to demand the same from the next generation."[49] Life story interviews gradually revealed more of Wilkins's memories of his past and of his father's struggles to maintain the family's prestige and status. Wilkins did not know much about his father's professional life until he was an adolescent. It was then that he began to learn that his father was not, perhaps, so "stunningly successful" as he had appeared to be on the surface. Like his two older brothers, David's father graduated from high school at the age of fourteen, got his B.A. from the University of Wisconsin, and arrived at Harvard Law School at eighteen. Returning to Chicago after finishing law school, his father joined the family law firm, which had been started by David's grandfather. Shortly after, David's grandfather and uncle left the firm for separate careers in Washington, D.C. Left working in the family firm in Chicago, David's father "hated every minute of it...doing the work of the 'traditional black practitioner...a solo practice in a small, out-of-the-way corner of Chicago, dealing with real estate, small black businesses, probate court.'"[50] David's family had a lot of prestige, but very little money. Nevertheless, all four children were sent to private schools, although there were times when David could not register for classes, at least temporally, because the fees had not been paid.[51]

Wilkins's mix of relative privilege combined with hidden struggle to keep up appearances left a legacy different from that of Ogletree's starker economic deprivation; moreover, his grappling with racial identity was also distinctive. Wilkins was light-skinned and could pass for white; he recalls having made a deliberate decision to "become black" after a racial incident he experienced as a fourteen-year-old left him feeling guilty. "I realized that I had been living in a cocoon." The debate team of which he had been a member was all white. "Interested in cementing this transformation to blackness," David decided to quit the debate team, "to sit at the black table," and to join the basketball team.[52]

Lawrence-Lightfoot notes aspects of Wilkins self-presentation as a Harvard professor that round out the spoken self-narrative. For example, Wilkins arrives for a class "wearing a black top hat, a long, flowing brown wool coat that reaches his ankles. Underneath is a dark blue, wide pinstripe Italian-cut suit...The clothes fit perfectly over his tall angular frame as he strides and gestures in front of the class...There is no way to talk about this man—his personae or the theater of his teaching—without referring to his 'threads.'"[53] Wilkins's students and Lawrence-Lightfoot are also aware that he owns a bright red Porsche "which everyone knows he cherishes" and that his office at the law school is filled with luxurious furnishings. His attention to his office furnishings, his clothes, and his car strike Lawrence-Lightfoot as significant as she interprets Wilkins's stories about his search for identity as an African American professional man, both imitating and differentiating himself from the paternal side of his family and especially his father.

Despite the similarity of their adult social positions, Ogletree and Wilkins traveled social, cultural, political, and psychological trajectories that were worlds apart. Ogletree defined his success as a lawyer and law professor at Harvard, for all of his ambivalence about it, as important in terms of his commitments to social justice; he emphasizes his connectedness with his roots despite (or perhaps because of?) the social distance he has traversed from them. Political motivations dating back to his coming of age in the 1960s and 1970s figure more prominently in Ogletree's account of his personal and political development than they do in that of the slightly younger Wilkins. Wilkins puts forth considerable effort to project and represent his success and to win the respect and empathy of his students. His story suggests that his motives include masking the status uncertainties and self-doubts that he reveals as key themes of his family history. In both cases, however different, the life stories point to the influence of lifelong experiences—including early family and subsequent intimate relationships—and political and pedagogic values on professional and career choices.

Other approaches to studying the trajectories of African American professional men could certainly isolate elements of biographical experience or institutional dynamics that in the aggregate are associated with intergenerational mobility or income variation, or political tendencies. But they could never get at the meanings and motivations behind career choices, nor the consequences of the different personal histories through which two men from such different backgrounds ended up in the "same" position, nor how they now occupy that position as unique individuals. What Lawrence-Lightfoot gains by eliciting and analyzing personal narratives is the possibility of a richer understanding of the human agent—as an individual constructed through social relations, acting from a variety of motives, acting in and on particular contexts, and changing over time. Of course, this richer understanding cannot be complete or definitive because motivation is complex and ambiguous; evidence of the unconscious or psychological dimensions of agency is elusive and difficult to interpret.

The Self as Narratively Constructed and Embodied

Personal narratives also provide the grounds for understanding the connections between the evolution of an individual's sense of self over time and lifelong practices of self-narration. Our discussion here draws on the work of narrative theorists across a range of disciplines. Paul John Eakin's remarkable interdisciplinary study of autobiography *How Our Lives Become Stories: Making Selves* brings together findings from neuroscience and psychology to inform his understanding of the autobiographical self ("the 'I' who speaks in self narrations…[and]…the 'I' spoken about"). Eakin's reading of neuroscientific evidence leads him to insist on the rootedness of a sense of self in the active construction through time of an individual's neurological system; in his view "the *bios* of autobiography and biography—'the course of life, a lifetime'—expands to include the life of the body and especially the nervous system."[54] Psychological evidence is presented to further argue that the key mechanism that creates continuity through time for this embodied self is *self-narrative*—stories about the self that take the body as their site and "make the connections" between present and past selves.

Following Jerome Bruner and other narrative psychologists, Eakin argues that "self narration is the defining act of the human subject, an act which is not only 'descriptive of the self' but *fundamental to the emergence and reality of that subject*." In framing his analysis of autobiography as a literary genre, Eakin also draws usefully on Ian Burkitt's critique of the social constructivism of Foucault and Jacques Derrida "for its emphasis on discourse 'at the expense of understanding humans as embodied social beings.'" Of particular interest to social theorists is Burkitt's emphasis on the embodiment of and socially learned quality of acts of communication including self-narration. In Eakin's view, this research points strongly to understanding acts of self-narration as simultaneously embodied in an individual and intrinsically social, based as they are on culturally learned behaviors that commence in infancy.[55]

This emphasis on embodiment resonates with the arguments of and debates among feminist theorists in a variety of arenas and reminds us of this additional aspect of feminist theory that has implications for conceptualizations of the self and agency. Differences between male and female bodies were key to Enlightenment debates about reason and citizenship alluded to earlier and have subsequently been critical to feminist debates about the Enlightenment's impact on women and gender.[56] They have been at the core of feminist philosophy and epistemology, feminist ethics, and feminist history.[57] Feminist scholars, as well as scholars who work on race and ethnicity, have become understandably skeptical about biologically based arguments; as a result they have tended to orient themselves toward social constructionist arguments that emphasize the discursive and cultural at the expense of the material. Kathleen Canning has recently summarized this debate, arguing for the importance of embodiment, while at the same time rejecting essentialist views of gender difference as simply rooted in bodies. Noting that "the repudiation of sex in favor of gender left sex inextricably linked to the body and stigmatized it with biologism and essentialism," Canning calls for approaches that recognize both the material and discursive construction of bodily experiences.[58] Both Eakin and Canning, then, suggest the importance of research techniques that reveal the dual construction of selves through processes that are both material and discursive.[59]

Among the various approaches to human agency in social theory, those of Dutch sociologist Norbert Elias and French sociologist Pierre Bourdieu best lend themselves to historicized, psychologically informed, and embodied notions of the self. Bourdieu's concept of *habitus* emphasizes practices that evolve within particular cultural contexts. For Bourdieu, habitus is defined abstractly as a system of internalized predispositions that mediate between abstract and largely invisible social structures and the everyday activities of individuals; habitus is simultaneously shaped by structures and regulated by practice.[60] Habitus has temporal depth; it can be understood as a lifelong learning process beginning in childhood and extending throughout the life course. Indeed, as Joel Pfister argues, "Bourdieu's concept of *habitus*...aims to supplant modern notions of the psychological self and debunk false dichotomies such as individual versus society (the individual, itself a mystified notion, could never stand apart from society in Bourdieu's view)."[61] Similarly, Ian Burkitt points to Elias's understanding of "the association between the development of the self and the *embodiment* of human beings, who, in the course of their upbringing, learn to discipline and control their own bodies in ways that are socially prescribed." Both Elias and Bourdieu emphasize learned processes of bodily self-regulation and interpersonal behavior, "the dispositions of a social class or group due to their common codes of conduct and the similar patterns of their upbringing" that produces "a level of the self and its understanding of the world that is not just textual or cognitive, but is grounded in the experience of the body."[62]

Picking up on and elaborating these themes in Elias and Bourdieu, we suggest that personal narrative analysis is an effective method of demonstrating how individual agency is operative in a particular context even while located in an embodied self evolving over time and over the life course. Indeed personal narrative analysis can effectively counter certain theoretical weaknesses in Bourdieu's otherwise rich ethnographic accounts, for example his vagueness about the relationship between the durability and the transformability of habitus. Bourdieu asserts that habitus is inculcated primarily by early childhood experience and that differences in habitus are based, in the example of French society, primarily on social class origins. Yet habitus is also transformed by subsequent experiences and is influenced by other aspects of the family setting; Bourdieu has little to say about the conditions of stability and plasticity of habitus. Further, although Bourdieu's theory of practice was intended to overcome the problems of French structuralism and the materialist determinism of traditional Marxism, his concept of habitus retains some of the deterministic qualities he sought to transcend. This problem becomes most evident in Bourdieu's discussion of "misrecognition." If social actors misrecognize the symbolic dimensions of power they unwittingly reproduce, then how does social change come about and what is its relationship to human agency? Finally, despite Bourdieu's enthusiasm to overcome the limitations of objectivism, he has little to say about the subjectivity of those he studies whether it is Algerian peasants or middle-class French academics.[63] Though he always carefully attends to social class and to culture, he pays scant attention to the complexities of the individual's subjective worlds, their feelings, emotions, and psyches, although recent publications reveal that late in his career he began to attend more to the psychodynamics of habitus.[64]

One example of a personal narrative analysis that suggests links between habitus, practice, and reproduction, and draws on the psychological in the process, is *Landscape for a Good Woman* by cultural and literary historian Carolyn Steedman.[65] Steedman's study combines a biography (of her mother) with her own autobiography. The biography revises and adds nuance to the historical portrait of working-class women, especially working-class mothers, and of the gender balance-of-power in the working-class household. The intimacy of the portrayal and Steedman's ability to draw on psychological dimensions of being mothered by a working-class woman, point to otherwise hidden agendas and complex motivations behind practices—motivations that are excluded from or denied by the more usual characterizations of working-class subjects and working-class cultural milieus. In the politically charged traditions of labor and social history so important to the production of working-class histories, analysts' own origins and orientations toward Marxist, materialist, and masculinist understandings of historical dynamics has led, Steedman argues, to an emphasis on interests, solidarities, and rational strategies. Psychological complexity was simply not on the agenda. In response, Steedman asks: "What becomes of the notion of class consciousness when it is seen as a structure of feeling that can be learned in childhood, with one of its components a proper envy, the desire of people for things of the earth?"[66] Steedman's willingness to delve into the often painful and hidden psychological aspects of her own mother's "minimalist mothering" opens up new possibilities for interpreting the relationship between working-class family life and adult class identities. Her account is rooted simultaneously in the material (her mother's desire for "the things of the earth") and the psychological (a complex mother-daughter relationship). Her focus on psychological dimensions of the acquisition of class identities and on the intersection between class and gender identities also reveal the effects of class-specific parenting styles across several generations, thus offering insights into some of the dynamics that transform habitus itself (e.g., the willingness—or not—of daughters in turn to mother). Analyses like Steedman's demonstrate the power of personal narrative evidence to operationalize subjectivities in a multidimensional way: Agency is embodied in persons who evolve in context; people's stories build upon their lived experiences over time and in particular interpersonal, social, cultural, and historical settings that they in turn continue to work through and transform in their present. In other words, they offer documentation of Bourdieu's claim that habitus is at once durable and transformable.

The Self as Constructed and Reconstructed over Time

Looking closely at the temporalities that structure personal narratives reinforces their value as documents of ongoing self-construction and social transformation.

Steedman's analysis involves a particularly complex interpersonal temporality, since the subjectivities she analyzes operate across two intersecting life courses—her own and her mother's. Temporality is an important dimension of personal narrative analysis, but it can emerge in a range of different registers. An analysis of the autobiography of Adelheid Popp, who was an activist in the pre–World War I Austrian socialist women's movement, provides another provocative point from which to examine temporal dimensions of the construction of agency in personal narratives.[67] Popp's story is recounted in Maynes's study of working-class auto-biographies, *Taking the Hard Road*. Popp, writing as a young adult autobiographer at the beginning of the twentieth century, recalled that when her family moved to Vienna around 1880, when she was ten, it was left to her to complete the residency registration because her mother could not write. She left the registration column labeled "children" blank because she "didn't think of (herself) as a child." According to Popp:

> When I'd rush to work at six o'clock in the morning, other children of my age were still sleeping. And when I hurried home at eight o'clock at night, then the others were going to bed, fed and cared for. While I sat bent over my work, lining up stitch after stitch, they played, went walking or sat in school.

As a child, Popp claims, she accepted her lot as unquestionable; only later in life was she "often overcome by a feeling of boundless bitterness because I had never enjoyed childhood pleasures or youthful happiness."[68]

Popp deployed a childhood story as a form of social critique—a not uncommon rhetorical device in German socialist autobiography of the late nineteenth and early twentieth centuries. However, in so doing Popp ironically presents herself as a powerful ten year old. She was contributing to the family's income; she could read when her mother could not; she helped the family navigate the Viennese bureaucracy. Moreover, Popp's comments underscore her ongoing reinterpretation of her childhood and her own sense of agency over her lifetime; only later in life did she learn that her childhood should have been different. The contrast between what ought to have been true of her past and what had been the case in turn contributed to her sense of agency and to her motivations as an adult. Like Popp, other members of the Austrian socialist women's organization saw themselves as motivated at least in part by their concerns about the situation of working-class families. For example, Popp's colleague Anna Maier alluded in her memoir to her dedication to winning mothers over to socialism "so that the children of the proletariat will in the future experience more joy in childhood than (she) had."[69]

Like Popp, many authors of personal narratives assume that childhood matters. Not all do. The role of childhood in accounts of the self raises huge comparative issues about not only individual understandings but also the evolution of genres and conventions of telling life stories, and the connections between the history of life stories and the history of the self. To offer a comparison involving a different notion of the narration of the self over time, early Chinese biographies include childhood stories, but these tend to be formulaic and perfunctory; childhood does not cause so much as prefigure adult destiny. For example, anecdotes of prodigious childhood feats of filial devotion served to establish a leitmotif of family virtue that characterized the entire life; there was no narrative logic that emphasized ongoing development from childhood through adulthood.[70]

Personal narrative analysis does allow for the possibility of understanding agency and its motivations as it operates and changes through time. One of the important questions to raise in using such sources is: For what analytic purposes does the temporal depth of the life story matter? What difference does it make, for example, if childhood is or is not part of the causal account that explains a life in history? Since, as we have been arguing, individual subjects and their self-narratives evolve in social context and in connection with one another, the probing of life history research needs to extend back far enough in time to capture the social-historical and individual dynamics relevant to the questions under investigation. Social scientists who collect personal narratives make a variety of different choices about how deeply to delve into their informants' life histories. Some are satisfied with accounts of motivations that restrict themselves to the recent past, whereas others find that they can answer their questions only by going much further back in time. Kath Weston, for example, writes in her book on contemporary lesbian identity in the United States: "Talk to someone in the United States about gender for more than twenty minutes and you're likely to walk away with a childhood story."[71]

For many analytic purposes, like those of Weston, social dynamics of interest to subjectivity, agency, and social action begin to be established in childhood. Indeed, in some cases, the process of telling a life story can itself jog self-consciousness that brings about awareness of changes in identity that have occurred over time but are rooted in the distant past. For example, for a number of the African Americans in Sara Lawrence-Lightfoot's books, which we discussed earlier in this chapter, agreeing to participate in her investigations created an opportunity for self-reflection and self-narrative. Their life stories suggest a doubled narrative of mobility—they record not only attributes and occupational accomplishments that have evolved over their lives but also transformations in the identities, categories, and orientations that they use to describe themselves and map out their course. This can be seen, perhaps most clearly, in accounts of relationships with family members or childhood associates, who appear in stories of the desperate search to flee from them, to differentiate oneself from them early in the life course, often followed later by the need to reconnect.[72]

The point here is that such narratives, like many German socialist narratives of the pre–World War I era or like Carolyn Steedman's story of working-class identity in twentieth-century England, retrospectively reconstruct the origins of salient adult subjectivities early in life—far earlier than the hero's or heroine's first encounter with the workplace, the Party headquarters, or the law school. Revealing a past as a child martyr was typical in German socialist memoirs of the industrial era; class exploitation was, in this analysis, first evidenced in terms of its negative impact on working-class family life and experienced by the historical subject-in-the-process-of-becoming and prior to the maturation of a level of class consciousness and accompanying political analysis that would have allowed for its more politically appropriate expression. Dimensions of African American subjectivity as related in adult personal narratives similarly involve the interplay of childhood stories and orientations with more recently acquired self-understandings. They also point to nostalgia for what has been lost or rejected in the lifelong process of self-construction.

Of course not every personal narrative analysis requires childhood stories to demonstrate the socially and historically contextualized and temporally ongoing construction of selfhood. Sociologist Jennifer Pierce's career trajectory interviews, for example, emphasize a different aspect of temporality—how self-narratives can change from one point in adulthood to another.[73] These interviews were conducted in the context of her research on the backlash against affirmative action in a northern California corporation, research that explores the interpersonal workplace dynamics that led to the marginalization of African American litigators among their predominantly white and male colleagues in the company's legal department. The work life histories she collected in 1989, and repeated in 1999, provide clues to the subtle, complex, and changing self-understandings of the attorneys she interviewed.

In contrast with white male lawyers' narratives of hard work producing professional success, the African American lawyers who all eventually left the legal department of the firm she studied (called Bonhomie Corporation) between 1989 and 1999 tell Pierce stories of marginalization, alienation, and then exit from the company. Randall Kingsley's narrative is one of these stories. His 1989 narrative began with a description of the opportunities opened up by affirmative action programs and policies in the late 1960s and early 1970s. In 1985, after he finished law school, he had applied for jobs in several big firms in employment law and ended up getting offered one position in the district attorney's office in Oakland and another in the litigation division within the legal department at Bonhomie Corporation. Both had good reputations for their affirmative action recruitment policies; he decided to take the position at Bonhomie because "the salary was better and the opportunities seemed greater." Despite Kingsley's initial note of optimism about the potential of affirmative action for changing "good ole' boy practices," his tone shifted as he began to describe some of the obstacles he encountered at work and his general feeling of being "set up for failure."

> Like the very first case I worked on. It wasn't in my central area of exper-
> tise, but Sam [the department head] encouraged me to take it anyway
> and said I should ask some of the more experienced attorneys to give me
> advice because that's what they're supposed to do...I was a little appre-
> hensive about taking this on because it was so far afield from labor law,
> my area of legal expertise. But, I figured okay, I will ask for help if I need
> it...You know how it is, in litigation, everyone is always really busy. So,
> when I first talked to Bill [a white attorney] about the case, he said he
> was busy, and I just thought, "Okay, he doesn't have time now." But then,
> he never did make time. And, he wasn't the only one who brushed me
> off...On the other hand, it was obvious to me that Todd [a new white
> associate] was getting all kinds of attention. I'd see them talking in his
> office, giving him articles from the library, taking him off to lunch. And,
> so I feel like I've been set up for failure.[74]

As Pierce learns in her second interview with Kingsley in 1999, he had left Bonhomie Corporation's legal department in 1993 and set up his own prac-tice to become, in his words, "a sort of jack of all trades." Although it would be inaccurate to describe him unambiguously as downwardly mobile—he was practicing law and considered himself to be "solidly middle-class"—within the stratification of the legal profession, he had moved from the top tier of highly paid corporate law to the lower strata of the lower-paying practice of the solo professional.

When asked why he had left Bonhomie, Kingsley explained that over time he had come to realize that the corporation's commitment to the motto "diversity is excellence" was an empty one. As he put it, "they don't really believe that. It's just assumed that if you are Black then you can't possibly be qualified for the job...In their heads, it went something like: 'minority' equals 'affirmative action hire' equals 'unqualified.' I don't mean everyone thought this way, but enough people did to make it matter."[75] After encountering a series of obstacles in his career at the firm—some described in his first interview—Randall decided to confront the head of the department.

> I said that I wanted to know what was going on. You know, because this
> was an incident of differential treatment. I used those words, "differential

treatment," very carefully. Oh, he got so mad. He started yelling, "Are you calling me a racist?" And then [later] he tells everyone else in litigation that I said he was a racist and they all start acting weird—really nice, but really defensive…Suddenly, Bill who is like, you know, a cold fish, is like, saying hello all the time and telling me how he was really busy when I stopped by asking for advice. And, how he was really sorry if there was any misunderstanding. And by the way, did I know that he belongs to the ACLU?…And Ralph, kept saying over and over that he really forgot that lunch date with me, "it doesn't have anything to do with [pause], you know…"

Q: It doesn't have to do with the fact that you are African American?

Yeah, that's what he meant, but he wouldn't say it. So after that they all started doing it. It's like they were just racing for innocence…And things just got weird. It seemed like either I did the wrong thing or people just reacted weirdly to me…And, so I decided to move on.[76]

Through the technique of reinterviewing, Pierce's analysis highlights the temporal specificity of self-understanding. Because Randall's narrative is told at two points in his career, 1989 and 1999, we are able to see how the build up of events over a period of time led him first to call attention to the problems in Bonhomie's legal department and, when they went unresolved, to decide on a different career course. In this movement over time and from one job to his current practice, we also see a shift and change in Kingsley's narrative about himself. The story he first tells about his time in the legal department at Bonhomie depicts him primarily as a victim of discrimination and unfair workplace practices. A decade later, however, Kingsley describes himself as content in his personal and professional life, a theme he embroiders after an animated description of a case he was working on:

Q: It sounds like you really enjoy your work.

Oh yeah, I love putting together all the pieces of a legal puzzle—figuring out how to make all the details work out best for my client. That's really rewarding. But, I am lucky, you know. The reason, I have such interesting puzzles to work with is because I work for myself. I am independent…I think one of the other advantages of working for myself has to do with time. I am ultimately responsible for my time. And, sure, I still have to bill hours to clients, but I decide when the work will get done. So, I might decide to go in early, and then take time off later in the afternoon to watch my son's little league game or one of my daughter's soccer games. Something I never could have done in corporate [litigation].[77]

Even though he makes less money—and may even be considered by some to be downwardly mobile—as a black man with a professional degree and a stable family life, he regards himself as a self-styled success. He appears to be more in control of his life and, in the new job setting over which he has more control, is less inclined to emphasize his status as a victim. By interviewing Kingsley at two distinct moments in his life, and in two different institutional settings, Pierce is able to capture both self-understandings rather than one or the other. Randall's changing personal narrative captures more of the complexity of his personhood, especially its temporal and contextual construction, and the contingency of his (and by extension, any) subject position.[78]

Memories, Histories

Finally, directly related to temporality, are questions of memory.[79] Memory emerged in academic study in the late nineteenth and early twentieth centuries originally as the domain of psychologists and philosophers.[80] Sigmund Freud and his contemporaries and later followers provided foundational inquiries into the process of memory formation and postulated theories about the relationships between subconscious memory, individual life narratives, and collective mythologies. Following World War I, discussions of traumatic memories and narratives captured the attention of other social scientists who began to place memory in social contexts. Maurice Halbwachs, notably, expanded on psychological memory studies, situating the processes of memory formation and recall into collective contexts, arguing that, analogous to language, memory is formed in and has no meaning outside of social relationships.[81]

Connections among memory, notions of the self, and personal narrative are close and multidimensional. In his summary of psychological work on memory, Paul John Eakin argues that of various reflexive understandings of the self posited in developmental theory, "the extended self—the self of memory and anticipation, the self in time—is the earliest to emerge, normally by the age of three"; for Eakin, "this self constitutes the foundation of the self represented in autobiography, providing a proto-narrative, temporal armature that supports and sustains our operative sense of who we are."[82] The social construction of the self in childhood is closely associated with learning how to construct self-narratives, which are in turn first articulated in what Eakin terms "memory talk" within the family, which includes photographs and the like along with stories told in conversations.[83] Moreover, like the sense of self, autobiographical memory is in his view an active, constructivist process: "our representations of reality—literary, psychological, neurological—are dynamic and constructed rather than static and mimetic in nature."[84]

But memory studies have other disciplinary genealogies beyond psychology and philosophy; other theoretical and methodological traditions of understanding memory are also relevant for personal narrative analysis. Beginning in the 1960s, as we discussed in the Introduction, social historians began to examine popular memory as a way to write "history from below"—especially those of the working class, women, and other marginalized historical actors. In this and other emergent historiographical fields, oral histories held promise for challenging official histories, as well as uncovering and attesting to individual and group oppression.[85]

Oral history pioneers also worked in Europe and the United States to collect sources that would enable a critique of hegemonic histories from the perspective of subaltern classes, women, or ethnic minorities. The best of the oral history pioneers offered nuanced and sophisticated models for writing a new sort of history based on collected memories. The work of Alessandro Portelli, among the founders of the oral history method in Europe, provides a case in point.[86] His groundbreaking work on oral history began in the 1970s with a study of local accounts of the 1949 death of Luigi Trastulli, an Italian laborer in Portelli's hometown. Portelli's method treats subjective memories as especially valuable for historians precisely because of their differences in content and emphasis from more "objective" written records (although he continually reminds readers about the fluidity between the oral and the written as, for example, court testimonies or interviews conducted for newspaper stories become frozen in written form).

At the heart of Portelli's method is the tension between what narrators report and "what actually happened" as he understands that from alternative accounts. Through such techniques, Portelli teases out the psychological reality and symbolic meanings of the stories people tell about themselves and their individual and collective pasts, meanings that he views as the real insights to be gained from research drawing on memories. The narratives themselves, according to Portelli, need to be considered as a work in progress: They change over the life cycle and they involve not just placing events in a narrative sequence but also figuring out which narrative sequences an event belongs in.[87] Memories and self-narratives based on them are shaped simultaneously by collective, often political, narratives and individual psychological needs.

Around the same time as the emergence of oral history among Africanists and Western "history from below," a cultural and political resurgence of interest in the memories and stories of victims of the Holocaust and other World War II–era atrocities led to a set of questions about history and memory: the analysis of traumatic memory; recalling and witnessing the past as therapeutic and as political action; the politics of public historical memorials; and the challenge and ethics of representing historical incidents of extraordinary violence. The literature around World War II, and especially Holocaust memory, pointed to the generational political implications for memory and led to enormous historiographical as well as popular controversies.[88]

Studies of individual and collective memory have grown in popularity as a research method, often in uneasy tension with more mainstream approaches employed in the discipline of history. The use of memories as historical evidence sparked ongoing discussions of reliability, veracity, and other epistemological concerns raised by historians accustomed to documentary sources. From a somewhat different angle, French historian Pierre Nora has led an attack on what he viewed as history's disciplinary colonization of (and antagonism toward) memory, although his thesis, which poses a stark opposition between traditional oral memory cultures and modern cultures of written history has been in turn criticized as romanticizing or exoticizing the former.[89] Nevertheless, the question to which Nora drew attention—that of the connection between forms of remembering the past and notions of time and history—has resonated widely. We will address these connections more fully in chapter 2, which focuses on the intersection of personal and historical narratives.

Subjectivity and selfhood are the special purview of personal narrative analyses; their exploration brings critical dimensions to the understanding of human agency. However, personal narrative evidence can never be taken as a transparent description of "experience" or a straightforward expression of identity. Pierre Bourdieu rightly called it an illusion to view individual biographical and autobiographical sources as in and of themselves deeper, truer, or more authentic than accounts based on other sources and methodologies.[90] Similarly, historian Joan Scott has argued that testimony from personal experience cannot be read as a transparent form of evidence, but rather is always produced in and through broader discourses that have been the focus of postmodern critique.[91] Moreover, personal narrative analysis, departing from much sociological, social psychological, and psychoanalytic practice, needs to historicize subjectivity itself. These expressions of skepticism do not lead us to conclude, however, that personal narrative sources are unreliable or uninteresting as evidence for social scientific inquiry. On the contrary!

Personal narrative analyses have the potential to theorize and investigate a more complex and interesting social actor—constructed through social relations, embodied in an individual with a real history and psychology, and living and changing through time. Personal narratives are complex forms of evidence that demand sophisticated analytic techniques that build on the recognition of their location at the intersection of the individual and the social. As we have argued, a personal narrative can document a subjectivity that has evolved along with and within a memory embodied in an individual who has constructed him- or herself in a specific social context through interpersonal relationships and psychodynamic processes. That self has been constructed through self-narratives, culturally shaped and interactive forms that yield operative self-understandings that evolve over time. A personal narrative document captures one form and moment in this ongoing narrative self-construction. The selves constructed through and revealed in such narratives are the sites of individual agency and of the particular motivations that ultimately govern both individual actions and self-narratives about them. In this chapter we have emphasized the individual and subjective dimensions of personal narratives. We turn, in chapter 2, to the intersections between the individual and the historical context in personal narratives and their analysis.

2

INTERSECTING STORIES

Personal Narratives in Historical Context

Lives are lived at the intersection of individual and social dynamics; life stories are correspondingly structured by multiple narrative logics and temporal frames—individual and collective. A life story is typically framed first in reference to the narrator's life course. An individual only directly "experiences" the events of his or her own lifetime, and most common conventions of life storytelling privilege this temporality.[1] The episodes recounted in life stories thus relate to a narrative sequence for which the life course itself provides the plot lines and the temporal frame.

At the same time, personal narratives are contextualized by, reflect on, and explore the individual's place in collective events and historical time. They evoke many additional narratives with their own distinct temporalities beyond the individual life. Of particular relevance here are those types of narratives that Margaret Somers and Gloria Gibson have termed *public narratives;* that is,

> narratives attached to cultural and institutional formations larger than the single individual, to interpretive networks or institutions, however local or grand, micro or macro—stories about American social mobility, the "freeborn Englishman," the working-class hero, and so on. Public narratives range from the narratives of one's family, to those of the workplace (organizational myths), church, government, and nation. Like all narratives, these stories have drama, plot, explanation, and selective appropriation.[2]

This means that beyond the time frame of the individual life course, narrators usually refer to a range of other temporal and historical frames—familial, institutional, and national—when they tell their "own" stories.

Moreover, the analyst adds still other historical and temporal dimensions relevant to the analytic project. For example, historian Michael Honey, the author of *Black Workers Remember* (discussed below), notes that his life history interviews with black industrial workers in Tennessee brought their personal stories into his own historical frames drawn from labor and civil rights history: "Remembering in a historical sense occurs not only through the voices of history's participants but through the work of the collector of stories."[3] He nicely captures the complex historicity that characterizes his and other personal narrative research. His interviews gave narrators the occasion and encouragement to historicize their lives—to set them in a framework of the collective events and historical transformations they understood themselves to be part of. At the same time, by bringing previously submerged perspectives into "public narratives" about the past, his and other analyses of personal narratives also have the potential to alter prevailing interpretations of the past. Attention to this multiplicity of narrative and historical temporalities and historical frames is a hallmark of effective personal narrative analysis for the social sciences.

Our argument here returns from another angle to the core theoretical problem that we introduced in chapter 1: understanding human agency as simultaneously individual and social. Paraphrasing Marx's claim that individuals make history under conditions not of their own making, Somers and Gibson assert that "all of us come to be who we are…in social narratives *rarely of our own making.*"[4] In chapter 1, we discussed variations in understandings of the self as these have informed social theory and everyday life practices of selfhood including authoring personal narratives. We also drew upon psychological and literary evidence to demonstrate the interconnections between individual subjects and the social relations and narrative practices through which they evolve and constitute themselves. We argued that personal narrative analysis, through its capacity to emphasize and problematize socially and culturally embedded subjectivities, provides insights to the understanding of human agency.

This chapter is closely related to the previous one, but we reverse the directionality of our lens: We move from a focus on personal narratives as sites of the expression of socially embedded individual subjectivity to a focus on social and historical context as an element of both the narration and the interpretation of life stories. Our point in this chapter is not to claim simply that history matters, but rather to argue that *analyzing personal narrative evidence demands attention to historical contextualization.* Conversely, personal narrative analysis *can illuminate the operation of historical forces and of public or historical narratives as they influence people's motivations and their self-understandings as historical agents.* We argue that personal narrative analyses that attend to historical context and problematize intersections between individual life stories and larger historical dynamics offer the most significant contributions to the reconceptualization of structure and agency, and their relationship. We would further argue that since lives are lived and personal narratives based on them are constructed within specific historical contexts, analysts need to understand and take into account these larger forces whether or not narrators themselves are explicitly attentive to them in writing or talking about their lives. Although some narrators of life histories are adept contextualizers of their own lives and frequently allude to historical dynamics and historical explanations in their life stories, the analyst always needs to interpret such contextualization (or the lack thereof) critically and to incorporate sources external to the narrative. Narrators of life stories, in other words, should be regarded as privileged but not definitive observers of their own historical contexts.

Interpreting Lives and Life Stories in Historical Context

Personal narratives both specify and are contextualized by particular historical moments; they, and the subjects they presume and help to construct, have emerged in historically specific cultural and institutional settings. How do analyses of personal narratives demonstrate this contextualization? Three examples illustrate different approaches.

An original and provocative case in point is Italian historian Luisa Passerini's *Autobiography of a Generation: Italy, 1968.* In this book Passerini undertakes a novel experiment in presenting a highly subjective and psychoanalytically informed approach to understanding human agency that at the same time embeds its analysis in a specific historical moment.[5] Passerini's book alternates autobiographical chapters based on her diary and notes from her own psychoanalysis with other chapters based on a set of life histories of participants in the Italian student movement of the late 1960s and early 1970s in which Passerini was also a participant. (The various documents and life stories date mostly from the 1980s; that is, after the heyday of the student movement.)

Passerini's reading of the life stories here is a very particular one. As she describes it in her chapter on the 1968 generation's early childhood experiences, she is reading for psychodynamic themes and symbolic associations that the narratives reiterate: "At the roots of our memory, in dozens of life histories, I find a rupture. Our identity is constructed on contradictions. Even those stories that emphasize the continuity of their own lives extract from the autobiographical material—as far as the formative years are concerned—recurring themes of division, of difference, of contrast." The bold claim to be writing "the autobiography of a generation" is based on the fact that Passerini interprets her own subjectivity in terms of what she had learned from life story interviews with participants in the 1968 movements, interviews that she had conducted in connection with a collaborative international oral history project: "I finished the interviews on '68. It's clear that the international book can't be a history of subjectivity...I will have to work alone on memory...I want to attempt a reading of these life stories, including my own. Take up the same thread from the other end. Talk about what I've seen in the mirrors held up by those I've interviewed."[6] Conversely, she uses her own autobiographical materials to interpret this wider history. For example, Passerini's chapter on the theme of "choosing to be orphans," which is based on the interviews with activists, is followed by her own diary notes recalling her political activities during the late 1960s: "We came together around a common vision of the world, a desire for the subversion and critique of respectability and for a break with it."[7]

The life histories gathered from former student activists point to a particular generational dynamic. For example, students who came of age in the 1960s, especially female students, rejected the bourgeois models of family and motherhood that had developed in Italy after World War II, models that were seen as consumer oriented and de-politicizing. Put succinctly by one narrator: "The best poster on the walls of my faculty, I remember it really distinctly, out of all the posters there: 'I want to be an orphan.'"[8] Passerini argues that the specific political and sociohistorical experiences of this generation, in conjunction with psychodynamic aspects of intergenerational relationships produced in the highly charged political and interpersonal milieu of their postwar family life, produced this cohort's unfolding stance toward the world. These elements were critical to accounts by former student movement activists of their behavior during the student movement and also in later years when they in turn rejected some aspects (e.g., its patriarchal culture) of the movement that had inspired them in their youth.

Passerini's self-analytic mode in the psychoanalytic chapters opens up deeprooted dimensions of subjectivity, motivation, and agency that would otherwise be virtually impossible for the historian or social scientist to observe or explore. As Joan Scott notes in her foreword to the book, "when viewed through the lens of psychoanalysis, what is rationally remembered is not a simple reflection of social position, economic structure, or political event; it is instead a way of selectively organizing experience to produce and explain one's self."[9] The methodological challenges still loom large. Although distinct analytic strands (the psychoanalytic narrative, autobiographical reflections, and collected oral life histories) inform each other and thematic resonances echo back and forth, Passerini never makes the connections explicit and perhaps she cannot. Passerini herself remarks that what attracts her about memory is its "insistence on creating a history of itself, which is much less and perhaps somewhat more than a social history."[10] Still, even if the argument is at times opaque, Passerini's project is a remarkable exploration of the intersection between her individual subjectivity and a sort of collective subjectivity of her generation.

The exploration of subjectivity in historical context is much enriched by Passerini's historicized psychoanalytic approach to explaining her generation's activism. But there are a variety of other personal narrative analyses that illuminate the interplay between individual subjectivity and larger historical dynamics. Historian James S. Amelang's book, *The Flight of Icarus,* for example, documents the articulation of artisanal identity in early modern Europe as seen in a variety of archivally preserved autobiographical writings.[11] Amelang does not restrict himself to autobiographies in the common sense of the term. He assesses a range of forms of artisan first-person writing including memoirs, diaries, family record books, spiritual autobiographies, personal chronicles, travel writing, and even autobiographical fiction.[12] Indeed, Amelang finds it necessary to examine this wide range of genres because, as he contends, the historical evolution of the forms or genres of self-expression is inseparable from the history of social identities and their institutional bases (a point we made in chapter 1 and to which we will return in chapter 3).

In Amelang's analysis, much attention is focused on the guilds, communities, and families that figure among the many sets of "allegiances," the dense networks of associational life in which artisans were enmeshed. He demonstrates the significance of such allegiances through detailed empirical analysis of artisans' daily contacts alluded to either in the autobiographical texts themselves or in other forms of documentation available through close scrutiny of local historical records. The institutionally based networks of family, friends, neighborhood, and trade and guild connections that made up the artisan's social universe were crucial elements in his (or occasionally her) personal cultural world, and they shaped his writing as well as his life. Amelang's research shows how personal texts such as autobiographical writings are simultaneously individual and collective products and how historically specific institutions play a key role in the construction of the subjectivities they document and construct.

Amelang's investigation of the cultural symbols evoked in the artisan writings sheds light on connections between self-imagining and specific cultural contexts. The mythological allusion in the title of the book signals the significance of widely shared cultural narratives in the plotting of early modern European artisan autobiography. The book's title was inspired by a seventeenth-century personal chronicle by Miquel Parets, a Catalonian tanner from Barcelona. The relevant passage, from the book's preface, reads as follows: "may this worthy ambition serve as a sun to illuminate my endeavors, rather than to cause me to plummet like Icarus...even though destiny assigned me to a lowlier sphere, it did not rob me of the wish to aspire to higher things."[13] According to Amelang, the Icarus myth was one of many classical literary models that informed the self-narratives of early modern Europeans of humble as well as more exalted origins. His interpretation suggests that the author understood his writing to be a bold, even transgressive, act that challenged social and cultural boundaries. The Icarus myth, then, in this and related usages, serves as an ambiguous class allegory that would have been familiar to Parets' audience—whether as a morality tale about the just punishment for pride or as an exhortation to attempt an ascent (and delivery from the labyrinth) even in the face of overwhelming odds. In either case, the artisan's use of the metaphor in writing about his own life illustrates how his sense of self depended on broadly shared cultural motifs as well as a specific institutional milieu, that were in turn located by him in a wider social and cultural hierarchy.

Michael Honey's *Black Workers Remember: An Oral History of Segregation, Unionism, and the Freedom Struggle* emerges like Amelang's study from the arena of working-class history, but in a very different context. It examines the interplay between individual agency and historical dynamics over the course of the twentieth century through oral histories of black men and women industrial workers in Memphis, Tennessee. Events in Memphis in 1968 became national and international news because it was there that Martin Luther King, Jr., was assassinated when he involved himself in support of a garbage workers strike that had been going on for several months. But *Black Workers Remember* is more about African American labor history in Memphis than it is about Martin Luther King, Jr. Honey presents the long history of black labor struggles, which he learned about from the stories of people who lived through them. Asking the question, "What was the role of black workers in labor history?" Honey found that he could not rely on the same sources labor historians use to document the history of whites in the labor movement. He turned to oral history as "the only available method for uncovering an active black working class in factories and other workplaces." Honey tells, largely in the workers' words, about the struggles of black workers in Memphis for decent wages, a union, and respect.[14]

In his interviews with blacks, Honey heard very different accounts of race relations in Memphis unions than he heard from white union officials. "The first black worker I located, Firestone shop leader Josh Tools, [when asked] whether his union had led the way in improving race relations...emphatically responded,

'Hell, no!'...Mr. Tools still became angry when he recalled how timid those lead-ers had been on race relations."[15] Working conditions and the union movement both institutionalized the racial divide. For example, one of the problems black workers faced at work and, for a while at least, in their unions as well was the construction of separate black and white job hierarchies, with lower wages for even the most skilled black job categories.

Black Workers Remember richly historicizes the particular form that race rela-tions and racialized working-class identities took in this setting in the industrial South, as well as the processes that changed them: the institutionalization of rac-ism through Jim Crow laws, the migration of workers from the countryside to the cities, the Depression and founding of the Congress of Industrial Organizations in the 1930s that provided black workers with resources for unionization they had not previously had, the postwar Red Scare that undermined communist cross-racial unionizing, the Civil Rights movement, and the labor activities and assassination of Martin Luther King—all of which had local as well as national res-onance. Honey's research shows how the black workers' civil rights activism was closely connected with their union-building activities and how both still manifest themselves in the political loyalties they articulate and in the scars they still show.

In his early interviews with Clarence Coe, for example, who had been active in unionization efforts since the 1930s, Honey found "one of the souls who had staked his life on the chance to break down the walls of Jim Crow through the American labor movement."[16] Coe's stories play a key role in Honey's revision of labor history from the perspective of black workers. Coe's memories provided not only new empirical evidence for the revision but also clues about the emo-tional dimensions of black labor activism, which still resonated for Coe even in his old age. In the final chapter of *Black Workers Remember,* entitled "Scars of Memory," Honey describes how, to his surprise, Coe opened up to him personally during their last conversation in ways he had not done before. (Coe died shortly thereafter.) As Honey writes:

> [Coe] spoke of his endurance of racism and segregation and told me about the many scars the past had left on him, about how painful his encounters with white racism had been to him emotionally...The scars of memory included the contorted faces of whites, how "they'd put that cheap dirty snarl on their face" or literally seem to jump back when they saw a black person...He told me for the first time in detail of how an older black worker tried to kill him [with a knife] when he upset the old order of things by trying to organize union...This scar [on his stomach], like his memories, kept alive the personal insults and attacks that he endured as a result of racism. It had dogged him all his days.[17]

It becomes clear that the pain of racism played a key role in motivating black union activism once the opportunity for organizing presented itself. Involvement brought risks, not only from whites but, as the episode alluded to above suggests, also from African Americans who did not approve of agitation. According to Honey:

> organizing the union was a life and death freedom struggle, one that required outside support [whether from the federal government or from divine sources]...but [black union activists] also had another kind of faith that sustained them. They were quintessentially American, in the sense that all of them had hopes that democracy consisted of more than words on paper..."All I wanted to do, [Coe said] was to live in a free country"...[they] used unions and the movement for civil rights to make that dream real.[18]

The somewhat different emphases in the stories told by women workers add an important additional dimension to the historical account of blacks in labor history. In their retrospective life stories women factory workers note, for example, the advantages they could give their children that would not have been available if they had to accept much lower-paying domestic work. In the present in which they recount their memories of work, they take great pride in their children's accomplishments. For the men Honey interviewed, however, their hard work did not provide the same feelings of accomplishment or pride in themselves. Indeed, quite the opposite was the case. If masculinity involved earning a family wage, one that was sufficient to support their wives and children as well as themselves, they rarely had that satisfaction. That this was important to these men is also supported by the widespread slogan I *AM* A MAN!, which was used in union actions such as the Memphis garbage workers strike; countering the demasculinization experienced at the workplace was a powerful incentive for men to become involved in the struggle for unionization and recognition.

In addition to his attention to differences between men's and women's stories, Honey also talked to workers of different ages. By interviewing younger workers, Honey was able to place some more recent stories into the long temporality of the union movement. For example, when Ida Leachman worked as a union organizer in the 1980s and 1990s, she found the task had become even harder and meaner with the antiunionism of the Reagan years. With subsequent globalization since then, union strength and benefits have deteriorated still further. Plant closures that were happening even as Honey conducted his interviews were making it harder to find jobs, and the problems of drugs, crime, and violence were adding to the harsh conditions of daily life, especially among the poor. The recent context, Honey suggests, is one in which black workers can make few gains.

More to the point, many workers interviewed by Honey expressed worries about the loss not only of the gains of the past but also of the organizational strengths and the organizing *history* that is crucial to motivating activists of the present and future. "As new generations struggle with the difficult tasks of organizing in a global and mobile labor market, the older workers who spoke their minds to me worried most about whether the lessons of the past would be lost."[19] Throughout the book, whether drawing from oral histories with men, women, or the younger generation of workers, Honey's attention to the historical context clarifies why these workers became involved in unionization efforts and how racism made their motivations and experiences distinct from white workers.

Despite the distinctive methodological approaches of each of these studies— Honey relies on oral histories; Amelang draws from autobiographical materials (broadly defined) from artisans in early modern Europe; and Passerini relies on autobiographical reflections, sessions with her analyst, and life histories with student activists—each points to the ways in which attention to both historical and individual dynamics, temporalities, and narratives illuminates human motivation. To further illustrate the importance of attention to interconnections between individual and historical frames in personal narrative analyses, we will now turn to two comparisons, each focusing on a pair of analyses of personal narrative evidence. The first pair of studies addresses the politics of sexual identities; the second pair addresses the social construction of mothering.

Subjectivities in Context: The Politics of Sexual Identities

The construction of gender and sexual identities is a rich arena for exploring the contribution of personal narrative analysis to the study of social action. During an initial phase, studies of gays and lesbians sought to bring to light the hidden history of social actors whose identities were often understood in categorical or essentialized terms. Recent analyses of sexual identity formation, however, have provided groundbreaking contributions to the reconceptualization and historicization of subjectivities and identity construction.[20] Among the large number of analytic studies that have appeared since the 1980s, sociologist R. W. Connell's *Masculinities* and historian Martin Duberman's *Stonewall* are particularly useful to discuss for our purposes here.

Connell draws from men's life histories that she elicited in several different late-twentieth-century Western social and institutional contexts such as gay communities, the environmental movement, and unemployed working-class youth to explore what she calls the "crisis tendencies" in power relations that threaten hegemonic masculinity.[21] In Connell's view, social spaces where the pressures for the construction of masculinity are high prove to be rich sites for unpacking the contradictions in hegemonic masculinity. Gay communities, in particular, are contradictory locations because patriarchal culture interprets gay men as lacking masculinity. Her chapter, "A Very Straight Gay Male," explores these tensions through the analysis of eight life histories of Australian gay men. Interestingly, the men interviewed in many ways resemble conventional straight men in their life trajectories and in their attitudes and expectations about gender. They had typical gender-conformist childhoods (they played football with their fathers), were often sexist and antifeminist ("I don't like extremisms of anything—the burn-bra thing sort of went over my head"), longed for committed long-term couple relationships, and were critical of men who openly flaunt their gayness. As Mark Richards, one of Connell's interviewees, says: "If you're a guy why don't you just act like a guy? You are not a female, don't act like one. That's a fairly strong point. And leather and all this other jazz, I just don't understand it I suppose. That's all there is to it. I am a very straight gay."[22] None of these men were involved in gay politics or expressed interest in social movement organizations. Connell argues that their conventional attitudes about gender and their lack of political involvement derive in part from their problematic engagement with hegemonic masculinity and from the stability of public institutional alternatives to it. In other words, because contemporary gay communities provide a space where they can be gay and be men, they do "not have to fight for their very existence as gay men, as earlier generations did."[23]

Part of what makes these life histories and their analysis compelling is Connell's insistence on agency, and ultimately, the choices these men make to become "very straight gays." Connell emphasizes the "agency involved in the journeying" and highlights change as a central theme in the life stories, in the "form of movement between milieus…The process of coming out, of establishing oneself as homosexual in a homophobic world, almost necessarily gives this structure to the narratives. The life-history is experienced as migration, as a journey from another place to where one now is."[24] For these men who grew up in small towns and rural communities with conventional childhoods, it is moving to the city that provides freedom for personal exploration. Furthermore, Connell rejects essentialist understandings of gay identity: In her argument these men don't "come out," but rather "come in" to an already constituted gay milieu. In other words, they establish their identities as gay men through their participation in an urban gay subculture.[25]

Although Connell makes this important claim, she provides little evidence about specific subcultural institutions in her analysis. In fact, once these eight men get to Sydney, she doesn't tell us much more about their lives, except in very general terms—"they experience gay sexuality as freedom, as something they really wanted to do."[26] In one life history, that of Alan Andrews, Connell mentions the man's first foray into the gay bar scene. However, we learn only that Alan found it to be a disappointing experience and had to learn to develop skills to find pleasure. Consequently, we don't know why this first encounter proved to be meaningful or formative to Alan or what happened to him afterward. Furthermore, though Connell provides some general historical context, "the rise of the gay and lesbian liberation movement," and mentions the institutionalization of gay subcultures and communities in the opening paragraphs of the chapter, her brief rendition homogenizes gay culture as if there were *one* gay community and subculture without any specificity, when in fact there are *many*.

Indeed, an important point of more recent scholarship in queer theory is its insistence on the diversity within the gay community, not only in terms of gender, race, and class but also in terms of sexual practices and understandings and presentations of the self.[27] Tremendous variety exists within gay communities in how gay men (and lesbians), to use sociologists Candace West and Don Zimmerman's phrase, "do gender."[28] Consider the performative differences between groups such as drag queens, transsexuals, leather guys, radical fairies, and butch and femme.[29] This opens up the question of how the men Connell interviewed become very straight gay men and not, for instance, drag queens. There is also a range of political activism within gay communities (related to issues such as HIV/AIDS, domestic partnership laws and benefits, decriminalization of sodomy laws, and hate crime legislation) and a spectrum of regional and national organizations, both progressive and liberal (e.g., Outfront Minnesota, the Human Rights Campaign) and more conservative (e.g., the Log Cabin Republicans). Given the range of possibilities, how did these eight straight gay men become apolitical while others did not? Because Connell provides little evidence about specific communities, institutions, and political organizations, and neglects to detail these men's participation in them, it is not possible to answer these questions. Connell argues that life histories can document "social structures, social movements and institutions" and that "life history methods always concern the making of social life through time. It is literally history."[30] The insistence that historical contexts and the institutions embedded within them matter is right on the mark, but the analysis must make these connections in concrete ways, in ways that sometimes push the analyst beyond the life story. Only then can we understand why and how context matters.

Martin Duberman's book *Stonewall* provides a vivid historical account of a group defined by their political activism—namely, participants in the Gay Liberation movement in the late 1960s and early 1970s in the United States—and of the historical moment that shaped their lives. In *Stonewall*, Duberman weaves together the life histories of two lesbians and four gay men who become political activists in the aftermath of the Stonewall riot in New York City in 1969. (The riot began when patrons at a gay bar resisted arrest in a police raid; the event marks the launching of the gay rights movement.) Duberman's choice of life history subjects reflects the diversity of gay communities, not only in terms of gender, but race (his interviewees are black, white, and Latino), political trajectories (some are more politically involved than others), and ways of doing gender (one is a straight-looking gay man, one is a drag queen, and another a butch lesbian). Duberman elicited a range of stories that speak from a variety of subjectivities and trajectories.

The life histories themselves are fascinating accounts of gender and sexual identity formation that effectively complicate theories of gender and heterosexual desire.[31] In childhood, both women—Karla Jay, a Jewish woman, and Yvonne Flowers, an African American woman—were gender rebels, impatient with traditional feminine roles. By early adulthood, they both begin to actively assert their lesbian identity. This assertion took form in an institutional context that is carefully specified. For example, Flowers's account suggests how the subculture of gay and lesbian bars provided an institutional terrain in which sexual identities could evolve in very specific ways. Describing her presentation of self in the lesbian bar scene in the late 1960s, Flowers says, "I cross-dressed primarily to take on the power of the other gender; and also to make a clear statement to women what my preference was and a clear statement to men that I was not available to them."[32] Personal rites of passage are carefully contextualized by Duberman's attention to historical detail. He investigates and describes the settings that were so critical to Flowers's evolving self-understanding. He moves from what Flowers has told him to what he has had to dig up about the settings and subcultures to which she refers:

> As Yvonne became increasingly comfortable with a lesbian identity, she continued to travel—much more than most—between several worlds that straddled racial and class divides. She spent at least as much time in the working-class bars and after-hours places of Harlem and Brooklyn as in the middle-class Greenwich Village clubs. A lesbian subculture seems to have developed earlier in Harlem than elsewhere, because blacks, knowing the pain of being treated as outsiders, had developed an attitude toward homosexuality relatively more tolerant than was characteristic of white heterosexual circles...Harlemites might ridicule stereotypic bulldaggers or drag queens, but in the twenties especially, bisexuality had a certain cachet in sophisticated circles.[33]

Mediating institutions are key sites of both identity formation and political organization. Duberman's account offers rich detail about the cultural and political institutions so important in the era of Stonewall. Stonewall not only brought lesbian and gay issues to national attention but also led to increased and diverse forms and sites of social movement organizing for these individuals.

> Yvonne…enrolled at New York University in Greenwich Village to complete her B.A. Billy, a gay male friend, took her on a tour of the Village clubs, and she quickly became a regular. She went occasionally to a few places on Eighth Street…but soon developed a fondness for Lenny's Hideaway and, somewhat later, the Grapevine, an interracial, upscale bar, just off Seventh Avenue, that had dancing and catered to both men and women.[34]

Karla Jay's "coming out" was made possible by her participation in the institutions of second-wave feminism—specifically within her consciousness raising group of the radical feminist collective Redstockings. But later, when Jay failed to get Redstockings to issue a sympathetic statement about the Stonewall riots, she decided to get involved in another organization, the Gay Liberation Front (GLF). Working with GLF, Jay felt:

> "like the religious fanatic who constantly searches for just the 'right' spiritual base—and is astounded to actually find it." Redstockings had come close, but GLF seemed to have the same devotion to social change, and without any attendant nervousness over lesbianism…Karla felt she had finally come home, and she plunged into GLF with all of her formidable energy.[35]

If the GLF became the emotional, social, and political space within which Jay defined her young adult identity, Duberman is careful to show that GLF did not provide the same sort of institutional home to all male homosexuals and lesbians. As an African American woman, Flowers approached GLF with more trepidation. "The absence of black faces confirmed her earlier sense that the gay movement had not succeeded in drawing—or perhaps had not even tried to draw—people of color. Yet at the same time, she was surprised to see at least a scattering of blacks present."[36] There were enough to keep her coming to meetings, but Flowers felt that the predominantly white gay movement did not understand racial issues. As a result, she and a number of other black lesbians eventually split off to form their own group, the Black Lesbian Counseling Collective, whose purpose was to "empower black lesbians to come out and organize."[37]

Duberman's attention to institutional and historical context and his inclusion of specific personal narrative evidence comparing the experiences of Karla Jay and Yvonne Flowers so thoroughly contextualizes these two women's stories that we are set up to understand how they came out of Stonewall and how it affected their lives. Readers can understand the role of specific institutions that they shaped and that in turn shaped their evolving self-understandings and actions. These specific identities, and the manner in which they provided grounding for motivated social action, cannot be fully understood without reference to the institutions and times in which they emerged. And to arrive at this level of understanding, Duberman had to attend to the specific historical contexts—the gay bars of Greenwich and the different ones in Harlem, the cultural history of responses to homosexuality in different class and racial communities, the social movement organizations through which gay identities were articulated—that played key roles in the lives he was seeking to understand. Both Duberman and Connell use personal narrative evidence to make significant contributions to the history and sociology of sexual identities; Duberman's study takes the additional step of locating the personal histories he explores within both a wider social-institutional context and a temporality of emergent GLBT (gay-lesbian-bisexual-transgender) politics.

Selves, Cultures, Histories: Gender and Mothering

Our second illustration of the importance of historical contextualization in personal narrative analysis draws upon two works that focus on gendered family dynamics and in particular on mothering. The gender and generational differences that structure family power relations are dimensions of critical theoretical significance. The two analyses we discuss here use personal narratives about socially marginalized mothers to explore family and gender relations in social and historical context. Both of these studies—Ruth Behar's *Translated Woman* and Carolyn Steedman's *Landscape for a Good Woman* (which we introduced in chapter 1)—are milestones in the arena of feminist personal narrative analysis; each makes significant feminist theoretical contributions concerning the reproduction of gender relations as well as rich empirical contributions. The point here, however, is to contrast the authors' approaches to interpreting and historicizing the personal narrative evidence.

Ruth Behar's book presents the life history of Esperanza as told in interviews with Behar, an anthropologist. Esperanza is a street peddler around sixty years old who lives on the fringes of society in a poverty-stricken region of rural Mexico.

Though Esperanza is marginalized economically, Behar's narrative highlights Esperanza as a strong, angry, and sometimes difficult woman who not only struggles to survive economically but also defies the conventional stereotypes of Mexican women as passive and subservient. Rather than submit to her husband's abusive behavior, Esperanza leaves him and supports her children on her own, thus defying the gendered strictures of the Catholicism that govern many dimensions of rural life.

What makes this account especially fruitful to feminist analysis is its complex understanding of one woman's motivations and agency in the face of economic and social marginalization. Throughout the narrative, Esperanza describes herself as full of *coraje* (rage). Time and time again, it is Esperanza's rage rather than any "self-interest" that propels her across the boundaries of traditional gendered norms. However, at other times in the narrative, Esperanza's rage serves to reproduce the very patriarchal structures she seeks to resist. For example, when discussing her daughter's sexual assault by her half-brother, Esperanza indicates that she suspects that she "may not have been totally innocent in the attack [and] beats her for good measure." As Behar suggests, "within a system of patriarchal law, women are always responsible for being abducted or raped."[38] Thus, in beating her daughter, Esperanza upholds masculinist norms about women's sexuality.

Esperanza's life story illuminates the complexity of women's agency under what sociologist Denise Kandiyoti has called "classic patriarchy,"—that is, a system that relegates formal authority to male household heads.[39] Esperanza is neither the passive subservient Mexican wife nor the "enlightened" feminist heroine of the story. Rather her rage enables her to resist patriarchal structures in some instances and reiterate its law in others. The narrative's focus on rage also highlights an understudied dimension of women's—specifically mothers'—motivations. Esperanza's rage shatters what feminist scholars Susan Contratto and Nancy Chodorow have called the "fantasy of the perfect mother"—a mother who lovingly and selflessly tends to the needs of her husband and children.[40]

Behar's study is effective in capturing the complexity of human agency, but less effective in historicizing it. The reader finds few clues in the narrative that place Esperanza's stories of her childhood, her adolescence, or her adulthood in historical time. Nor is there any allusion to her grappling with economic, political, or social changes that occurred in Mexico during her lifetime and shaped Esperanza's options or understandings. Most of the explicit conceptualization is left for the book's last chapter. Given the lack of historical specificity, the patriarchal structure that frames Esperanza's actions seems eternal, impervious to resistance or change. What emerges from the narrative is a story of a strong personality, but one seemingly isolated from history.

Carolyn Steedman's biographical/autobiographical study *Landscape for a Good Woman* is, in contrast, saturated with historical context. Steedman explores the position of her working-class mother and herself in a specific social and historical context—working-class and formerly working-class circles of twentieth-century Britain. Steedman offers us an interpretation of human agency that considerably complicates prevailing representations of the British working-class mother. In popular fictional narratives of working-class life in England and in much working-class history, "Mum" is usually seen as the heroic and self-sacrificing heart of her family. She is subservient to her husband and yet beloved—the family's emotional center.

Feminist revisionism has certainly undermined this image. For example, historian Ellen Ross's study of working-class motherhood in London has offered evidence of a far less subservient wife and mother who often engaged in legal and physical combat with her spouse to get what she felt was owed to her and her children.[41] But Steedman's pained portrait goes even beyond Ross's critique to offer a more starkly unsettling revision. Her own mother's "minimal mothering" was barely adequate to meet the threshold to which socialization and psychoanalytic theories have drawn attention—namely, mothering adequate enough so as to assure that daughters grow up with the desire and capacity to mother in turn. And the sources of Steedman's mother's inadequate mothering lay not so much in stark material deprivation as in her envy of the wealthy and her desire for fine things. Steedman's mother pursued her own desires, in stark contrast with the image of the self-sacrificing mother of legend. The things that she wanted—fine clothes, a New Look coat, a skirt made from yards and yards of fabric—she understood to be the ticket for a woman to "pass" for what, in class terms, she was not. In a classic reversal of the image of self-sacrifice, Steedman's mother even economized on her children's food, though not to the point of threatening her daughters' health, to save for the things that fulfilled her own desires.

Steedman eventually reveals that her mother had always been aggressive in pursuing what she wanted, in shaping her destiny with the few tools at her disposal. Once she had determined that the man who became Steedman's father would provide her with her best ticket out of the textile mill town life of her own mother and grandmother, she used a pregnancy to tie him to herself. Her children, from the start, were elements in her personal strategy for self-improvement. In contrast with the usual gender exchange postulated by anthropological theory, whereby women are "exchanged" by men, Steedman insists that her mother made her own bargain: She was "both bargain and bargainer."[42] Like Esperanza in Behar's *Translated Woman*, Steedman's mother has a strong will. The historical framework Steedman provides allows us to see what options were available to her mother and, given those options, what she chose to do to get what she wanted. We understand that however much an "individual" Steedman's mother was in her steadfast pursuit of the desires that motivated her, she was also a product of the historical possibilities of her time and situation.

Like Duberman, Steedman works to supply this historical context even while disclaiming the possibility of writing general "history." She claims rather to be telling stories from the working-class margins—stories about her life that her mother had told her "in bits and pieces throughout the fifties":

> something else has to be done with these bits and pieces, with all the tales that are told, in order to take them beyond the point of anecdote and into history...what follows in this book does not make a history (even though a great deal of historical material is presented). For a start, I simply do not know enough about many of the incidents described to explain the connections between them. I am unable to perform an act of historical explanation this way.

Despite this disclaimer, Steedman does write history albeit of a novel sort; she uses the work of historical contextualization to better understand her mother's life (and her own very different life). One poignant example is provided when Steedman describes a research trip north to investigate details of her mother's early life:

> As a teenage worker my mother had broken with a recently established tradition and on leaving school in 1927 didn't go into the [weaving] sheds. She lied to me though when, at about the age of eight, I asked her what she'd done, and she said she'd worked in an office, done clerical work. Ten years later...practising the accomplishments of the oral historian, I talked to my grandmother and she, puzzled, told me that Edna had never worked in any office, had in fact been apprenticed to a dry-cleaning firm that did tailoring and mending. On that same visit, the first since I was four, I found a reference written by the local doctor for my mother who, about 1930, applied for a job as a ward-maid at the local asylum, confirming that she was clean, strong, honest, and intelligent. I wept over that, of course, for a world where some people might doubt her—my—cleanliness. I didn't care much about the honesty, and I knew I was strong; but there are people everywhere waiting for you to slip up, to show signs of dirtiness and stupidity, so they can send you back where you belong.[43]

In this passage and others like it throughout the book, Steedman reconstructs elements of the story that her mother leaves out or misrepresents. These elements reveal important insights about the web of power relations and the set of cultural presumptions that growing up in a working-class mill town in early twentieth-century England entailed, a milieu from which her mother had sought to escape when she "cut herself off from the old working class by a process of migration, by retreat from the North to a southern county with my father, hiding secrets in South London's streets." Steedman knows that despite her mother's flight to a new life, she had "carried with her her childhood." The history of that childhood, and the changing contours of working-class childhood in twentieth-century England more broadly, form an important context for the interpretation of Steedman's mother's story.[44]

The Play of Historical Narratives within Personal Narratives

The focus of our discussion so far has been on the importance of reading and analyzing personal narratives within specific historical contexts. Here we will turn to a slightly different argument, moving from our discussion of the historical contextualization necessary for personal narrative analysis to a consideration of personal narratives as forms of circulation of historical narratives, or counter-narratives.

Historians have pointed to the relationship between historically specific forms of historical thinking and related understandings of social action and agency. In the context of Western history, so the argument goes, the period of the French Revolution and its aftermath saw the emergence not only of new notions of the self but also of a new understanding of history and the individual's relationship to the past: "the ability of contemporaries to conceive of themselves as historical products of specific periods opened the way for them to think of themselves as active agents."[45] Narrators may incorporate broader public or historical narratives into their life stories; they may utilize them in strategic ways; they may undermine or contradict them. In any case, alertness to the presence or absence of such narrative frameworks can produce provocative analytic results.

Anthropologist Vincent Crapanzano's *Waiting: The Whites of South Africa* provides an example of a case where narrators deploy historical narratives in their own stories, generally, as Crapanzano suggests, to strategic ends. The book examines the effects of apartheid as a set of rules and institutions from the perspective of those who benefited most: the English-speaking and Afrikaner-speaking whites of South Africa. Written and researched in the 1980s before apartheid was dismantled, the book offers profound insight into the understandings of the then-dominant classes and how they at once justified their racial privilege and made sense of racial inequality in the face of the world's disapproval.

In Crapanzano's analysis, these complex, multilayered life stories tell us not only how whites regarded others, but implicitly how they defined themselves in terms of these real or imagined others: "The Afrikaner who asserts that the English are hypocrites is implicitly declaring himself, the Afrikaner, a non-hypocrite. The white who says Coloureds have no sense of time is saying that he has a sense of time."[46] ("Coloured," under apartheid, was the official classification of all people deemed to be mixed racial heritage.) Crapanzano carefully contextualizes his interview evidence in terms of the history of the colonization of South Africa by the Dutch and the English as well as the consequences of the first and second Anglo-Boer War (1880, 1899–1902). He thus provides a cultural and historical framework for understanding the ongoing antipathy between the Afrikaners and the English, as well as of their shared disparagement of Coloureds and blacks, and their political deployment in the 1980s of widely circulating narratives that evoked and kept alive old historical resentments.

These life stories are not only informed by essentialist racial narratives; they are also linked to histories of national and religious identities. They are often grounded in accounts of the Boer Wars and each group's sense of their rightful belonging in South Africa. Moreover, Afrikaners situate *their* South Africa within a "symbolic geography" wherein Western Europe and the United States represent extreme cultures whose mistakes, they insist, they will not repeat. As members of the Dutch Reformed Church, Afrikaners speak of themselves as "God's chosen" (in opposition to the British) and see their role in South Africa both historically and contemporarily as one of establishing and maintaining "a new social order in which racial purity is guaranteed, as are harmonious relations between different racial and ethnic groups."[47]

The life stories are also constructed in response to yet another particular set of public narratives about South Africa as a racist society circulating internationally in the 1980s. During the era when Crapanzano was collecting the stories, the United States as well as many countries in Western Europe considered or deployed economic sanctions against South Africa to register their opposition to and condemnation of apartheid. In this context, whatever questions Crapanzano, an American, posed to his interviewees, their answer presumed that opposition to apartheid was his real interest. As one Afrikaner tells Crapanzano:

> "You killed off your Red Indians," he says. "Your Blacks are a minority. Ours are the majority. We're the minority"…"How can you condemn us for Soweto when you have the South Bronx"…He is shocked by miscegenation [in the United States], distressed by racial hatred

("We do not hate the Black man; we know his place"), and offended by those who condemn him without hearing him out. Above all, he is wounded by those, in America and in Europe, who know nothing about his country and who are surprised to learn there are white South Africans.[48]

A response to these international narratives about South Africa as a racist nation and his resentment for being condemned by those who do not understand is reflected by yet another white South African:

You people from overseas are always putting pressure on us to change. You Americans and your President Carter. Waldheim! [the former Austrian president] He's the worst of the lot...And the United Nations—it's a kaffir [derogatory Afrikaans term for blacks] organization. You don't understand. We have lived with the kaffirs. We fought against them, taught them, take care of their health, educate them, and uplift them. We want to change too and we are changing...but you can't go too fast. That's what you people from overseas don't understand...You talk about giving one man one vote. That's nonsense. It didn't work for the Coloured...When will *you* have a Black president?[49]

As Crapanzano's thoughtful analysis reveals, Afrikaner- and English-speaking white South Africans' personal stories are constructed within and against many other kinds of public narratives—including both nationalist narratives of racial difference and historical progression, and international condemnations. Beneath these, Crapanzano suggests, the central preoccupation and underlying feeling that emerges from the life stories is white South Africa's sense of "*waiting for something, anything, to happen*" (emphasis in original), signaled not only in their personal, racial, and political anxieties expressed in relation to the past but also in their fears about where they stand in relation to other nations in the 1980s and in the ominous future.[50]

Here Crapanzano provides an important model for analyses of historical memory. In an essay on the topic of research on historical memory, historian Peter Fritzsche maintains that much of the literature on collective memory is insufficiently critical of the construction of those memories: "The use of the idea of the collective myth obscures its own historical origins; it silences other social identities; and it misunderstands the opportunistic deployment of this idea by elites." Crapanzano's placement in political and ideological frameworks of the "collective memory" he encounters in South Africa provides an example of the critical sensibility that Fritzsche advocates.

Personally significant counternarratives—that is, self-narratives pitted *against* official or hegemonic narratives—can also figure in the construction of the subject positions from which personal narratives are told. In these cases, public historical narratives are not inscribed in personal stories but rather contradicted by them. The subject position is built, to some extent, around this contradiction. Such narratives also connect the historical and the personal, but in ways that create a tension between the two.

A good illustration of this sort of analysis is provided by historian Dorothee Wierling's work based on analysis of life history interviews conducted with members of the cohort of East Germans born in 1949.[51] Wierling demonstrates how these personal narratives undercut official public narratives in revealing ways. In particular, Wierling argues that the official history of the Nazi era in postwar East Germany that celebrated "anti-fascist heroes" and victims of "capitalist fascism" in the German Democratic Republic's (GDR) ritualized commemorations at the Buchenwald concentration camp was related in a very contradictory way to the more emotionally salient and private memories of GDR childhoods that came to the surface in life histories Wierling collected in the 1990s. These "49ers" even "remember" suffering that they were too young to "really" have experienced. Narrators recalled their early childhood identification with their parents (some of whom had been Nazis), remembering them more as the real "victims" of the war and postwar political and economic sufferings. Moreover, the inculcation of the official history through such rituals as required Buchenwald concentration camp visits—a component of the official coming-of-age ceremony in East Germany—sometimes backfired, generating fascination with violence rather than the intended identification with the victims. Wierling uses this subtle analysis of the interplay between personal narratives and public narratives to suggest the dynamics of what she terms the "return of the repressed" in the form of previously unspeakable shows of sympathy for or fascination with the Nazis that later resurfaced in East German neo-Nazism. As Wierling puts it, "In the GDR too, the past had many potentials."[52]

Peter Fritzsche also discusses this interplay between family memories and historical narratives in his essay on recent historical works on the history of memory in Europe. He is interested in a number of issues, including understanding how "the nation, in particular, can be usefully thought of as a memory system that enabled individuals to recognize their lives in nonrepeatable, historical time." He discusses several recent works that take a variety of approaches to the study of historical memory, all of which nonetheless see important connections between private memories and public commemorations of the past.[53] Fritzsche discusses the work of Jay Winter on forms of commemoration of French soldiers killed in World War I for example. According to Fritzsche, Winter's analysis suggests that for all of their prominence, the public commemorations were not the most significant. Instead, mourning:

> was not an official or state act, and it did not perform a state claim on private bodies…"that meaning was highly personal." The most poignant illustration of the private claims on the public was the massive disinterment of soldiers' bodies from battlefield cemeteries and their reburial in local graveyards. Only in France was reinterment permitted, and an astonishing 40 percent of the 700,000 identified bodies went back home at state expense. The dead were reburied as the sons of fathers and mothers, not of the Fatherland. The war was remembered, Winter concludes in a related article, "overwhelmingly as an event in family history."[54]

Fritzsche points out, however, that for all of the intimacy of the family mourning that Winter uncovers, "the argument is not conclusive because the sight of the dead did not automatically create a site of memory"—that is, family reburials involved private rituals but they were not simply an alternative form of historical commemoration. Behind and enabling the private family mourning there still lurked "the authority of 'social scripts,' which resisted innovation and routinely disallowed particular stories." That is, the French state, in subsidizing and enabling the acts of family mourning also influenced their ritual performance even in "private" and thus influenced their historical meaning.

To illuminate this point further, Fritzsche discusses a contrasting example where such social scripts and official support for private mourning was lacking—Catherine Merridale's work on remembrance of the victims of Stalinism in Soviet Russia—which provides "a superb illustration of the difficulty private memories had speaking for themselves and the ease with which they were contaminated by national projects of remembrance." According to Fritzsche:

> There is unquestionable poignancy about the "proscribed memories" of the Stalin era—"tales of arrest, disappearance, lost parents, orphans" that were "kept alive as family secrets, private narratives rehearsed in kitchens." But, Merridale argues, "family secrets" crumbled at the touch: not only did the state destroy photographs, burn letters and diaries, and make it dangerous for relatives to safeguard what had become state's evidence but in addition "personal grief had no wider framework, no mirror in which to observe itself." Although Merridale does not quite want to say it, potentially subversive memories of the Stalin years seem to have vanished easily without witnesses to give them credence or narratives to provide them structure. The implication of Merridale's research is that even the most traumatic personal memories had

difficulty finding terms of articulation when they were not spoken for by more embracing—and selective—national renditions.[55]

These studies reveal that even the intimate personal memories and rituals of mourning can be evoked, or repressed, by official narrative frameworks and institutions, especially, of course, in situations of war or atrocity or other forms of political contention where the stakes are high. Personal narrative analyses can sometimes recapture these processes through careful attention to the circulation or suppression of public narratives in personal stories.

This question of the construction and circulation of historical narratives in and through personal narratives is taken up in a most provocative fashion in Amitav Ghosh's *In an Antique Land: History in the Guise of a Traveler's Tale.* The book chronicles Ghosh's attempts to reconstruct the life history of a twelfth-century slave, "Bomma," who worked for a North African Jewish merchant named Ben Yiju who traveled as a trader between Tunisia and India. The book alternates between the twelfth century and Ghosh's own time in the late twentieth century, between chapters that write this long past history and chapters that analyze Ghosh's field notes and interviews with Egyptian villagers written during his dissertation research visits.

What initially captured Ghosh's imagination about this obscure slave's history is that Bomma, like Ghosh himself, was an Indian who spent time in Egypt. Although Ghosh travels to Egypt with a different purpose and in a different historical epoch, parallels among his alternating chapters make it clear that Ghosh, like Bomma, is a stranger in Egypt, an outsider whose nationality and religion mark him as different. As the Egyptian peasants ask Ghosh time and again: "Is it true what they say about you? That in your country they burn the dead?...is it true that you worship cows?" As Ghosh reveals, it is not possible for him to be unmoved by such queries; they inevitably evoke his childhood memories of riots between Muslims and Hindus that followed Partition in India.[56]

These vignettes from his own personal biography and from his fieldwork set the stage on which modern religious strife takes place between Muslims and Jews and between Hindus and Muslims. But in his historical research on the twelfth century, based on Ben Yiju's correspondence, Ghosh uncovers a past very different from his present, one where diverse peoples moved around and sometimes came together to work, to trade, and, even to live as families. (Indeed, the site where Ben Yiju's correspondence was discovered was on the grounds of a major Jewish synagogue in Cairo—a place of worship that seems anomalous today.) Ghosh finds for instance that Ben Yiju left Egypt to live in Mangalore, India, for seventeen years. Ben Yiju worked with a diverse network of associates in India: Muslim expatriates, Hindu Gujarati of the trading caste, and the Tulunad of the landowning caste as well as Jewish and Muslim merchants in Egypt. Ben Yiju marries an Indian woman in Mangalore, a slave girl named Ashu whom he grants manumission and who later accompanies him back to Egypt with their children.

This historical tale provokes parallels with the story set in the 1980s. The more fluid if not unproblematic identities of the older world have hardened in present-day encounters. In one of the most painful moments of his fieldwork, Ghosh is publicly humiliated in an open air village café by an older man who says contemptuously and loudly that the people of Ghosh's country "burn their dead." On this occasion Ghosh loses his temper and launches into a heated argument about his country that escalates into a debate about the military prowess of India and Egypt: "in our country, we've even had a nuclear explosion," Ghosh vehemently concludes. Later, he laments this encounter: "I felt myself a conspirator in the betrayal of history that had led me to Nashawy [in Egypt]; a witness to the extermination of a world of accommodations that I had believed to be still alive, and in some tiny measure, still retrievable."[57]

Ghosh does discover a residue of this past, however, a remnant of Ben Yiju's world, in an Egyptian village's annual festival at the tomb of a Jewish holy man whose followers still come from Israel every year to commemorate him. On the way to the train station, Ghosh asks his taxi driver to take him to this site, and when he and the driver finally arrive, they encounter armed guards and are subsequently taken to the police for questioning. As it turns out, because Ghosh is not Israeli, the police suspect that he may be a terrorist and are baffled by an Indian's interest in visiting the tomb of a holy Jewish man. As Ghosh writes:

> There was really nothing I could point to within his [the police officer's] world that might give credence to my story. The remains of the small intertwined histories of Indian and Egyptian, Muslim and Jewish, Hindu and Muslim had been partitioned long ago. Nothing remained in Egypt to challenge his disbelief…I had been straddling a border unaware that the writing of History had predicated its own self-fulfillment.[58]

The borders drawn around nation-states and the impositions of modern categories and conflicts have all but erased historical memories of a different time, when connections among the religious worlds of Muslims, Jews, and Hindus, while hardly smooth, were nevertheless routine.

Ghosh's analysis is meticulous in its attention to the specific contexts of the parallel historical narratives. But even more innovatively, it also calls attention to the construction and circulation of historical narratives in his own life story in the present and in the personal narratives he collected during his field research. Throughout the book, Ghosh struggles to incorporate and to resist the analytical categories and stories he has inherited and to find another, more usable, past. As the book's subtitle, *History in the Guise of a Traveler's Tale*, suggests, in traveling to other times and places we are always putting together stories about ourselves and others—trying to make sense of our contemporary world and of the past. Ghosh's traveler's tale reconstructs a story about the lives of Ben Yiju and Bomma that in turn historicizes his contemporary narratives; he also demonstrates how he, as a social scientist, reconstructed it within the constraints of existing records, sources, and histories (not of his own making).

Embedded in Historical Context but Not Reducible to It

In the last section, we moved from a discussion of personal narrative analysis operating within historical frames to personal narrative analysis as a means of contributing to or criticizing historical frames, or even as a source of historical counternarratives. Before we turn, in chapter 3, to a discussion of various genres of personal narrative evidence, it is important to make one last point about historical context that returns to and echoes our arguments in chapter 1. Alertness to the role of historical and institutional context is critical to the effective analysis of personal narratives, but it is not sufficient. To put our point bluntly: Individuals are shaped by their contexts but never reducible to them.

This point is made explicitly, for example, by Austrian historian Norbert Ortmayr in his book *Knechte* (farmhands). The book has two parts. The first section offers the reader three edited autobiographies, all of them written by men who were born around the closing years of World War I and served as farm servants throughout their adolescence and young adulthood.[59] The second section is a detailed sketch of the sociohistorical context that shaped these servants' lives. We learn, for example, about how family structure and landholding patterns as well as ecotype and farm size influenced the number of servants in any given locality and also the quality of their lives. Ortmayr demonstrates that two different agrarian regimes produced the unusually high proportions of farm servants that characterized Austrian rural society until the late twentieth century. Both the older Alpine herding systems and the newer market-oriented large grain farms of the lower altitudes met labor demand through hired live-in male and female servants rather than by either full-wage laborers or family labor. We also begin to understand why the illegitimate status of two of the narrators was so characteristic of the agrarian class system in which they lived. Ortmayr describes the farm labor system as precluding landless young people from marrying while throwing them together as farm servants in relatively unsupervised settings free from control or protection.

The continual change of employers, as disruptive as it was in the lives of younger servants, also takes on new meaning as we learn about its role in the prevailing system of agrarian social relations. Servants could negotiate a new deal for themselves every year or two and could to some extent use the occasion to refuse to renew a contract or even to spread the word about a male employer's brutality or a wife's stinginess with the food. Thus, despite the bleakness of the stories the servants tell, it becomes clear that their descriptions of individual decisions to move from farm to farm can indeed be read as strategic actions, as agency.

While carefully contextualizing the stories, Ortmayr nevertheless resists the temptation to "explain" them completely through context. The individual variations in the emotional content, motivations, and subsequent life opportunities of the three men serve as a reminder that no fate can be read simply from social position. The stories present interesting differences despite their tracking of men's lives begun in similar positions. Richard Pucher's is the fullest and also the bleakest rendition of the abuse that was often the servant's fate. For the illegitimate and abandoned Leopold Sekora, on the other hand, the painful pursuit of an explanation for his mother's actions is but an intermittent motif in a generally untroubled recounting of his adventures. And Felix Nobäuer—the legitimate child of a religious family—offers yet another version of what it meant to live the servant's life in rural Austria in the interwar era. As Ortmayr so aptly observes, all three may have been "dealt the same hand"—and not a very good one—in their young lives, but each played that hand in a different way that cannot be explained by context alone.

Social and historical contextualization is crucial for understanding lives. Still, as Ortmayr insists, the individuality of each narrator is not fully explained by it. Bonnie Smith makes a similar point in her introduction to *Confessions of a Concierge: Madame Lucie's History of Twentieth-Century France:* "Madame Lucie's life poses as many questions as it answers because of the intractable nature of human experience; her life demonstrates why historical writing can never be exclusively theoretical, why the questions "who" and "how" must constantly be reopened. Like Mme Lucie, each individual can at any moment mess up all theory or disturb our answers." Madame Lucie was the concierge in the apartment building where Smith lived when she was doing research in Paris for a book on the history of bourgeois women: "Madame Lucie…was as far removed from my historical agenda as possible. Her narrative demands on my time interrupted the progress of my other work, and the meanings she suggested were at that particular moment largely gratuitous—the product not of the public and analytic history I practiced but of the private stage on which she played out her life." In their conversations, Madame Lucie seduced Smith with her stories about her past and thus asserted herself as a life story narrator. But she was not one, like those of many other oral history projects, chosen because she represented something in terms of the analyst's historical frame. Instead, she was always something of an enigma, "a bit of historical serendipity, totally non-utilitarian as, in a way, all life is; as, in a way, all history is."[60] Madame Lucie's story in some respects demonstrated familiar social-historical patterns of twentieth-century Parisian and French life (for example, the occupation of concierge as a path to assimilation and upward mobility for immigrants from the provinces). Still, Madame Lucie's uniqueness kept asserting itself through her story, to the extent that it challenged Smith's comfort with generalization. The subtitle of Smith's work, *Madame Lucie's History of Twentieth-Century France,* reflects this discomfort. In short, the *Knechte* and Madame Lucie are individuals with distinctive subjectivities even while they live their respective histories. The arguments we have made in this chapter must be read in connection with that of chapter 1. The value of personal narrative analyses lies in their potential to see people and their actions as both individual and social, and to understand human lives as governed simultaneously according to the dynamics and temporalities of the individual life course and of collective histories.

3

THE FORMS OF TELLING
AND RETELLING LIVES

In a 2001 cartoon, Zippy the Pinhead articulates a view about the connection between literary plots and life:

> [Zippy]: Claude! Tolstoy says there are only two stories: "Someone goes on a journey" and "A stranger comes to town"!
>
> [Claude]: Oh yeh? That's…uh…fascinatin'…
>
> [Claude]: Well, I'm headin' down to th' Pep Boys store…Indy 500 winner Juan Montoya's gonna be there signin' special cans of STP Engine Flush!
>
> [Zippy]: The end!![1]

Here, Zippy reduces plot to an exaggerated minimum, of course, but the point remains. The circulation of plotted stories reflects and structures how people talk about their lives. Just as no life story is disconnected from its social and historical context, we argue in this chapter that the ways in which life stories are told are connected to available genres, tropes, and plots. Every form of telling a life story draws on rules and expectations about writing and storytelling, literary conventions, rhetorical strategies, and ideas of what is interesting or important to readers and listeners. The specific shape and content of any life story are marked by these cultural norms and by the models for personal narratives that prevail at the time and place of its telling.[2] Part of the job of historians and social scientists interested in life stories is to be attuned to questions about the narrative forms and conventions through which stories unfold and are presented.

Such considerations, once regarded as the domain of literature, are increasingly apparent in social-scientific readings of personal narratives as well. While constraints of genre seem perhaps most applicable to analyses of more formal texts like autobiographies, they also pertain to other forms of personal narrative. The most popular forms of personal narrative evidence among social scientists—namely, elicited life stories or in-depth interviews—typically follow interview schedules or protocols written by the researcher. But even the narratives produced under such formal control cannot be presumed to be innocent of generic influences. Within whatever range of freedom the interview format allows, narrators of life stories will shape what they tell by drawing on their understandings about what lives and life stories are supposed to be like.

Nevertheless, each form of personal narrative evidence—oral histories and life history interviews elicited by researchers, memoirs and autobiographies, and such forms as letters, diaries, and journals—raises somewhat different formal considerations, so we discuss each of them separately. Our focus will be on the literary influences that shape personal narratives as told or written by narrators, rather than on the literary influences that affect the analyst's "write-up" of the personal narrative evidence. Here, the focus is on the narratives themselves, and we argue that the most effective analyses of personal narratives pay close attention to how specific genres and their rhetorical modes shape the life stories that compose the personal narrative evidence under consideration. In other words, *what are the particular conventions for each genre to which the analyst needs to be attentive?* What are its rules, its temporal constraints, and its explicit or implicit narrative logic? What generic considerations or models shape the choices narrators make in selecting events and details when they tell their stories? And who is their presumed audience? The particular forms that life histories, autobiographies, diaries, or letters take, the audience for whom narrators are writing (or speaking), and the conditions of their production inevitably shape the structure of an account, what is included in the text, and what is not. To analyze personal narrative sources effectively, analysts must not only carefully consider these questions, but explicate as fully as necessary how they are reading their sources in light of these issues. As we will demonstrate, analysts who neglect these considerations often miss the nuances and complexity of the sources upon which they draw.

In the final section of the chapter, we examine *hybrid forms* of personal narrative analysis—that is, analyses that depend on considerable autobiographical material about the analyst. In contrast with the genres we discuss elsewhere in the chapter, these studies are at once a particular generic form and a method of analysis. What makes them distinctive is that the author serves the double role of narrator and analyst. Our discussion of these forms thus serves as a bridge between the focus on genre in this chapter and our discussion of the relationship between narrator and analyst in chapter 4.

Oral Life Histories and Life History Interviews

We begin our discussion of genre with oral life histories and interviews because these are the predominant forms of personal narrative evidence employed in social science research and among historians who use personal narrative evidence. As alert oral historians and ethnographers have noted, oral forms of self-narrative follow their own particular logics, conventions, and rhythms that, once noticed, can serve as a guide to interpretation. Sometimes the significance of an event or memory emerges from the manner in which it is related, the style, cadence, or "velocity," to use Alessandro Portelli's term, "the ratio between the duration of the events described and the duration of the narration."[3] Events or developments that are exaggerated are likely either of special significance to the narrator or masking something s/he prefers the listener not to notice or question. Oral narratives share these features with adjacent oral cultural forms such as folktales, fictional models, proverbs, and stereotypes—which often supply the literary motifs around which self-narratives are organized and the facts of a life are plotted.

Many oral historians and interviewers have noted similar phenomena; that is, that in eliciting facts about people's lives they get answers that are shaped in terms of the cultural conventions of storytelling, often reflecting the sharing, telling, and retelling of self-narratives in many settings and over a lifetime.[4] To discuss the implications of the role that notions, models, and social and cultural practices of storytelling play in how people talk about their lives in interviews, we turn to the work of historians Luisa Passerini and Alessandro Portelli and anthropologist Ruth Behar.[5]

Luisa Passerini, in *Fascism in Popular Memory: The Cultural Experience of the Turin Working Class,* writes about the themes used by socialist women she interviewed to portray themselves:

> The self-representations of the subjects given in answer to our questions follow recurrent narrative forms…"Memory of self" does not, then, refer to the psychological aspects that are at the root of self-representations… Instead it refers to the transmission and elaboration of stories handed down and kept alive through small-scale social networks—stories which can be adapted every so often in a variety of social interactions, including the interview…the personal memory combines with the collective

memory, and individual mythology turns into a tradition shared by a family, a circle of friends or a political group.[6]

For example, Maddalena Bertagna, born in Turin in 1884, described herself "as the person who breaks the rules." Bertagna's story involves a strong sense of membership in her family and closeness with her father in particular. Bertagna claimed, "We were born Socialists. We were born Socialists! My dad was already one," which Passerini sees as demonstrating "links between family, love and political relationships." Another working-class woman, Anna Bonivardi, born in 1904, remembers that at sixteen she participated in strikes and demonstrations: "My dad taught me that way...we were already born like that." Another woman explained "why she always felt herself to be anti-fascist: 'Well, you see, my dad was already that way. I was born on May first and so I was a Socialist from birth'"[7]

Passerini notes that these women's characterizations of themselves as a "born rebel" or the "rebel girl" suggests a connection that goes back generations. "If, on the one hand," Passerini argues, "autobiographical material and family traditions are selected out of the necessity to legitimize new forms of behavior, on the other hand, they echo storytelling conventions." Passerini identifies several different storytelling traditions in the life history narratives she collected: "We were born Socialists," irreverence, reference to women's traditions, choosing poverty, and social mobility, among others. What is notable in Passerini's discussion of narratives of self-representation is their particular historicity, the gradual shift in the story themes to adapt to the emergence of communism or fascism in Turin, historical experiences through which the older narrators had lived. Passerini's familiarity with these traditions suggests that analyzing narratives of the self cannot be adequately done from some abstract or formulaic template. Individual life histories are both composed with reference to particular cultural formulas and responses to ongoing historical events.[8]

Alessandro Portelli, in interpreting the oral histories he collected in his hometown of Terni, Italy, insists on reminding his readers of their narrators' cultural contexts. "An oral speech act," Portelli argues, "to a higher degree than a written one, is implicitly social, because it requires an audience...A more explicit social element is the presence of motifs, theme, and patterns of plot and performance which can be compared with other stories told in the same environment."[9] The oral and narrative characteristics of the stories as well as their connections with previous storytelling experiences, adjacent genres, and audience expectation all figure into Portelli's discussions. In analyzing a life history interview with Valèro Peppoloni, the "Best Garbage Man in Town," for example, Portelli notes that:

> The story...has a very tight and recognizable structure. Though it was a long, spontaneous interview, Peppoloni never lost control of the

pattern. He had certainly thought about this for a long time, and had told his stories over and over…but never as a coherent whole, at one sitting. The interview gave him a chance to connect coherently a repertoire of stories that had been told many times, but separately.[10]

Portelli then discusses one exemplary recurring motif—a boyhood story of stealing fruit—that appears in Peppoloni's account as well as in others Portelli collected. Portelli compares Peppoloni's tale of stealing apricots with similar stories told by two other narrators (Iginio Vella and Alvaro Valsenti) because the comparison tells us "how each narrator connects [such stories] with his own personal growth":

> Vella's is the tale of a youthful escapade: you haven't been a child unless you've stolen fruit at least once…On the other hand, Peppoloni's stripping of the apricot tree…prepares his future awareness of social injustice which, at this stage, is still implicit…Finally, Valsenti also describes himself at length as an unruly, daring, working-class street urchin…However, he places the habit of stealing fruit in a broader context of class relationships symbolized by his topography…making a statement about the invasion of the urban center and institutional space by working-class "ghetto" kids.[11]

Portelli's careful discussion of literary motifs that circulate in local oral culture allows him to recognize both a shared symbolic structure and individual variations of it from story to story, as well as special characteristics stemming from the story's orality.

Esperanza, the subject of Ruth Behar's *Translated Woman* discussed in chapter 2 also presented a "storied self" par excellence, one that builds on her location in a very particular local culture of stories. Behar was fascinated by Esperanza's capacity as a storyteller; she noted that many anthropological accounts of Latin Americans have focused on political economy, but none approached it through women's stories. The term she and Esperanza use—*historias*—has the ambiguous double meaning of *stories* and *histories*. Esperanza's fascination with stories, and her skill at interweaving old stories with her life story, eventually moved to the center of Behar's "translation," pushing other analytic considerations to the side: "Her story suggests that a woman from the margins of the other America can also be a thinker, a cosmologist, a storyteller, or even a novelist working within that embedded literary tradition which, in the absence of schooling and access to the means of production, consists of the living stories that she and her mother have lived and told, and the stories that her daughters have yet to live and tell."[12] Esperanza's sense of self and her self-narrative were inseparable from her practices as a storyteller. Behar's analytic role, defined as translator, brings not just or primarily Esperanza's literal words, but also her culture and the particular tradition of storied selves from which Esperanza described her life, to Behar's world of Western social science.

The influence of culturally specific storylines on how people talk about their own lives and respond to interview questions about their life histories, even in highly literate cultures, is well illustrated by the example of the coming-out stories that have been the focus of several recent sociological and historical studies.[13] In *Masculinities,* also introduced in the previous chapter, sociologist R. W. Connell discusses this plot's form and its variations:

> Alan offers a classic coming-out story passing through six stages. *Prehistory:* growing up in a country town; a relaxed, conservative family; no particular tensions. *Preparation:* adolescent uncertainties—liking to be with girls, but not getting a girlfriend; sex play with a boy friend, who backs off. *Contact:* aged 19, he stumbles across a beat (a venue for semi-public encounters, like the American "tea-room") and has sex with men. Then he goes looking for beats, gets better at it, has a "wonderful" sex-laden beach holiday. *Acknowledgment:* aged twenty, "I finally came to the conclusion I was gay, and went to my first gay dance." *Immersion:* does the bars under his own steam, has multiple relationships. *Consolidation:* aged 22, meets Mr Right, and settles into a couple relationship; gets more gay male friends, joins some gay organizations and comes out to his parents.[14]

Connell goes on to argue, however, that despite general awareness among gay men of these conventions, despite even their presumptions that they had coming-out stories to tell, events in their own lives proved messier. Connell's point is not just that there is always a distance between a generic model and a particular example, but more so that the analyst needs to identify where the generic models don't fit and therefore produce problems in the telling, setbacks and uncertainties that prevent the plot from moving along as it is supposed to. Connell's aim is to underscore the social elements that shape the stories and to demonstrate that "coming-out" stories are simultaneously individual stories and stories of finding a particular subculture and its institutions that encourage the stories to be told. The continued support and reinforcement of the story by these institutions is necessary to keep the storyline, and the identity, straight (well, actually, gay).

Acknowledging key cultural elements and conventions that affect the life stories people tell, while also identifying fissures and inconsistencies in their stories, are key methodological devices used elsewhere as well; for example, in the analyses of lesbian life stories by sociologist Arlene Stein and anthropologist Kath Weston.[15] For Stein, such stories circulate because they have played an important role in the politics of sexual identity. According to Weston, however, such stories, while politically significant, are inherently unstable. Many lesbian life stories, she suggests, are motivated by the idea that "the more consistent, the more 'natural,' the more authentic, the more convincing. Stories about growing up gendered can help her claim a timeless sexual identity as a dyed-in-the-wool lesbian." But, Weston goes on to ponder, "Could it be that childhood memories chronicle something more complex than simply 'crossing' between two fixed gender positions, or staying put?"[16]

The subcultural circulation of coming-out stories may be unusually influential in negotiations of gay and lesbian subjectivities and political identities. Analysis of them in these studies highlights connections between the models embedded in stories in circulation and the ways people think, and then talk about, their individual lives. Coming-out stories are perhaps more specific to a particular social group than other plot devices in contemporary North American culture, but the more general point is well made by them.[17] The plots that circulate—in fictional and nonfictional forms—and the ways people tell stories about their lives in particular institutional or political contexts, influence the life stories they tell in more formal interview situations as well. In collecting and analyzing life histories, it is important for analysts to be aware of both the standard plots and recurrent motifs in circulation, and also the ways in which each teller departs from or dismisses them, even while using them, or having used them, to think with. Before moving on to other genres of personal narrative, we should note that one of the main features that distinguishes oral histories and interviews from most other forms of personal narrative evidence is the close involvement of the analyst in its production and the complex relationship between the narrator and the analyst. This dimension will be addressed in chapter 4.

Autobiographies and Memoirs

As a written genre, autobiography is also liable to the influence of literary conventions and constraints. As we noted in chapter 1, histories of autobiography have also linked this form of personal narrative with historically changing and culturally specific notions of the self.[18] Autobiography is therefore a particularly interesting form of narrative for the study of subjectivity, meaning, motivation, and individual agency. But any study that uses autobiographies for purposes of social-scientific or historical analysis needs to recognize their social, cultural, and historical specificity, and the influence on them of literary conventions.

In standard histories of the genre of autobiography, writers such as Rousseau and Goethe are often cited as influential models; they are seen not merely as creative individuals, but in writing an autobiography as emblematic figures giving literary form to a new kind of social consciousness. Despite the fact that neither of these two influential autobiographers lived a typically middle-class life, the Western autobiographical form they helped to pioneer resonated with emergent European bourgeois masculinist notions of agency. They did not tell their stories in the same way or with the same emphases. For example, Goethe was far more interested than Rousseau in historicizing his own life, in describing in detail the spatial and cultural settings of his youth; Rousseau, conversely, focused more relentlessly on his own subjectivity. But certain key impulses were shared. By describing their developmental process of becoming an individual (with attention to youth and education in shaping personality), by presuming this kind of a story as worth telling for the insights it provided about motivation and subjectivity, and by deliberately attempting to shape how "the truth" of one's life is interpreted by contemporaries and by later generations (through an imagined audience), the two authors and the genre they helped to shape became part of the broader historical creation of the Western bourgeois personality.[19] Their widely circulated autobiographies left their stamp on the genre and influenced readers and writers far beyond their immediate times and milieus.

Historians and theorists of Western autobiography point to generic characteristics that have come to define this genre of personal narrative and its evolution over time. Typically, theorists of autobiography see it as a genre that tells a verifiable personal story written retrospectively from a single moment in time about the incidents of life that the author deems important for the reader to understand his or her motivations and actions. Theorists often draw a useful distinction between autobiography and memoir along the lines of temporal depth and narrative aim. Whereas a *memoir* can be limited to describing or explaining a particular phase of a life or a limited range of (often public) activities—for example, diplomatic ventures or theatrical performances—the *autobiography* ranges more widely thematically and temporally to fulfill its promise to explain the development of a personality.[20]

Of course genres are flexible and mutable, and writers of autobiography, like oral storytellers, are always negotiating between generic models and their own unique opus. Still, these generic characteristics set up writers to produce and readers to expect certain kinds of texts, containing specific kinds of truth claims, through what French sociologist and theorist of autobiography Philippe Lejeune so provocatively has characterized as "the autobiographical pact":

> I of course became aware of the fact that autobiography could not merely be defined by its form (a narrative) or by its content (a life), for fiction could imitate both, but by an act, which made it utterly different

from fiction, and that act is the commitment of a real person to speak of himself or herself truthfully. This is what I called the "autobiographical pact"…An autobiography is not a text in which one speaks the truth about oneself, but a text in which a real person says that he or she is speaking the truth about himself or herself.[21]

Moreover, as historian Peter Fritzsche points out in his discussion of literary theory of autobiography (here drawing on the work of James Olney), autobiography is a self-conscious form of narration; it is " 'a second reading of experience' which is 'truer than the first because it adds to experience itself consciousness of it.'" However, Fritzsche continues, its indirect relationship to experience is revealed through its apparently narrative character since "narratives, whether or not they are written down, are constructed; they require repeated readjustments over time, and thus they incorporate the memory of remembering and with it the knowledge of the partial, unstable, and tendentious nature of narrative."[22]

Finally, literary studies of autobiography also point to changing models that inform their narratives. In her history of American autobiography, Diane Bjorklund argues that four ideal-typical models of the self have structured changing forms of autobiographical self-representation in the United States: tales of religious conversion, self-development, the psychological self, and the sociological self.[23] Each of the models of the self embedded in autobiography emerges in historically specific contexts and affects how individuals see themselves as actors and subjects in their autobiographical writings. While the specifics change in different cultural or historical settings, the general point is significant: Autobiographers typically write their life stories within the framework of one or more general plotlines drawn from among the limited number of plausible ones available in circulation.

These characteristics of the genre of autobiography (or memoir) must be considered in interpreting them as evidence. Social-scientific and historical analyses of written autobiographies are relatively rare compared to analyses of oral histories and life history interviews.[24] Nevertheless, such analyses do reveal possibilities and pitfalls that are thrown into relief in comparison with those of oral life histories and interviews discussed above.

James Amelang's *The Flight of Icarus,* introduced in chapter 2, offers a good example of the role of the generic qualities of autobiography in a historical analysis based on these sorts of texts. As we have already mentioned, Amelang notes the play of particular metaphors of the self in the autobiographical writings of early modern European artisans—metaphors drawn from other cultural forms through which they thought about their lives. In discussing the Icarus myth and other classical references, Amelang shows how these stories crossed back and forth between elite and popular culture, although sometimes with different valences. These references to "high culture" demonstrate that early modern European artisan authors prided themselves on their learning and felt the need to display it in their self-narratives and the models they chose to emulate. Their autobiographical writings were often driven not just by the desire to be remembered by familial descendants and in their own occupational milieu but also by the need to "witness" more publicly a claim to a place in history, a way of "inscribing, and ensuring, the author's sense of value, of being worth something."[25]

The point here is that to properly read and analyze documents such as artisan autobiographies, it is important to recognize the literary and cultural, as well as the social, universe in which they were written and the literary models that inform them. Amelang argues that the adoption of particular literary forms, styles, and allusions was for highly literate artisans part of their project of self-creation and self-expression, a component of artisan identity in this era that would be overlooked by historians inattentive to form. One might wish that Amelang had taken his point a step further. His analysis falls short at times in its insufficient attention to how *particular* genres of what he lumps together as "autobiographical writings" (memoir, personal chronicle, or family chronicle) might be differentiated from one another, given their distinctive implications regarding temporality and audience.[26] There are moments in the analysis when attention to the differences between, for example, family record books and chronicles would have paid off, since the former are the result of periodic entries into a ledger and the latter are generally constructed retrospectively at a particular moment in time. Nevertheless, Amelang's painstaking research into the social and cultural world of early modern artisan autobiographers hammers home the connections among generic qualities of self-narrative, social positionality, self-understanding, and historical agency.

Another empirically rich historical study of European autobiography is the analysis by historian Gunilla-Friederike Budde of around four hundred late-nineteenth-century German and English middle-class autobiographies and other personal narratives.[27] Budde's work is careful and, at times, provocative. One ingenious methodological possibility that she pursues with striking results is the comparison of a small number of girls' *adolescent journals* with *autobiographical accounts of adolescence* written by middle-aged women (indeed, in several cases, by the same authors). She finds a significant difference in the representation of the years between school leaving and marriage in these two different genres of personal narrative. The autobiographies typically reconstruct a life story emphasizing the fulfillment of a life centered on child rearing and the normative bourgeois gender division of labor. The journals, in contrast, track a psychic journey often taking girls between school and motherhood from a critical refusal to adopt the lives of their mothers to an anxious fear of their inability to live up to that pre-scribed role. These two genres of personal narrative caught women at different points in the life course and also reflected the diverse emphases and selectivity of contrasting genres—the more immediate and future-looking journal attests to a different reality from the backward looking and self-justifying autobiography. It needs also to be noted that the possibility of such an explicit cross-generic com-parison is rare, especially for historical populations. All written forms of personal narrative are far more common for educated classes than for others; journals, in particular, tend to be the product of relatively leisured daily lives.

There is plenty of food for thought in these and many other areas that Budde's book explores. In comparison with Amelang's alertness to the literary qualities of the autobiographical writings he studies, however, in Budde's analysis there are only occasional asides addressing how the images that emerge have been shaped by the literary nature of the sources. The interesting strategy of using cross-national comparative evidence to highlight and assess what is and isn't peculiarly German or English about what is reported makes much sense. Still, it is not always easy to sort out milieu or national differences from differences stemming from the variant national histories and characteristics of the autobio-graphical genre itself. A closer discussion of the sources, their selectivity, and the auspices, forms, and motives of autobiography in the two countries and over the time period during which the texts were produced would have added a crucial dimension to the analysis. Budde's use of these sources in the absence of such a discussion raises some questions about how they are best to be read and for which purposes they are the most analytically useful. For example, Budde points to a contrast between German male autobiographers' complaints about the stark discipline and rigid curriculum of their secondary schools versus English male authors' complaints, which are mainly about their forced separation from their families. She hints at the possibility that, beyond the institutional differences underlying these portrayals, there were also influences stemming from the liter-ary models of and political discourses about schooling that may have shaped how these years were recalled and written. Nevertheless, without closer attention to how individual texts operated in these particular political cultural contexts, the analysis falls short of its full potential.

An important form of autobiographical writing from the point of view of his-torical analysis and among interdisciplinary scholars in African American studies and other fields is the *slave narrative*.[28] Like the other forms of autobiography we have discussed, slave narratives were shaped by the particular rules and con-ventions of their context. They have also provoked contentious methodological debates.[29] A thoughtful and pertinent analysis of some of these texts is provided by historian Walter Johnson in his book *Soul by Soul: Life Inside the Antebellum Slave Market*.[30] He uses slave narratives along with other sources (such as letters from slave owners, accounts written by visitors, Acts of Sale, traders' slave records, advertisements, and legal dockets) to examine the commodification of slaves from the perspectives of different participants in the process: slaves, slaveholders, and visitors to the South.

What makes Johnson's book especially innovative is his drawing on multiple perspectives through which to read these various sources with an intent "to assess their asymmetric information, expectations, and power, to search out their mutual misunderstandings and calculated misrepresentations, to investigate what each has at stake and how each tried to shape the outcome."[31] In his discussion of the slave narratives, Johnson is careful to emphasize the ways this particular genre was shaped by the conditions of its production, specifically that of southern slavery and organized antislavery. On the one hand, slave narratives are "incomplete accounts" because they are written by those who escaped slavery and not those who remained enslaved. On the other, ex-slave narrators depended on white northern abolitionists who had access to editors and publishers who, in turn, had their own agendas and philosophies to pursue. "'Give us the facts,' Frederick Douglass was told, 'we will take care of the philosophy'"[32] As Johnson reminds us, the imposition of this northern abolitionist philosophy along with assumptions about what a moralistic bourgeois audience might want to read often supplied a narrative of "ideal slaves" as "saved souls," one that glossed over the anger, dissimulation, suffering, and brutality of actual slaves' lives.

Further, echoing Portelli's approach to oral history, Johnson makes clear from the outset that he does not intend to read these autobiographical accounts as unmediated or transparent, but reads them instead for what he terms "symbolic truths." He observes:

> Some incidents appear so often that it seems certain they are stock figures drawn from the reading of other narratives rather than actual experiences. These include the idea that illiterate slaves holding books for the first time would put them next to their ears to hear them talk, or that an escapee seeing a steamboat or a train would run away, thinking it was the devil. But these stock figures have a truth of their own to tell: they gesture at the way the world looked to people whose access to information and technology was limited by their owners and the threat of violence. Whether or not every one of these stories was true (and we know some were), collectively they tell a truth about people forced by their slavery into a doubled relations with their bodies and their children.[33]

Johnson's careful reading of these documents, his attention to the limitations of the slave narrative genre, and his understanding of the "symbolic truth" contained therein provide a useful model for the analysis of "dubious" forms like autobiography.

Letters, Diaries, and Journals

The intermittent forms of personal narrative—letters, diaries, journals, and the like—have not been of central interest in our discussions in this book for several reasons. First, they have been far less used in social-scientific and historical work than the other forms of personal narratives we have been emphasizing. Second, and more important, since they focus on the events of a single day at a time (or other relatively short periods), they typically lack the temporal framing based in a self-reflective and retrospective narrative stance that we find most useful for the analysis of socially embedded subjectivity and agency. In comparison with other forms of personal narrative, letters (and to some extent diaries) have what historian Liz Stanley has called "a flies in amber quality"; that is:

> Letters are strongly marked by their quotidian present...Letters also do things with and to time: when a letter is read, its reader of course knows that time has passed and the "moment" of its writing has gone; but at the same time, the present tense of the letter recurs—or rather occurs—not only in its first reading but subsequent ones too. Letters thereby share some of the temporal complexities of photographs: they not only hold memory but also always represent the moment of their production.[34]

Nevertheless, we discuss examples of studies that work with letters and diaries to demonstrate how they have been used and to note particular issues of genre involved in using such sources in personal narrative analysis.

Liz Stanley's thoughtful framework for theorizing letters notes several of their relevant characteristics as genre; they are *dialogical* (a form of communication among two or more people); *perspectival* ("their structure and content changes according to the particular recipient and the passing of time"); and *emergent* ("they have their own preoccupations and conventions and indeed their own epistolary ethics").[35] Moreover, Stanley notes, unlike an interview protocol or a published memoir, letter collections are typically fragmentary, incomplete even as texts; researchers must work with "what remains."[36] The relationship among the correspondents, of course, also matters, in terms of what is taken for granted, what is said and not said. Letters thus have an "obstinate" and often elusive referentiality, at the same time that they cannot be taken at face value to represent a real-life relationship. Letters, Stanley insists, "construct, not just reflect, a relationship, develop a discourse for articulating this, and can have a complex relationship to the strictly referential."[37] Although letters can indeed be intimate, they have often been written with at least one and perhaps many readers in mind. Series of letter exchanges over time can provide some of the same insights as other forms of personal narrative; they have been a mainstay of biographical studies for this reason. Persuasive analyses of letters must pay close attention to the aims and conditions of letter writing and to their generic qualities.

A classic sociological study of U.S. immigration that draws extensively on letters as evidence is William I. Thomas and Florian Znaniecki's book *The Polish Peasant in Europe and America*.[38] Originally published in five volumes between 1918 and 1920, the study begins with a vision of peasant life in Poland in the mid-nineteenth century and ends in the Polish immigrant community of the Chicago of Thomas and Znaniecki's day. By examining letters written by Polish immigrants to their families, letters written to local community newspapers, newspaper articles, charity organization records, and court records, these influential sociologists make an argument about continuity and change in Polish communities as migrants moved from Eastern Europe to their new lives in the United States.[39] In their discussion of the letters as forms of evidence, they emphasize the generic conventions of a predominant "fundamental type."

> We call this type the "bowing letter…." The bowing letter is normally written by or to a member of the family who is absent for a certain time. Its function is to manifest the persistence of familial solidarity in spite of the separation…In accordance with its function the bowing letter has an exactly determined composition. It begins with the religious greeting…Finally, come greetings, "bows," for all the members of the family or from all the members of the family if the letter is written to the absent member. These elements remain in every letter, even if the function of the letter becomes more complicated; every letter, in other words, whatever else it may be, is a bowing letter, a manifestation of solidarity.[40]

To support their broader argument about maintaining family solidarity in the midst of social change, Thomas and Znaniecki reproduce in the book a series of letters, either written by Polish immigrants to their relatives in Poland or from families in Poland to relatives in the United States. Most peculiarly, as in "the Wróblewski series," which contains letters written from Walery in Poland to his brothers in the United States, each series contains only one side of the correspondence. Thomas and Znaniecki open each section with a general argument about the function of the documents, then include a series of letters over time from a particular family member, and finally, insert footnotes to explicate the significance of the details contained therein. Consequently, most of the work of contextualization and translation is removed from the main text and relegated to footnotes.

By reprinting the letters in their entirety without analysis in the text—other than the general introduction provided in each section—Thomas and Znaniecki create the impression that the letters can be taken more-or-less at face value. The footnotes serve as annotations to the text, providing some useful context in one letter, a translation of a word or phrase in another, and details about a family member mentioned in yet another. Rather than reading these letters critically for both what they reveal and what they might not, Thomas and Znaniecki treat "bowing letters" as relatively transparent reflections of the Polish peasant's life in the Old World and in the United States. Thomas himself regarded documentary evidence as a more "reliable" form of evidence than interviews because he considered the former less likely to distort peasants' lived experiences. Given the epistemological presumptions of empirical sociology in the early twentieth century, their treatment of letters as "objective" evidence is perhaps not surprising. As a discipline at that historical moment, sociology was intent on establishing itself as a "scientific" field searching for general laws and principles of social organization that relied on "objective" evidence.[41] Nevertheless, by treating the letters as objective data, Thomas and Znaniecki do not adequately address the literary, generic, and cultural dimensions of the letter form; they instead treat it as a report of actual behavior. While they note the convention of "bowing" in the letters and realize that it has a symbolic significance, they nevertheless fall into the trap that Stanley cautions us against: of reading letters uncritically as empirical evidence, in this case, of real-life familial solidarities.

Thomas and Znaniecki also fail to discuss the limitations of having only one side of the correspondence for each series of letters. What might be missed, for instance, without the Polish immigrant letters in the Wróblewski series? As this series reveals, Walery tells his brothers in one letter about an argument between their father and his brother Feliks (who is also in Poland) that involved "knives and axes" and results in Feliks and his wife leaving the family farm and complaining that they have been "wronged" by the father who refused to let them manage the farm and by Walery himself who sided with his father. Walery concludes the letter by writing:

> I hear that they plan a lawsuit against my father for indemnity in their pretended wrongs…Please write your opinion about this affair. Perhaps this letter will find itself among the documents of Feliks. [You will

concert with Feliks against me and send him this letter.] But I don't believe it.

I remain respectfully yours, but writing always the truth.[42]

The story of family divisiveness, and the bad feelings that accompany it, continues in several of the letters—though it is never clear how the immigrant brothers in the United States replied to Walery. Are they surprised by the arguments between their father and their brother, Feliks? Do they offer advice or support to Walery? What do the existing letters reveal about the dynamics of epistolary relations in the context of the face-to-face relations of those family members on either side of the ocean? And, with respect to Thomas and Znaniecki's broader claims, how does this exchange support their argument about the significance of maintaining family ties in the peasant community?

An analysis more sensitive to the generic characteristics of these letters, along the lines suggested by Stanley in the context of her own work as editor of collections of letters, would have led to a richer and better justified analysis. We need to know more about who was writing to whom and the many reasons for and aims of writing these letters. For example, the initial volume contains letters from over fifty families; however, there is no discussion about whom this sample might include and exclude. Obviously, illiterate peasants were not included. But what about those who were literate and did not write "bowing letters"? Were they also interested in maintaining family ties by other means? Furthermore, while the letters collected display many of the ceremonial functions of "bowing letters," many of them also concern requests for money as well as details about family divisions and conflicts.[43] We also need to know about patterns of change over time and variation among individual letter writers as well as about the overall contours of the genre. Given their idealized vision of peasant family life in the nineteenth century, Thomas and Znaniecki were perhaps reluctant to consider the complexity of the correspondence and its place in a wider social and cultural context; as a result, their analysis of peasant migrants is less rich than it might have been.[44]

Persuasive analyses of letters attend to the aims and conditions of writing, including, for example, the nature of the relationship among the correspondents. Shula Marks's *Not Either an Experimental Doll* uses letters well in this instance to understand how seemingly personal and subjective experiences such as mental illness are rooted in social circumstances.[45] This work is based, among other sources, on letters exchanged among three South African women between 1949 and 1951: Mabel Palmer, a middle-aged white teacher; Violet Sibusisiwe Makhanya, a Zulu social worker who had trained in the United States; and Lily Patience Moya, a Xhosa schoolgirl. The intense exchange of letters offers a brief but vivid record of the three women's relationships. The letters are written at a crucial moment in Moya's development (when she was fifteen through seventeen years old). Moreover, Marks was able to follow them up with research into Moya's future, including into records of her subsequent mental illness. The letters become precious evidence about the social contextualization of mental illness, and an individual trajectory toward it. As Marks observes:

> The correspondence between Mabel Palmer, Lily Moya, and Sibusisiwe Makhanya helps to move us beyond the aridity of an unpeopled political economy, to the ambiguities of everyday life. Through it we see the overarching constraints of social structure on human agency, and the complex relationships of individual psychology to a culture-bound social order. If what is precious in the letters is the personal and the idiosyncratic, it is nevertheless possible through them to show that "the private lives, even [the] obsessions of...individuals, far from being simply psychological quirks or even aberrations, flowed directly from their social situation of these...individuals."[46]

Marks's understanding did not emerge from the letters alone, however, but through her careful analysis of them as shaped by the constraints of letter writing in a particular setting and set of relationships. The exchange of letters, as is true of all such exchanges, is comprised of individual documents that are sporadic and strategic. Marks often has to fill in the gaps, to try to figure out through other records what relevant incidents sparked particular comments in the letters without being revealed by them. Lily's position of dependency means that she more often than the other two has to be guarded in her writing. For example, despite Lily's "duly submissive" response to a patronizing and dismissive letter from her patron Mabel Palmer, we learn that her behavior at the school seems to have changed dramatically as a response to the letter. Filling in the gaps is easier for the older and better-known women than for Lily. We are ultimately left with questions and uncertainties, about which Marks herself comments. Nevertheless, Marks's genre-sensitive reading of the evidence does allow for the provocative exploration of the subjective as an element of historical dynamics.

Letters can also illuminate the cultural ideals that guide different social categories of people in coming to and defending their own decisions and actions as well as those of others. A thoughtful example is historian Walter Johnson's *Soul by Soul: Life Inside the Antebellum Slave Market.* As discussed earlier, Johnson relies on a variety of personal narrative sources—slave narratives, slaveholders' letters, and accounts written by visitors to the South. As in his discussion of slave narratives, Johnson is attentive to the conditions in which people produce letters and what these kinds of sources can tell us about slaveholders and their social world.

Such letters are doubly revealing, for not only do they memorialize a single performance of the self but reveal the terms which made that performance intelligible, the cultural register of the roles upon which their authors drew as they sat down to write. The letters thus recapitulate accounts of slaveholding selves that were likely to surface in other circumstances—conversations, gossip, fantasy, folklore and so on. The letters are full of striving sons, masterful patriarchs, anxious brides, and dutiful wives, all of them recognized social identities available to antebellum whites as they tried to make themselves make sense to someone else. And, they are full of talk about slaves—slaves described, desired, bought, and brought home.[47]

One interesting contradiction that speaks to the "cultural register" of the roles slaveholders drew on is the moral distinction they made in letters and elsewhere between themselves and slave traders. While most antebellum Southerners justified slavery through an insistence on their benevolent paternalism, they condemned slave traders whom they regarded as dishonest, "coarse," "ill-bred," without conscience, and miserly. Of course, slaveholders still sold slaves, and as the letters and other sources reveal, they often lied to their slaves about their intent to do so. How then did they explain their decision to sell one of their slaves? In Johnson's careful reading, slaveholders justify their actions through a "narrative of economic necessity." Compared to the slave trader who sells slaves to make a profit, slaveholders sell them only when they are compelled to do so by a debt, crop failure, or some other kind of financial loss. Such a narrative sleight of hand not only reinforces the boundaries between the roles of slaveholder and slave trader but also absolves the former of moral responsibility for their actions while vilifying the latter as a "Southern Shylock" or "Negro Jockey."[48]

One final example of an analysis of a body of letters is drawn from Mary Jo Maynes's work on the history of girlhood and selfhood in late-eighteenth and early nineteenth-century Europe. Like Johnson, Maynes uses letters and other sources to examine changing notions of consent, choice, and contract. The moment of deciding to marry (or, more rarely, not to marry) plays a key role in her analysis. "How," Maynes asks, "were highly modern marriages of convenience among the new industrial elite reconciled with cultural values and an economic ideology that increasingly emphasized individual choice?"[49] Maynes focuses her analysis where the documents are richest—that is, on marriages of girls from families of property and education—although she draws on other types of evidence to demonstrate the class variations in the construction of young female selfhood through discourses and practices around marrying.

Many educated women of the Enlightenment era were prodigious and renowned as letter writers; some women intellectuals wrote almost nothing but letters. Like all forms of personal narratives, their letters present their own challenges to the historian. The following example points to the ambiguities of "choice" in a setting where young women's choices were heavily constrained. It is drawn from an intensive correspondence around 1780 among three educated upper-class young German women, and the example highlights the difficulties discussed by Liz Stanley of working from fragmentary epistolary sources.

Maynes's interest in a particular letter was sparked by a brief excerpt from it in Olwen Hufton's masterful history of European women, *The Prospects Before Her*. "Musing on her marriage to a dull professor at Göttingen," Hufton writes:

> Caroline Michaelis commented in 1781 on how she had been led into a match, as were other German girls of her class and temperament: "My brother gave me in marriage to the man he had marked out for me since childhood, his best friend who loved me from that time. In this marriage I fulfilled the wishes of my family, my friends, and his, and for a long time my heart was in agreement with them. Guided by those powerful motives I made my choice."[50]

The construction of "choice" here was so "provocatively ambiguous" as to lead Maynes to follow up on this excerpt to figure out how best to read Michaelis's letter.

Putting this excerpt into the context of the correspondence of which it was a fragment, however, only made her "choice" more ambiguous.[51] The woman in question was Caroline Michaelis Schelling (1763–1809). She began her life-long epistolary career in her teens. Her early correspondence (up through her first marriage at age twenty-one in 1784) is nearly all with her friends Julie von Studnitz and Louise Stiehler Gotter. In letters to the former, Caroline focuses on reportage about events and travels; although always lively and witty and quite warmly personal, they do not offer personal confidences to the extent that her letters to Louise do. In letters to Louise between 1780 and 1781, Caroline continues what appears to be an ongoing discussion about her troubled relationship with a young man named Link. In June 1780 she wrote:

> Far from me are all those ideas such as found in novels! I feel that I could prefer Link to all others. I know that he is worthy of the preference I grant him...Difficulties on both sides could prevent our union. My father doesn't know him; would he turn over his daughter for whom he feels so much paternal love, to a stranger? Link is certainly quite wealthy, but dependent on his uncle and will cede to his will. I know all of this and am reconciled. If it is good for me to find happiness in this

way, then God will unite us; if it's not good, he will separate us...I am not so novel-struck to say that I would never want to marry anyone else but him.[52]

Caroline may deny having ideas "found in novels," but the dilemma she describes parallels that of a romantic heroine. Six months later, her tone was angrier and less patient:

> The old uncles and aunts always and forever cause problems. I wish they would for once leave young people in peace...Imagine—poor Link has such an abhorrence of his uncle who unfortunately has to serve as his guardian...What's going to come of this? Soon I will be sending you an advertisement for a novel entitled *Der alte Onkel* which I intend to publish by subscription...I laugh about this, but really I am like one who forces her lips to smile with tears in her eyes.

She writes to Louise that she will not write to Link because that would be inconsistent with her "duty"; moreover, "she doesn't want to deceive her good parents or her dear brother." By July of 1781, she is reporting to Louise that she has "completely freed herself from her passion," that Link is gone from her life. He might be dead, or unworthy, or miserable, but he is, in any case, "lost as far as I am concerned."[53]

Over the next two years, Caroline's letters are filled with her thoughts on the latest novels she has read and on theater pieces she has seen, with comments on her views about education and politics, and also with more personal concerns. She is worried about her brother, with whom she is very close, who is in America serving as a doctor for the Hessian troops, and her younger sister who is involved in an inappropriate romantic relationship. She refers to her former infatuation with Link only in veiled allusions. Maynes cites a letter of November 1781 to Louise in which Caroline now terms her relationship with Link not "love" but "self deception" and remarks that "if I were truly my own master and could live in a proper and pleasant situation, I'd prefer not to marry at all, and look to be useful to the world in another fashion."

To Caroline's great relief, her brother announces his imminent return from America in 1783. Then, in February of 1784, in what Maynes now recognizes as uncharacteristically stilted language, she announces to Julie (in the first letter quoted above) her imminent marriage to her brother's best friend. And to complicate things even further, Maynes finds a surprising letter to Louise after her brother's return in which Caroline describes her brother's current state and her joy and relief at having him back. She remarks: "So this is the brother who loves me so much, and I him, that the two us have been up until this point dearest in the world to each other. He claims that I will always be so to him, but I didn't want that; and in three weeks I will no longer be able to say out loud to you that he means the same to me."[54] After the marriage, Caroline and her husband move in with her brother and his wife.

Through her analysis of the epistolary evidence concerning Michaelis's decision to marry, Maynes makes it clear that these sources, however rich, cannot be interpreted definitively. Hufton provided a defensible reading of one of the letters. Putting that letter in the context of Michaelis's wider correspondence, and also reading it in terms of its style and form, makes clear that it was not a simple report of an arranged marriage similar to that of "other German girls of her class and temperament." Indeed, the letters leave themselves open to a variety of interpretations. In terms of the problem of choice and agency, the analysis of the body of letters unsettles any simple notions of agency, and instead helps to historicize and complicate what that might mean.

Just as the analysis of letters is enriched by attention to their generic qualities and cultural context, so too is that of diaries and journals. We begin with a definitional and theoretical reflection, again from French sociologist Philippe Lejeune:

> For me, a diary is "a series of dated traces"…But the diary is first and foremost a life practice and a writing practice…millions of diaries are written and only a few are published…Can we be sure that the few published diaries are representative? No, in fact we can even be sure that it is the reverse. For instance, in France, 85% of published diaries are written by men, whereas it is a well known fact that most diarists are women. Moreover, published diaries tend to be those of writers or well-known people or war memoirs. The ordinary life of unknown people is grossly underrepresented."[55]

Here Lejeune demonstrates his approach as a sociologist of literature; his impulse, before any social-scientific analysis of the evidence of diaries, is to characterize them as a genre of texts produced under specific social and historical circumstances. Laurel Thatcher Ulrich's prizewinning book *A Midwife's Tale* offers one example of the interpretive possibilities inherent in well-contextualized diaries.[56] Of course, historians have used diary evidence before. To offer one frequently cited example, the diaries of the seventeenth-century Londoner Samuel Pepys are often called on to provide evidence about many aspects of everyday life and politics in that era.[57] But Ulrich's study goes well beyond the usual mining of diaries for empirical information; she uses the diary to illuminate social actions of a woman on the margins of the official historical record. Like other effective personal narrative analyses, Ulrich's book contextualizes the diary with extensive research into the surrounding culture. We learn, for example, that the diary's author, midwife Martha Ballard, recorded her own presence at 60 percent of the births in her community of Hallowell, Maine, during those decades of the eighteenth century when Ballard was the town's midwife. Nevertheless, the only public record of her existence in the town is a two-line obituary in the local paper. Analysis of the diary offers the possibility at getting at the subjectivity and agency of an otherwise obscure woman.

The diary form involves its own unique constraints, but Ulrich's work demonstrates how under some circumstances it is still possible to analyze this genre most effectively. In Ballard's time, a diary was more likely to limit itself to recording the weather and the performance of household chores than it was to disclose intimate thoughts. By the nineteenth century, especially among members of the educated middle classes of the transatlantic world, diaries had become "intimate companions" with whom one shared secret or undeveloped ideas, longings, and observations.[58] These are the sorts of personal narrative documents, alluded to earlier, that Gunilla-Friederike Budde was able to compare so effectively with later autobiographies to discern altered aspirations and gender grievances between adolescent and middle-aged European women.

Diaries are also at the center of historian Joan Brumberg's *The Body Project,* a history of American adolescent girls' feelings toward and understandings of their bodies. Obviously, the form of the diary makes it useful for research on subjective perspectives on a variety of topics, and especially topics not often discussed more openly. According to Brumberg, "old diaries are a national treasure, providing a window into the day-to-day routines of family, school and community. They also recapture the familiar cadences of adolescent emotional life, and they provide authentic testimony to what girls in the past considered noteworthy, amusing, and sad and what they could or would not talk about."[59] Brumberg uses diaries and other sources to document what was usual or imaginable to discuss in different settings about the topic of the female body—that is, what could be discussed in more public media such as advertisements, as opposed to a private genre such as the diary—and how this changed over time in the United States. Brumberg draws on brief excerpts from the diaries throughout the book. Although the brief excerpts tend at times to be, ironically, somewhat disembodied (i.e., not easily connectable with authors recognizable as whole persons), she provides a series of effective biographical vignettes at key junctures in her argument. These vignettes, for example the story of "The Slimming of Yvonne Blue," are richer portraits that place the diary excerpts in a biographical narrative that gives fuller information about the narrator's setting and events of her life course around the point in time when the diary excerpts were written.[60] In these vignettes, Brumberg also tracks the narrator's temporal development as recorded over time in the diary.

As with the other forms of personal narrative, analyses of diaries must recognize their rootedness in specific, and generally very limited social milieus and phases of the life cycle as well as the changing conventions that affected what they were expected to reveal and conceal. Brumberg does talk about her sources and the understandable difficulties of collecting and working with diaries; she does not focus much on the question of how the selectivity in terms of which adolescent girls did and did not write diaries affects her analysis, nor how the sociology of the genre did or did not change over time. She does use other sources that, for her analytic purposes, counter potential limits inherent in the genre. In the chapter on skin, for example, she pointedly includes skin color as one dimension of the quest for "perfect skin." But the apparent rarity of African-American girls' diaries makes it hard for her to do the same sort of analysis based on diaries that is possible for middle-class white girls. Instead she relies on such sources as memoirs, ads, and letters to the editor.

Hybrid Forms of Personal Narrative Analysis

We have already mentioned several important personal narrative analyses that combine autobiographical narrative of the analyst with personal narratives of others. Note that we are not talking simply about self-positioning. Indeed, most self-reflective analysts include some autobiographical accounting in their write-ups, if for no other reason than to clarify their stakes in the project and their relationship to the narrators whose stories they often collected personally. We will discuss strategies for and approaches to self-positioning in chapter 4. Here, we call attention to the contributions of several works in which the analysts draws on autobiographical insights far more extensively and pointedly than what such positioning normally entails. In these hybrid forms, the analyst's autobiographical narrative is intrinsic to the analysis.

In an example we have called on frequently because of its self-reflexivity about many of the issues that concern us, Carolyn Steedman's study *Landscape for a Good Woman* combines elements of a biography of her mother with autobiography.[61] As a double narrative—the mother's and the daughter's—it demonstrates the power of a personal narrative analysis to make sense of the realm of possible choices and decisions narrators make in particular contexts in specific and intimate auto/biographical detail. The intimacy of the portrayal uncovers otherwise hidden agendas and motivations that are denied in more usual characterizations of working-class "interest" and reveals more complex psychodynamics and more contradictory motivations than are normally ascribed to working-class subjects.

Similarly, Luisa Passerini's *Autobiography of a Generation* alternates analysis based on oral history interviews with notes from Passerini's sessions with her psychoanalyst. As we mentioned in chapter 2, Passerini's book, like Steedman's analysis, opens up the dimensions of the construction of subjectivity, motivation, and agency that are otherwise almost impossible to explore. Like Steedman's analysis, Passerini's account rests heavily on her own personal experiences and her willingness to reveal them in intimate ways. In both cases, the resulting analysis necessarily stops short of being definitive or replicable for the precise reason that it draws so heavily on the highly subjective experiences of its author. Nevertheless, we would insist, such studies as these also demonstrate precisely the richness and the unique and distinctive contributions that can be drawn from analyses based upon well-contextualized subjective evidence.

Amitav Ghosh also employs various forms of personal writing as analysis in his *In an Antique Land*.[62] As we discussed in chapter 2, Ghosh challenges the limits of biography by writing about a subject about whom the documentary sources are nearly silent. But, at the same time, he also writes a "travel memoir" based on ethnographic field notes (themselves a form of personal narrative, of course) later amplified with other sources. Using the memoir form allows the interactions between Ghosh and his informants/friends in Egypt to complicate his analysis in interesting ways. First, his place as an active participant in the field research allows him to present himself as "Other" through the eyes of those Egyptian villagers and also to compare the questions they put to him with those he puts to them. Those interactions are intrinsic to the ethnographic research process. Moreover, the juxtaposition of "displaced" people and their analytic categories for understanding each other in the ethnographic present is juxtaposed with the very different categorizations of the world of Bomma, the medieval slave, and his Jewish master Abraham Ben Yiju.

Ghosh self-consciously adapts the traveler's tale genre as an ideal in which to present both of his related projects. First, they both problematize the interpretive work and the imaginative leap it takes to communicate while traveling. By implication, it suggests that similar leaps are at work in the intersubjective interpretations we make as ethnographers or as historians. These interpretations are pieced together through archival materials, fieldwork and interviews, and conversations with academics and others who help to make sense of them. Whether we travel geographically, as Ghosh does, or historically, as he does as well, we are always putting together stories about ourselves and about others—trying to make sense of our contemporary worlds and of our past. Travel, then, is an important metaphor in the construction of Ghosh's personal narrative; the formal choice of "a traveler's tale" fits his vision well.[63] Travel as metaphor and form of personal narrative writing contrasts in interesting ways with the metaphor and form of translation used by Ruth Behar. Both obviously involve an attempt at intersubjective understanding across difference. But the act of translation attempts, never with complete success, to fully render one culture into the terms of another. In a successful work of translation, moreover, as it is usually understood, the translator ideally recedes into invisibility. A travel memoir, on the other hand, keeps the traveler's subjectivity close to the surface. The reader never loses sight of his or her mediation of the relationships and situations described. In both forms, it should be noted, the presumed audience stays home.

In sociology and anthropology, there has been an increasing interest among a number of scholars in writing in related forms often termed "auto/ethnography."[64] Like the other hybrid forms of analysis we have discussed, these scholars are interested in narratives of self-inscription, but rather than studying "others," they write critical ethnographies of themselves, or themselves in relation to others. Informed by developments in postmodern, feminist, and postcolonial theory and methods, auto/ethnographers build on recent reconsiderations of the uses and meanings of personal narratives to examine the ways in which selves and social forms are culturally constituted through biographical genres.[65] For example, in *Final Negotiations: A Story of Love, Loss, and Chronic Illness,* sociologist Carolyn Ellis writes about the painful loss of her partner who struggled for many years with chronic illness and her own struggle to write a sociological book about the same topic. In weaving these two narratives together, Ellis's aim is to make sociology, a discipline that typically emphasizes the general rather than the specific, "an intimate conversation about the intricacies of feeling, relating, and working."[66] Similarly, Ruth Behar's objective in her collection of personal essays, *The Vulnerable Observer,* is to write "an anthropology that will break your heart." She rejects the search for universals and objective "truths" in favor of the personal and the subjective. Part of the inspiration for these essays was the need to write a different kind of anthropology that could address, for example, the emotional dimensions and personal experiences that characterize and shape fieldwork.[67] What makes these works distinct from an autobiography or a life history is the narrator's attempt to turn the ethnographic gaze on his or her own life and work. In this respect, like Steedman, Ghosh, and Passerini, auto/ethnographers are at once narrator and analyst.

A final interesting example, which the author describes as a memoir, is economic historian Deirdre McCloskey's *Crossing: A Memoir,* an account of her personal journey from male to female.[68] It is a sharp-eyed analysis of the enactment of gender, an analysis that is uniquely informed by the author's experience with performing both masculine and feminine personae. In McCloskey's case, the social world in question is that of late-twentieth-century American and European academics and their personal and professional-institutional networks and relationships. McCloskey does not discuss gender abstractly, but rather through the specific ways men and women in these milieus understand and perform it. The friends and colleagues who surround McCloskey are essential to first his, and later her, self-understanding at every juncture. Relationships with women, often quite romanticized here, are a big part of McCloskey's story. Her Dutch and American *vriendinnetjes* (girlfriends) and more formalized groups like *Damesnetwerk* (women's network) offer models of femininity, emotional support, and feedback on gender performances. They literally help shape McCloskey's feminine ideal and eventual feminine persona.

Many of the significant friendships originated in professional ties—colleagues, students or former students, wives of students and colleagues. The degree of acceptance or rejection by friends, family, and colleagues plays a critical role in McCloskey's experience of transition. The institutional responses to the gender crossing are also a central part of the story. For example, McCloskey was arrested twice in November 1995, in response to court orders her sister requested in order to prevent her from proceeding with surgery. The second arrest occurred while McCloskey was in Chicago at the annual meeting of the Social Science History Association of which she had been president some years earlier. In response, the Social Science History Association passed a resolution condemning the seizure of their former president, and then rescheduled the session honoring McCloskey's scholarship. "This was unusual. Academic associations are usually timid, which is better illustrated by the Speech Communications Association, meeting in San Antonio, to which Dee was scheduled to fly on Sunday. The Communications people heard about his commitment and canceled his participation."[69]

Here, there is also a connection between gender identity, institutional culture, and intellectual predispositions. Economics, McCloskey argues, is a particularly "macho" discipline. Its practices are gendered. There are interesting, if imprecise, parallels between McCloskey's crossing from male to female and her increasing skepticism about certain of the epistemological foundations and methodological claims of this most positivist of the social sciences. Moreover, the reception by audiences of McCloskey's arguments was altered by Donald's decision to cross, and by Dee's, and then Deirdre's, increasing femininity.

McCloskey's analysis of her gender crossing offers keen insights into the operation of gender. That McCloskey's gendered identity is strongly held and at the same time socially constructed is explicitly revealed through the memoir of which McCloskey is both narrator and analyst. Her sense of agency is clear and powerfully expressed (she prevails in her determination to cross in the face of strong opposition); nevertheless, as the author makes clear, she could never have crossed "alone." Indeed, crossing would have no meaning outside of the experiences, relationships, and institutions that endow gender with content and meaning. This is obviously an unusual narrative in many respects; like the other examples of "hybrid" genres of personal narrative evidence and analysis we have discussed here, McCloskey's story reveals insights otherwise well beyond the realm of social science. And like many other adept analyses based on personal narrative, this one too shows how human agency is distinctly individual and thoroughly social.

At the same time, McCloskey's analytic memoir underscores how difficult it is simultaneously to be narrator and analyst of a personal narrative. Such an approach entails disclosures that some analysts might well find compromising or difficult. Moreover, there is a real problem in distancing from each other the two subjective stances involved in being simultaneously narrator and analyst. As we will discuss in chapter 4, one key element of the analysis of personal narratives is its intersubjective methodology—whatever genre of personal narrative is involved, the analyst to one extent or another must think him- or herself into the mindset of another person and use the personal narrative evidence to develop a facility in understanding how the narrator sees the world. Intersubjectivity, we will argue, is central to the knowledge creation that happens through the analysis of personal narratives. Hybrid genres can to some extent mimic this intersubjectivity, and even bring new depths to the process, but they can never benefit from intersubjective encounter in the more usual sense.

In this chapter, we have argued that the most effective analyses of personal narratives pay close attention to how genres and their rhetorical mode shape life stories and explicate precisely how analysts are reading their sources in light of the generic characteristics of their sources. As we have shown, the particular form personal narratives take (whether as oral histories, autobiographies, diaries, or letters), their temporal dimension (in historical time and the point in which they are written in the narrator's life cycle), and the conditions under which they are produced all shape both what is included in the text and what is not. Letters, for example, are individual documents often written sporadically and with strategic aims for specific audiences. They also have a much more limited temporal dimension than other personal narrative sources—such as autobiographies or oral histories—do, and excerpting fragments from a larger stream of correspondence can bring pitfalls. Autobiographies and oral histories, in turn, are constrained by other generic considerations. For instance, each of the four models available for autobiographical self-representation that Diane Bjorklund identifies (tales of religious conversion, self-development, the psychological self, and the sociological self) encourages the writing of particular kinds of narratives and not others.

In addition, careful attention to when in the narrator's life course a personal narrative source is written has implications for the tenor of the story told, and for what is included in the story and what is not. And finally, the presumed audience for personal narratives as well other conditions of their production have implications for the shape of a life story. As Walter Johnson points out in *Soul by Soul*, the fact that slave narratives were written in conjunction with white northern abolitionists who had not only access to publishing houses and other realms of influence but also particular philosophical and political objectives and audiences in mind meant that slave narratives, as a generic form, tend to emphasize some themes and experiences, while erasing others.

Failure to consider the questions raised by the generic qualities of personal narrative evidence creates a number of problems for personal narrative analysis. Analysts may draw dubious conclusions by reading their sources uncritically or may overlook the significance and meaning of contradictions and inconsistencies in the life stories of their subjects. As a consequence, opportunities to provide more complex and nuanced readings can be missed. The hybrid forms we discussed raise a particular set of questions about genre, but they also introduce new questions about the relationship between narrator and analyst and its significance in shaping personal narrative analysis. We now turn in chapter 4 to a discussion of this relationship.

4

PERSONAL NARRATIVE RESEARCH AS INTERSUBJECTIVE ENCOUNTER

Critiques of positivistic epistemology in the social sciences have challenged the notion that social scientists can be objective observers whose research produces universally accepted truths. Even in the realm of philosophy of science, recent discussions have tended to emphasize that the acceptance of scientific truth claims is based more on shared practices and tacit agreements within communities of scientists than on universal and objective criteria. This claim is certainly all the more pertinent in the social sciences, where research methods are far from unobtrusive or disengaged. In these discussions, feminist critiques in particular have emphasized the need to acknowledge the positionality of the researcher, an epistemological and methodological imperative nicely summarized by anthropologist Lila Abu-Lughod, who argues that scholars should recognize "that every view is a view from somewhere and every act of speaking, a speaking from somewhere."[1] The critique of positivism does not undermine all forms of social-scientific truth claims; nor does it justify the response that, methodologically speaking, anything goes. Instead, alternative epistemologies have emerged that focus on the production of "situated knowledges"—that is, understandings of the world that recognize that knowledge is always produced from a specific social location and always aimed toward a specific audience or audiences. These epistemological insights have particular relevance for our focus in this chapter: the interpersonal or intersubjective relationships between the narrators and the analysts of personal narratives and the consequences of these relationships for the construction and interpretation of personal narratives. As we use the terms in this context, *interpersonal* relationships involve actual meetings or direct communications between narrator and analyst; *intersubjective* relationships involve attempts to understand another person's subjective take on the world, and these can develop even where there is no direct contact between narrator and analyst (as in the case of reading an autobiography or personal papers or using life history interviews gathered by someone else).

Personal narratives emerge in institutional and historical contexts and are mediated by culturally specific narrative conventions; moreover, they do not exist apart from the social processes through which they are created. In many cases, though not all, the personal narratives used in social science come into being specifically through a research process that involves two or more *interested* parties; where research involves interviews, these would include the life story narrator or subject and the interviewer and/or analyst. Careful attention to this relationship is important because it inevitably shapes the form and content of personal narratives and their analysis. To paraphrase historian Susan Geiger, researchers undertake particular responsibilities when they use what they have learned from collecting or eliciting people's life stories—among others, the imperative to be clear about (1) *how* they have come to know what they know and (2) *where* they are situated in the act of creating knowledge.[2] The specific epistemological and methodological implications of the intersubjective character of knowledge production and the interpersonal relationships often entailed by personal narrative research raise a set of questions we will address here: How do analysts discuss and assess the interpersonal relationships through which they produce personal narrative analyses? How do they handle the multiple positions and agendas involved? What elements of these relationships hold the greatest consequences for the knowledge produced?

To address these questions, this chapter problematizes the interpersonal and intersubjective relationships involved in working with personal narrative evidence. Beginning with the relationships through which scholars elicit life stories, we examine the implications of different kinds of relationships for both the stories that are told and their subsequent analysis of them. This involves not only the original interviews or evidence gathering but also the transcription, editing, and/or publishing processes. Important considerations include the positioning and motivations of narrator and analyst; their varying situations, constraints, and rewards; and the different intended audiences that often distinguish the narrator from the analyst. Whether a social scientist works closely with the life storyteller or in some other fashion, detailing the subsequent analytic process is important because it ultimately affects the form and content of the final version of the story. Although we start with stories collected by analysts, some of these concerns, we suggest, pertain to the use of preexisting narratives such as diaries, letters, or autobiographies as well. Even where the analyst is not

directly involved in producing the narrative, analysis still involves intersubjective engagement—a way of knowing that requires attention, acknowledgment,
and critical examination.[3]

We also explore the intersubjective dimensions of analysis and interpretation.
Here, we consider the extent to which narrator and analyst are speaking the same
language; that is, the extent to which the concerns and uses of implicit or explicit
categories of analysis are shared and how this matters. Whatever the answers, we
suggest, the questions need to be posed. This process is analytically necessary, but
it has implications for the interpersonal relationships involved because it often
necessitates probing areas of uneasiness or disagreement between narrator and
analyst. Finally, in the last section of this chapter, we consider how researchers have
dealt with complicated aspects of the relationship between analyst and narrator.
We look at cases where highly emotional or ethically troublesome matters—lies,
secrets, silences, or embarrassments—intrude into narrator-analyst relations.
Given the interpersonal character of much personal narrative research, these
issues all raise ethical as well as epistemological dimensions that often overlap.

Positioning the Analyst

Personal narrative analysis can never be disconnected from the analyst. This is
patently obvious in the case of the auto/ethnographic and autobiographical
forms (discussed at the end of chapter 3). As historian Luisa Passerini writes in the
first chapter of *Autobiography of a Generation: Italy, 1968:* "I conducted my first
interviews with the protagonists of '68. The interviews plunge me into my own
past: as I listen, the film of what I was doing at the time unreels."[4] In Passerini's
study the relation of analyst to the life stories and storytellers is especially apparent and close, for the generation she is studying is her own, and she even includes
autobiographical evidence in chapters drawing on diary extracts and notes kept
from her own psychoanalysis. But even where this is not the case, and where, as
is far more common, the analyst is not explicitly part of the story, personal narratives are usually the product of interactions among a number of people including
the analyst. An oral life history, for example, results from the interaction between
two people—in the words of anthropologist Marjorie Shostak, "one with unique
personality traits and particular interests at a particular time of life, who answers
a specific set of questions asked by another person with unique personality traits
and interests at a particular time of life."[5]

Life stories collected in the context of ethnographic study are similarly joint
productions. Ethnographers who have documented their own positionality vis-
à-vis the individuals or groups they study or whose stories they collect thereby
illuminate and enrich their findings. Anthropologist Faye Ginsburg, for example,

in reflecting on her fieldwork in Fargo, North Dakota, was forthright in discussing the complexity of finding a strategy of self-positioning that would enable her to interview both the pro-choice and the pro-life activists whose social movements were of interest to her. Initially, she thought that being young, single, Jewish, and from New York City might pose unbreachable barriers to communication with Fargo's women activists, most of whom were married, Christian, and from rural or small-town backgrounds. While not denying the difficulties, Ginsburg nevertheless reports that:

> Much to my surprise, the fact that I was in many ways "culturally strange" to Fargo occasionally served to my advantage. Interviews frequently ended with curious questions regarding Jewish holidays, customs, and ceremonies. Had I been a member of a Christian denomination, I would have had to negotiate my way through inter- and intra-church conflicts in town and my questions about religion and frequent "church-hopping" would have been viewed with some suspicion. As a single woman, my queries and interest in people's feelings about marriage, birth control, motherhood, and the like were treated as natural curiosity; responses were often framed as if I were being counseled for my own future conjugal happiness.[6]

Ginsburg's insights about the significance of a researcher's positionality—as well as her recognition that the people whose stories she elicited were as curious about and eager to analyze her as she was them—underscores the importance of attentiveness to the multiple positionalities and perceptions involved in personal narrative research and to how they influence the resulting narratives.

Ginsburg's research account emphasizes surprisingly open encounters based on an unexpected degree of mutual respect. Not all encounters are like this, of course. Sociologist Jennifer Pierce's ethnographic study of two San Francisco law firms placed her in very different positions vis-à-vis the various groups with whom she worked.[7] She generally developed different types of relationships with lawyers than with paralegals, and different kinds of interactions with women than with men. These relationships, in turn, influenced the kinds of career stories she elicited. As she writes:

> As a white woman, a feminist, and a former paralegal, I had entrée to the world of woman paralegals that a male sociologist may not have had...my multiple statuses, particularly as a former paralegal, made it easy to find interviewees—most women eagerly volunteered—and in some cases led to shared understandings about the difficulties of this work world. On the other hand, as a woman, I also faced a number of obstacles to my research. Male lawyers did not regard me as a peer,

> as they might have with white male researcher…some male attorneys
> may have been less forthcoming in their interviews with me than they
> would have been with another man. [And others,] in an effort to please
> me, may have presented themselves as more critical of the adversarial
> role…As a consequence, my writing about the work world of male liti-
> gators may appear to be flatter, less detailed, and perhaps even less inter-
> esting than my writing on women legal workers.[8]

Pierce's open discussion of her positioning demonstrates not only that specific
gaps in "knowing" are unavoidable but also how attention to self-positioning can
enrich an analysis—if only by encouraging the acknowledgment of the limits of
what can be known through any particular research relationship—and indeed
becomes part of the knowledge produced through intersubjective research.

Feminist geographer Richa Nagar explores many relevant dimensions of the
researcher-narrator relationship in an account of her fieldwork in Dar es Salaam,
the capital of Tanzania, in the early 1990s. Nagar's research focused on identity
politics among South Asians in Dar. Her commitment to fieldwork that included
the collection of a large number of life histories as well as participant observation was based on her belief that methods involving self-reflexive interpersonal
encounters "can be a form of resistance to dominant ways of acquiring and codi-
fying knowledge." As a geographer, she was attentive to the processes involved in
navigating within and across Dar's many Asian and African communities, with
their particular spaces, boundaries, markers of identity, and hierarchies of power.
As she put it "Dar es Salaam became a kaleidoscope of social sites for me, as
I traversed its segregated gendered, classed, raced, and communalized spaces in
the course of my daily life. With every turn of the kaleidoscope, I was conscious
of my changed position, both geographically and socially."[9]

Nagar details how her own position came to play a role in the research relationships she developed and subsequently in the stories told to her. She discusses
the interpersonal and ethical, as well as methodological, dimensions of her complex positionality:

> Some things about me were quite apparent to almost every Asian with
> whom I interacted—I was a single woman in her mid-twenties, from a
> lower-middle-class Hindi family in India, doing Ph.D. research…Other
> aspects of my background I revealed in diverse ways, depending on
> the context…People's imagined and symbolic connections with geo-
> graphic regions…played an important role in defining their attitudes
> toward me.
>
> Gujarati speakers, who formed about 90 percent of the Asian pop-
> ulation of Dar es Salaam, easily guessed my Gujarati ethnic origins…

> My Hindi accent, however, often required me to clarify that although my family has retained a "Gujarati" identity…my first language is Hindi/Urdu…the doubtful state of my "Hinduness" allowed me to come closer to non-Hindus, particularly Muslims.[10]

Nagar's ambiguous identity allowed her to move among the various Asian communities of Dar; nevertheless, in each encounter, people's presumptions about her identity shaped the relationship and the research. As she came to learn more about how she was perceived, she found herself adjusting her behavior and her appearance so as to maximize her acceptance among the diverse groups with whom she interacted. Nagar grew increasingly attentive to how she dressed, since codes of dress were closely connected with each of the various communal identities. "My confrontations with dressing," Nagar writes, "were continuous":

> Although *salwaar kameez* (loose fitting pants worn with long shirts) and Western dress were popular among the Hindi women in their young and middle ages, it was only a *sari* or a *bindi* (dot) on the forehead that automatically branded a woman as a Hindu. Most Goans saw both *sari* and *salwaar kameez* as "old fashioned" or "too Indian" and the majority of Goan women wore Western-style dress. Among Sikhs and Ithna Asheris, *salwaar kameez* with a *dupatta* (long and wide scarf to drape over head and chest) was the most popular dress although *hijaab* (veil) was practiced in public places by Ithna Asheri women.[11]

Nagar adopted the *salwaar kameez* as her most usual form of dress because it had been among her ways of dressing and so did not feel dishonest and, although it marked her as "old fashioned" in some Westernized communities, it did not really exclude her from, nor did it mark her as an "insider" in, any one community. She notes that she was "aware of how easily many Ithna Asheris, Sikhs, and elderly Hindus granted [her] trust and respect on the basis of [her] being dressed properly." Nagar notes the comic side of her struggles with dress; for example, the day when she went to an interview with a Westernized young Goan man wearing the pants, T-shirt, and tennis shoes she knew would make him more comfortable with her, but carrying in her bag not only her tape recorder and notes but also the *sari*, blouse, petticoat, *bindi*, and footwear she would change into for a Hindu celebration she was attending later in the day.[12]

This constant attention to self-presentation, and her alertness to the fact that interpersonal research involves perceptions and strategies on both sides, brought Nagar rewards in terms of her ability to navigate the complex communal spaces of Dar and the generally warm welcomes and cooperation she met with in all communities. And it clearly demonstrated both the richness and the contingency of this form of knowledge production. But the method raised problems for her as well. She found it difficult to keep silent when people with whom she was developing a rapport voiced opinions she found objectionable; for example, when an Asian expressed racist attitudes toward Africans. These attitudes, too, however, were part of what she was trying to study. As she became closer to some of the people she was interviewing, even developing friendships with some, she found herself debating such opinions with them rather than just recording them.[13] Nagar's growing awareness of how her performance of identity shaped her research also fed into her ethical concerns about the possibility that the knowledge she would take away might be seen as a "betrayal" of trust. As a researcher, Nagar was always aware that the communities she studied "were heterogeneous not only in terms of 'race' and class, religious, sectarian, regional, and linguistic affiliations, but also in terms of their access to power." Her research goals and her political commitments to expose and critique these power relations collided with the relationships of trust that she had developed, and she worried about using "the words of several community leaders, husbands, and wealthy women and men in contexts where they might not have liked them to be used."[14] Although she never masked her role as a researcher nor hid her own interests from the people with whom she interacted, she was constantly aware of how perceptions (and misperceptions) of her and the trust they invoked shaped what people told her.

While not the same as conducting interpersonal narrative research in face-to-face settings, research based on preexisting personal narrative documents can also provoke significant intersubjective encounters as part of the learning process. Barbara Laslett, in her autobiographical essay in *Feminist Sociology: Life Histories of a Movement,* writes about her "relationship" with the prominent early and mid-twentieth century sociologist, William Fielding Ogburn, about whom she did biographical research. Ogburn was an outspoken advocate of science in sociology, which for him meant objectivism, quantification, and the absence of emotion. Although Laslett never met Ogburn—he died in 1959—she was trained in the Ogburnian tradition at the University of Chicago where she obtained her undergraduate and graduate degrees.[15]

Laslett began her research with the implicit question "How did we get this way?"—referring to the narrowness of vision and practice that Ogburn's ideas about sociology seemed to exemplify. It therefore came as a surprise when she learned in the course of her research that Ogburn had not always been "this way." Early in his career, he had sympathies with socialism, had undergone psychoanalysis in Washington, D.C., around 1919, was widely read in the psychoanalytic literature, and had taught Freud's works.[16] When active in the Social Science Research Council between 1924 and 1941, he supported the use of psychoanalytic approaches in sociological research. For example, he recommended financing psychoanalytic training for John Dollard, author of *Caste and Class in a Southern Town,* a classic in its time.[17]

Ogburn's feelings about the need for sociology to become more scientific and more quantitative became stronger over time, although in practice he did less quantitative research than he had earlier in his career. After his retirement, thinking back to his earlier life, he described his intense feelings about statistics. "The feeling of devotion and loyalty was very strong…My worship of statistics had a somewhat religious nature. If I wanted to worship, to be loyal, to be devoted, then statistics was the answer for me, my God." The irony, of course, was the discrepancy between the emotional intensity of his feelings about statistics and his wish for emotions to be eliminated from scientific life. For instance, he described a meeting of the Census Committee on Demography in 1948 as "One of the most enjoyable meetings I have ever attended…curiously there was no emotion discernable on the surface or underneath…I hate discussions…which are supposed to be scientific, that become emotional. For emotion and science do not go together, to my way of thinking."[18]

What ultimately drew Laslett to this life story, however, was not solely the ideas about emotion and science that Ogburn espoused, with which she strongly disagreed, but trying to understand why he held them as a person who was an individual living in a particular social and historical context, and what that might tell us about the connection between the individual and the social. Ogburn provided part of the answer himself in an undated typescript: "My father, planter and merchant, died in 1890 when I was four. Then began my long struggle to resist a dear mother's beautiful but excessive love. To the successful outcome, I attribute my strong devotion to objective reality, my antipathy to the distorting influence of emotion."[19] This typescript offered clues that, along with other documents about Ogburn's life, allowed Laslett better to understand the patterns of Ogburn's career choices, priorities, and values. Fearing the influence of emotion on science, he came to see the necessity of maintaining a strict separation between emotion and objectivity, a view that he promoted in his teaching, writings, and professional activities.

The change in Ogburn's thoughts and actions, Laslett argues, was understandable in terms of his family and professional history; the historical context in which he lived, including changes in the occupational structure and gender and class relations; and the new professional goals of sociology as a science in the first half of the twentieth century in the United States.[20] While these conditions may have produced a rhetoric about science for the times, it also contributed to Laslett's understanding of why the separation of personal and professional life developed then. Being able to understand the subjective as well as institutional context through which Ogburn came to his claims about the need for a strict separation between science and emotions, which he espoused in his personal writings and in his professional demeanor, influenced Laslett's thinking about connections between scientific knowledge and feelings. Moreover, her work also underscored how personal narrative research could demonstrate the nature of connections between the individual and the social.[21] Although Laslett's research did not involve direct contact between narrator and analyst, her account of the research process reveals dimensions of intersubjective engagement.

To offer a final example, in discussing her stance as interpreter vis-à-vis the nineteenth century, working-class French and German autobiographers whose published works she analyzed, historian Mary Jo Maynes noted: "As a motivation, mine is certainly no less intrusive or directive than the aims of earlier editors to tell about life in the depths or to capture workers for solidarism or socialism... I have certainly made judgments. As is no doubt apparent, I like some of these authors immensely and find others of them pompous and self-serving... Some of the autobiographies evoked anguish in me, some admiration, still others, laughter." While acknowledging the role of intersubjectivity in her analysis, Maynes goes on to express the hope that she has managed "despite [her] far from disinterested perspective... to have been evenhanded." She notes her effort, even when criticizing or second-guessing autobiographers' accounts, to "give them a hearing and to understand their own assessments of their life and choices." The suggestion is that even when the personal narratives that are the focus of analysis preexist, and their narrators are long dead, it is still necessary for scholars to reflect on how their subjective responses to the personae behind the narrative may ultimately influence their interpretation of a text.[22]

Producing Life Stories

In her insightful analysis of the diaries of the Victorian house servant Hannah Cullwick, Julia Swindell reveals the central role that Arthur Munby, Cullwick's employer, played in their composition. Munby not only requested that Cullwick write the diaries, but directed her to provide details about the "dirty work" she did as a housemaid, descriptions that appealed to him as he pursued his cross-class relationship with Cullwick. By bringing to light Munby's position in relation to the diaries as "reader and editor/author," Swindell's analysis serves not only as a caution about reading any personal narrative as transparent but also as a reminder that analysts need to pay attention to the interpersonal processes through which personal narratives get told or written.[23] In chapter 3 we discussed generic constraints that shape life stories told in various forms. Here we explore a slightly different set of issues about interpersonal and intersubjective dynamics that affect the production of personal narratives. How is a life history produced? What conditions affect who speaks to whom in interviews and what they reveal, or hide? How and to whom are diaries, autobiographies, and letters written? How are personal narratives edited, preserved, or published by their authors and/or other interested parties? Attention to these questions is important in conducting personal narrative research because they inevitably shape the form and content of the narrative.

Marjorie Mbilinyi's essay "'I'd Have Been a Man': Politics and the Labor Process in Producing Personal Narratives" calls explicit attention to various aspects of interpersonal relations in life history work. Mbilinyi carefully elaborates the stages of production that she and Rebekah Kalindile, a member of the Mpata clan in Tanzania, went through to produce Kalindile's life history. Mbilinyi conducted a series of interviews in 1985 with the aid of Tuasajigwe Sambulika, a translator. After transcribing the interviews, she went back in 1987 to work with Kalindile jointly in the process of revision. During the process, they went through the transcript together word for word with Mbilinyi reading it slowly aloud until a question was raised by either one of them. As they discussed each episode together, Kalindile provided corrections, revisions, and further elaborations.

In discussing the writing of life history, Mbilinyi suggests that "the most creative stages of the process are those in which the producer and the life historian directly interact with and confront each other...The dialogue becomes an invitation for each to reexamine the life history, as a story, and to produce a clear, more critical understanding of the past and the present."[24] Certainly, such a dialogue is highly labor intensive, and, as Mbilinyi reveals, this one provoked disagreements and conflicts along the way. Nevertheless, the description of the process is valuable in that it documents how the dynamics of the research relationship influenced the published life history. This process of co-revision brought out elements of the story that had not at first been apparent. For example, Mbilinyi discusses a serious disagreement she had with Kalindile. In her 1985 trip to Kalindile's village, Mbilinyi had criticized Kalindile for teaching young women in her village "that the church taught women to 'turn the other cheek' and be subservient to men."[25] Two years later, in revising interview transcripts together, Mbilinyi learns she had seriously misunderstood the meaning of Kalindile's counsel. Fearing that direct or open confrontation with their husbands might endanger young women, Kalindile had advocated more indirect, covert tactics of resistance. When Mbilinyi queried this, saying, "'So, you don't mean that you should agree with everything [a man says], except as a tactical move?' She [Kalindile] replied, 'Exactly! You *fool* him'" (emphasis in original). Furthermore, though Mbilinyi was initially unaware of this misunderstanding, Kalindile was not. As Kalindile reports, "I said at the time, 'We don't understand each other.' I said, 'My goodness, this child has no brains!'"[26] Mbilinyi's account of the dynamics of their relationship throughout the stages of production clarifies how and why Kalindile's understanding of resistance becomes part of the published life history and its implications for the revised analysis.

Ruth Behar also documents the process that brought about the life history of Esperanza in *Translated Woman*. In the introduction Behar notes that life histories are of course always "translated" or mediated in the first instance by their narrators and are never simple reflections or reports of experiences. "Calling a life history a text is, in one sense, already a colonization of the act of storytelling... I have tried to make clear that what I am reading is a story or set of stories that have been told to me, so that I, in turn, can tell them again, transforming myself from a listener to a storyteller."[27] In the case of Esperanza's story, Behar alerts the reader to the many steps entailed in translation: The story moves from spoken to written word, from Spanish to English, and from one cultural context to another. Behar also describes how she constructed the text and her reasons for doing so. Because her intent is to keep Esperanza's voice at the center, she retains Esperanza's narrative ordering of the events in her life. Further, in her thinking about how to give form to the book—as a testimonial or as a more conversational mode of storytelling—Behar decides to do both because this more closely captures the form of Esperanza's narrative as it changed over time.

Behar's insights into the complexities of the "translation" of a life story are valuable and stand among the book's most important contributions. There are some instances, however, where even more detail about the construction of the text would have been useful. For example, Esperanza's narrative in parts 1 and 2 of the book is presented seamlessly, as if there were no prompts or queries from Behar. Surely, Behar posed questions along the way, but she does not share with the reader the questions, prompts, or interjections that undoubtedly shaped the narrative. In describing how to shape Esperanza's stories into a book, Behar recalls feeling "like a filmmaker with reels of her story before me that I had to assemble using filmic principles of montage and movement. As I undid the necklaces of elegant sentences and paragraphs of prose, as I snipped at the flow of talk, stopping it sometimes for dramatic emphasis long before it had really stopped, I no longer knew where I stood on the border between fiction and nonfiction."[28] Behar mentions that she decided reluctantly to take sole responsibility for transcription and editing. Although Behar's discussion of the final narrative form and chronology for the published version of Esperanza's life story provides some clues to the rationale behind her editorial choices, the logic of her analytic imposition of order upon Esperanza's words is not fully described. Our point here is not that Behar's choices weren't justifiable; certainly there is no one correct rationale for or process for editing collected personal narratives. This depends on the analyst's aims, audiences, and agreements reached with narrators. Our point, rather, is that full attention to these processes enhances the value of life histories as evidence for social scientists and as documents of subjectivities.

While both Mbilinyi and Behar, to varying extents, describe the relationships involved in producing personal narratives they publish or analyze as scholars, such discussions are often minimal or absent in other life history studies. Often the publishers of oral life histories have a general audience in mind and therefore see details of process as unwelcome intrusions upon the narrative as story. Narrators themselves may prefer a more literary presentation, or one that masks the extent of the editorial intervention of the interviewer. Life stories that do not attend to the issues that concern us here can still provide marvelous evidence for social-scientific or historical analysis, but questions always remain about whose voice is being recorded, the relative power of the two parties involved in shaping the narrative, and the impact of the research setting on the story told.

A helpful example in this regard is *Lemon Swamp and Other Places,* a life history of Mamie Garvin Fields as told to her granddaughter, the sociologist Karen Fields. As we learn in the introduction to the book, a packet of old family letters describing Charleston in the 1890s that Mamie Garvin Fields presented to her three granddaughters one Christmas prompted Karen Fields to ask questions and record conversations with her grandmother about her life. Eventually, they began thinking about producing a book, and in the summer of 1978, they spent mornings and early afternoons recording more interviews.

Both women are listed as authors of *Lemon Swamp* and they shared copyright. Karen Fields transcribed the tapes and her grandmother read and corrected the transcripts, "adding recollections as she went along."[29] The introduction, written by Karen Fields, also includes a brief description of the revision process:

> Upon reading certain passages, Grandmother would say, 'We must add this'—if for example, we had neglected the accomplishment of some respected local person. Or she would write, 'Let's leave this out'—if, on mature reflection, a comment seemed too strong, or if an observation threatened to resurrect some long-dead sentiment that she deemed well-dead. "Why?" I would demand. Discussing the reasons why showed me aspects of belonging to a Southern community that would not have occurred to me to ask about, while showing us both differences between our standpoints.[30]

Although Karen Fields alludes to their method of production in this brief passage, and even suggests that—as in the other cases we have discussed—attention to this process casts light on the knowledge she and her grandmother jointly produced, she does not offer many examples or specifics about what they decided to add to the text or what they decided to delete. What kinds of comments, for instance, did her grandmother think were "too strong?" What kinds of sentiments were deemed "well-dead"? Like Esperanza's story, this narrative is presented seamlessly, with no reflection about possible silences and gaps in the story hinted at in the references to "long-dead sentiment." While it is likely that Mamie Garvin Fields was legitimately protecting her own privacy (or that of others) in asking for these deletions and that Karen Fields remains silent on this issue in respect of her grandmother's wishes, for our purposes it would nevertheless be useful to know in general terms what kinds of gaps in the life history such editing might have produced. If, for example, these deletions concerned sensitive topics such as sexuality, making that clearer would not just alert readers to arenas considered sensitive but also would explain the absence of attention to such topics in the life story.

In a related vein, this passage also suggests that editing the manuscript together illuminated some differences in perspective and aims. However, it is not clear whether the process of editing consistently privileged Fields's or her grandmother's perspective (or some combination of the two) and how such editorial decisions might have shaped the final manuscript. In some ways, this project is similar to Mbilinyi's; in fact, Mbilinyi mentions *Lemon Swamp* as a model for her own work with Kalindile. However, unlike Mbilinyi, Fields does not specifically explain how editorial decisions were made in the end nor how disagreements were resolved. For Karen Fields's purposes in publishing this rich life story, and no doubt even more for Mamie Garvin Fields's purposes, such omissions made sense. But a social-scientific reading of the story would have been enriched by a greater alertness to the dynamics of the interpersonal encounter that produced it.

As a final illustration of strategies regarding narrator-analyst relationships in the editing process, Judith Stacey made an interesting choice in publishing her study *Brave New Families*. She decided to offer her chief informants, Pam and Dotty, the working-class women among her interviewees with whom she was closest, the opportunity to have the last word in her book. In Stacey's words:

> Out of gratitude for their having granted me permission and the where-withal to write it, out of concern for the book's potentially hurtful effects on them and their kin, and in the dialogic spirit, I granted Dotty and Pam the right to control its closing words...Dotty unenthusiastically indulged my "noble" impulse, but claimed few grievances with my rendition of her family.

For Pam, it was quite a different story. Pam's provocative closing words are both reassuring in their confirmation of Stacey's trustworthiness as an analyst even while they remind readers of the elusiveness and open-endedness of any rendition of a person:

> Well, at first it frightened me, it disturbed me, because I thought, is this me? You know, here I am being taken at my word, is this the real me? And it took me awhile to realize that, yes, it is me, but it is only a part of me...And I was thinking, if Christ is more important than his teaching, which is something that the pastor was saying in church Sunday...I was thinking, are we more important than our words or deeds?...no matter what you ever painted about me, I would be more important than that, and I would be different than that. You know. You know, you could never capture me.[31]

This response, and Stacey's willingness to record it at the end of her book, points to an epistemological approach that departs from typical social-scientific presumptions in many respects and moves toward an alternative epistemology better suited to the collection and interpretation of life stories—one that recognizes intersubjectivity and contingency in knowledge production.

Multiple Agendas

Despite their complexities, personal narrative evidence can be especially useful for understanding agency precisely because it highlights the construction of accounts and explanations of activities through intersubjective encounters involving multiple perspectives and agendas. Researchers have scholarly purposes in mind in seeking out life stories, often framed or overlain by the requirements of the academic institutions that employ them, about which they are forthcoming in varying degrees. The narrators of life stories also have agendas in agreeing to talk or deciding to write their stories. Personal narrative analyses are enriched by attention to these different and often competing agendas because they tell us about the social processes involved in and having consequences for the production of knowledge.[32]

The motivation for some narrators is simply the opportunity to get a hearing—often in their later years in life—an opportunity to reflect on their life's accomplishments or to set the record straight after conflicts or misunderstandings. Historian Michael Honey, author of *Black Workers Remember: An Oral History of Segregation, Unionism, and the Freedom Struggle*, believed that the eager collaboration of the narrators with whom he worked was central to the success of his project. Honey, who is white and was a graduate student during most of the time he was doing his interviews, was struck by the willingness of so many black workers, men and women, to open up to him. As he explains, "The main reason black workers proved so willing had to do with their own objectives. This was their own story, in their own words, told from their point of view. They wanted the world, or someone, to know about the struggles they had waged and the conditions they had endured. Most of them expressed surprise and pleasure that others cared to know about their lives."[33] Of course their willingness to talk to Honey also depended on their relationship with him, his personal background, and his political commitments. As he tells us in the opening of the book:

> My search for this history in a sense came out of my own family's union, ethnic (Acadian and English), and working-class origins, which sensitized me to the economic roots of racial injustice. My work as a community and civil liberties organizer in Memphis and the South during the early 1970s also kindled a curiosity to learn, as songwriter and union organizer John Handcox put it, about "those who fought and died before." As a witness to continuing racism in my own era, I became increasingly inquisitive about its roots: how deep they went, whether they could be untangled, who had sought to do so, and to what extent they had succeeded. I continue to unearth the roots of racism and plant other roots, and my search for these hidden narratives became part of that continuing effort.[34]

Honey's longstanding political commitments and personal background as well as his willingness to listen, really listen, to what the men and women he spoke with said about their experiences in the labor and community struggles in Memphis all served to facilitate the process of gathering these hidden narratives. He wanted to listen, and his narrators wanted to tell their stories. Through these oral histories Honey was able to recount the history of black labor and black labor activism in the industrial south throughout the twentieth century.

Many other analysts have reported similar reactions from the people whose life stories they collect. For example, in describing the fieldwork she did in writing *Nisa: The Life and Words of a !Kung Woman*, anthropologist Marjorie Shostak describes her own goals as she recalled them years later: "Armed with the life histories of Cora Dubois (*The People of Alor*) and Oscar Lewis (*The Children of Sanchez*), I went, in 1969, to the Northern fringe of Africa's Kalahari Desert in Northwestern Botswana to begin a twenty-month stay with the !Kung San (Bushmen). My goal was to collect life histories, a vehicle through which I hoped the people's experiences, thoughts, and feelings might be expressed."[35] She reconstructed what may have motivated the narrator Nisa's decision to tell her story to the anthropologist:

> Nisa...reveled in the knowledge that she was teaching me the "truth" about life, while others, she would explain, often taught me "lies"...But

there was more. Nisa responded to our talk as though she appreciated the chance to contribute to something "bigger" than was typically asked for by the anthropologists...During the very first interview, she expressed this concern directly: "Fix my voice on the machine so that my words come out clear. I am an old person who has experienced many things, and I have much to talk about."[36]

By explicitly addressing her own motivations as well as Nisa's in pursuing this project, Shostak provides a self-reflective framing for the life history that she had previously published based on Nisa's story.

That said, this eagerness on the part of many narrators to go on record does not suggest that the relationship is subsequently simple or straightforward. Consider again, for example, Marjorie Mbilinyi's relationship with the life-history narrator and coauthor Rebekah Kalindile. Mbilinyi lays out the different situations, views, and agendas of the two co-authors and the conflicts that ensued despite their shared will to create a life story. "Kalindile's World" is contextualized by a brief history of her locality and its social and economic history under British rule and independence. "Mbilinyi's World" centers on the analyst's formative years at the University of Dar-Es-Salaam, when as an American expatriate she participated as an intellectual in the postcolonial government's experiment with African socialism. Coming from different places, the two collaborators in the oral life history also had somewhat different, if at times overlapping, goals (both, we should note, relayed through Mbilinyi's retrospective perceptions). One of Mbilinyi's main goals was:

> to portray women as active makers of history, not passive victims, but also to increase our awareness of the way that women's actions and consciousness were limited by objective conditions beyond their control...What were Kalindile's [motivations]? I gradually realized that she perceived the narrative as both a testimonial about the oppressions experienced by women in the context of family and community, and a way of preserving Nyakyusa tradition and culture and handing it down to others.[37]

The incident mentioned above—when Mbilinyi misinterpreted a comment by Kalindile but did not know this until two years later—resulted to some extent from the competing agendas that motivated the two women. According to Mbilinyi:

> I...had to reexamine my mechanical notions about "feminist" behavior in the context of the contradictions existing in Kalindile's world and in mine. Why had my interpretation of her work made Kalindile so angry? She had correctly perceived that my criticisms of her teaching

called into question the purpose of her life as she understood it. One way
that she had coped with the pain and humiliation of being a woman, a
wife, and a mother in Nyakusa society was by being an organizer and
a teacher of women in the church…I had come along and dismissed
her life's work as the furthering of women's enslavement.[38]

Only because Mbilinyi and Kalindile decided, each for her own reasons, to continue to work together despite their anger and disagreements did the nature of
Kalindile's views about strategies for women's empowerment clearly emerge.

Richa Nagar's work with personal narratives, discussed above, also demonstrates the complexities and possibilities for collaborations involving very
different agendas. Nagar is critical of two common tendencies she sees in
fieldwork-based research in the global South, especially but not limited to the
feminist work that is the focus of her own interests. First, research agendas and
publication priorities are primarily or exclusively driven by academic requirements; second, often from fear of appearing to be judgmental or Eurocentric,
researchers might shy away from highly sensitive topics such as domestic violence that may nevertheless be of great importance to the narrators whose stories
they collect. Instead, Nagar suggests, researchers should "accept the challenge of
figuring out how to productively engage with and participate in mutually ben-
eficial knowledge production."[39] As she and Susan Geiger argue in an article on a
related theme, it is important to address the question of how scholars "produce
knowledges across multiple divides (of power, geopolitical and institutional locations and axes of difference) in ways that do not reflect or reinforce the interests,
agendas and priorities of the more privileged groups and spaces."[40]

The Analytic Process: Speaking the Same Language?

This challenge of negotiating competing agendas is echoed in the analytic process
as well. One of the rich insights of *Lemon Swamp*, discussed above, comes from
Karen Fields's straightforward acknowledgment of the differences between her
analytic frame and her grandmother's:

I began my part of *Lemon Swamp* with a mental map showing historical events and processes, a map strongly colored with discrimination,
violence, economic pressure, and deprivation of civil rights. Notwith-
standing the respects in which I am a Southerner, I tended to operate
with a Northerner's "sociologism" about the South, that is, with an abstract
schema lacking the texture of lived life. By contrast, my grandmother dealt

in actual people and places, in the choices that she or her neighbor confronted, in what a man or woman did given a particular circumstance.[41]

While analysts aim to understand the narrators whose stories they elicit or find, and to respect their voices, the analytic categories central to social-scientific research are not usually phrased in the terms of a common vocabulary. This observation raises a number of important questions for analysts of personal narratives. To what extent do analysts share with life story narrators an understanding of concepts and categories? Or, are analysts imposing categories that don't make sense to narrators? When and how does this matter?

Nancy Chodorow addresses these questions head-on in her essay, "Seventies Questions for Thirties Women: Gender and Generation in a Study of Early Women Psychoanalysts," in which she recounts the difficulties she encountered in interviewing women psychoanalysts, many of whom were politically active Jews, who came of age in the 1930s. Compared with most other women of that era, these women were highly educated. They traveled widely, spoke at international conferences, wrote books and papers, and conducted professional lives even as they cared for families. Drawing from her own theoretical interests, Chodorow's interview questions focused on the centrality of gender in their lives; she asked them, for instance, how they thought that being a woman had influenced their professional lives? To her surprise, the interviewees often denied the relevance of gender to their public lives and insisted that they had not encountered problems as women. They had been more interested in social democratic politics and antifascism, and frequently emphasized their Jewish identity as having been more central to their self-understandings. Initially Chodorow was dismayed that they did not see things as she did, and they could not relate to her analytic framework. As she writes, "How could the early women psychoanalysts be unattuned to gender, in a field that makes a theory of gender so central? Could one be a woman psychoanalyst without noticing the theory of femininity?"[42]

Over time, however, Chodorow began to realize that she was imposing categories that she, as "a hyper-gender sensitive 70s feminist," found important, while her narrators who had come of age in a different time and place were telling her something quite different. Working through this insight, she begins to relativize and expand her own understanding of her gender consciousness and of the varieties of gender consciousness and self-understanding available to women of different eras and milieus. "I came to see that my ideas, as well as those of my subjects, were rooted in our different social and cultural conditions, that differences in women's interpretation of a situation may be understood not only in terms of structural categories like race and class, but also historically, culturally, and generationally."[43] Theoretically, she uses this insight to develop a more historically situated and less absolute theory of gender. Chodorow's revised concept of gender proposes it as more or less salient in different arenas, at different times of life, and in relation to other aspects of social, historical, and cultural organization.

Chodorow's critical examination of her misunderstanding (somewhat like the angry confrontation between Kalindile and Mbilinyi) resulted from an attempt to impose her analysis on these early women psychoanalysts' life stories. In Chodorow's case, this misunderstanding crossed generational lines, whereas in Mbylinyi's case, it crossed the boundaries of generation, class, and culture. In both situations, in their initial attempt to squeeze narrators' stories into preconceived conceptual schema, analysts failed to listen to the specific complexities of storytellers' lives they were told. And, in each case, the analyst's ability to work through the misunderstanding produced a more astute analysis as well as more robust analytic categories.

Categories need to be open to revision, then. This is not to say that taking personal narratives seriously as social-scientific evidence about agency, motivation, and subjectivity means taking them at face value. Nor does it mean that analysts must always agree with narrators' interpretations of their own lives. Where there is disagreement, we are suggesting, analysts are responsible for acknowledging it, for explaining why they chose one interpretation over another, and, to whatever extent is possible, for querying their own analytic categories vis-à-vis the terms in which narrators relate their own histories. In both of the examples cited here, the analysts came to a fuller understanding of the agency of the narrators because of their willingness to reconsider their initial interpretations. In developing the concept of gender salience, Chodorow paid careful attention to what narrators told her and she explains the reasoning behind her eventual interpretation. By expanding her theoretical conception of gender consciousness, she develops a term that is more sensitive to her narrators' self-understandings. At the same time, because she explains why she chose this term, she leaves open the possibility for other interpretations of the evidence they offer to her and she demonstrates how her revised analytic categories in turn helped her to make sense of the stories.

Crossing geopolitical boundaries in personal narrative research brings even greater challenges. These are raised clearly in Richa Nagar's report of the provocative complaint of a feminist activist in India in a discussion with Nagar about her research: "[Suppose] you tell my story in a way that makes no sense at the conceptual level to me or my community, why would we care about what you have to say about my life?"[44] Another pointed example of an analyst who takes special care in trying to relate her own categories with those of her narrators is provided in historian Susan Geiger's *TANU Women: Gender and*

Culture in the Making of Tanganyikan Nationalism, 1955–1965. While conventional accounts of nationalist movements in Africa, and the Tanganyika African National Union (TANU) more specifically, tend to focus on men's contributions, Geiger uses the life histories of women participants in TANU "to confront the biases, silences, and resulting distortions found in existing histories of the period of Tanzania's nationalist movement."[45] Her explicit concern with how women understand nationalist politics comes through in the way she chooses to present interview material in the text. Rather than use short snippets from a variety of interviews to make points, Geiger uses lengthy excerpts—sometimes several pages long—from her narrators, and then uses their words to make connections to her broader theoretical concerns about gender and nationalism. For instance in her chapter "Activists and Political Motivation," she uses long excerpts from eight life histories, and then directs the reader to notice that:

> Several themes emerged in these interviews [with urban Swahili women]. Women were drawn by notions of "dignity," "the right to rule ourselves," "the right to decide what we want to do," "equality among all persons, regardless of race, gender, or educational background," and "lack of discrimination in any form." They juxtaposed these positive goals of independence and self-government against conditions of colonial exploitation, both generalized and specific, which women readily identified as arbitrary controls, racial discrimination, inequalities and hardships, lack of access to education and jobs, and a failure to accord Tanganyikans the respect all human beings deserved.[46]

As Geiger concludes, TANU's commitment to end sex discrimination resonated with women who sought for their children, and especially their daughters, the education and jobs they themselves had been denied under German and British colonial rule. Furthermore, they drew upon TANU ideology to challenge aspects of gender oppression in their own families.

> Throughout their interviews, women referred to their experiences of restriction and lack of freedom in marriage; their feelings that women were not regarded as competent or fully human by men; and their sense that this situation was unjust. Women quickly realized the possibility of using TANU as a movement that stressed not only equality for all people, but the need for men and women to work "side by side" as an aspect of "respect and dignity" necessary to challenge their social situation.[47]

By grounding her analysis closely in the words and perspectives that emerge in the life stories she collected, Geiger develops an original understanding of African nationalism and of motivations for participation in nationalist movements. Nationalism in Geiger's interpretation did not simply represent Tanzanian men's historical triumph over imperialism, but also women's actions through their organizations and networks to implement ideas about equality and dignity. As they made clear in their stories, TANU women understood, as their husbands usually did not, that those ideas meant women's equality and dignity too. Like Chodorow, Geiger came out of the process of collecting life stories with a different notion of a critical analytic construct—anticolonial nationalism—than she had when she started, a revision inspired by listening to life story narrators. Her analytic categories are the product of a negotiation.

Analysts do not always have to come to shared understandings about concepts and theoretical language with life story narrators. As Karen Fields noted, sociologists generally draw on abstract theoretical frameworks to interpret life histories; this is an intellectual impulse that an analyst legitimately brings to a research setting, but it should not overpower the story or the storyteller. To the contrary, any effective use of analytic categories and concepts depends on the connections they make to what life story narrators actually say.

Sociologist R. W. Connell's analysis of men's life histories provides a good example, especially her life stories of men in the Australian environmentalist movement who, according to Connell, are attempting to "reform their masculinity to produce a new, non-sexist self." As Connell notes, the effort to remake masculinity is a challenge in a still patriarchal culture. None of the men she interviewed were "born feminist." In fact, all of them had conventional childhoods with a working father and stay-at-home mother. Each got involved early on in competitive sports, learned to value traditional male career paths, expressed homophobia, and suppressed their own feelings. Each of them reports reaching a point in his life, however, when he decides through his encounters with feminism or social movement activism to renounce the conventional trappings of masculinity. For some, this means leaving a career for an alternative life, for others it entails opting for a feminized occupation (e.g., nursing), and for still others it involves developing relationships with women that call for greater emotional openness and honesty. Their disengagement with what Connell terms "hegemonic masculinity" has not been an easy process. As Danny Taylor, one of Connell's interviewees put it, "It's hard not to be aggressive sometimes."[48]

While "hegemonic masculinity" is not a term used by her narrators, Connell's careful attention to the details of their lives and their self-understanding reveals the connections to her terminology and in turn specifies her concept through the use of concrete examples. Furthermore, Connell also uses the life histories critically to interrogate other analytic frameworks and to remind readers how in real lives these categories are often fluid and negotiable. For example, in contrast to traditional Freudian theories which suggest that the successful resolution of the Oedipus complex for boys is a definitive identification with the father, Connell's narrators describe a more complex and contradictory process where change is ongoing and identities are often in flux. Some identify with older brothers rather than their father; others identify with important women in their lives; and for still others, identification shifts and changes over the life course. Rather than trying to fit narrators' lives into a preexisting conceptual framework, Connell emphasizes instead the "agency involved in the journeying" and highlights change as a central theme in the life stories.[49]

Lies, Secrets, and Silences in Personal Narratives: Methodological and Ethical Dimensions

The main power that life history narrators have in the research relationship is the power to talk or write about their lives, or to remain silent; to reveal truths as they see them, or to distort or lie about them. Their interest, if they are at all inclined to tell a life story, is to have theirs be the version of history preserved, and told to a well-chosen, relatively influential, or well-connected listener or other selected audience. Of course the temptation or the unconscious tendency will be there to omit painful or embarrassing incidents. And, as oral historians have learned, until a story is committed to the tape recorder or the written page, it is a living text that changes with the circumstances and the audience, "always a work in progress."[50] Still, the fact that texts are works in progress does not mean that there is no difference between truth and falsehood in the telling. Historians, sociologists, and anthropologists who use personal narratives are increasingly interested in the literary aspects of life stories, to be sure. But in contrast with literary scholars, for whom literary characteristics are of prime importance, social scientists and historians address the problem of assessing the truth value of claims made in the context of personal narrative research projects with considerable interest and urgency.

In chapter 5 we will address the kinds of analytic truth claims that can be made persuasively on the basis of personal narrative evidence. Here, in the last section of chapter 4, we will examine questions about truth and falsehood, secrecy and disclosure, as they relate to the specific research relationships between narrators and analysts of life stories. Methodologically self-reflective oral historians such as Susan Geiger, Luisa Passerini, and Alessandro Portelli have offered guidelines for thinking about how the research relationship affects which aspects of a life story are emphasized and which are silenced, distorted, or misremembered.

Their thinking acknowledges the subject status and agency of narrators and the reality that, even where narrators are not knowingly dishonest, their life storytelling is motivated, even as the collection of their story by an analyst is motivated.

Portelli offers a number of telling examples based on his own experiences collecting life stories and other oral history materials. One in particular emphasizes the extent to which the two-sidedness of the research relationship affects the knowledge produced. He recounted an experience that:

> taught me that there are always two subjects to a field situation, and that the roles of "observed" and "observer" are more fluid than might appear at first glance...In June 1970...I met Trento Pitotti and recorded his repertoire of folk songs. Trento was by far the best folk singer I ever met, and he knew many religious, ritual, and lyrical songs. He also sang some "topical" songs, music-hall style, from the 1930's and 1940's. Only one blemish marred my delight and the "perfect" tape I took home that night: two of Trento's topical songs (both interesting and previously uncollected) were unmistakably Fascist.
>
> I liked him anyway. So a year later, when I happened to be driving past Labro, I dropped by to say hello. We talked a while, and it turned out that, far from being a Fascist, Trento was a politically active Communist...I asked him why, then, he had sung those Fascist songs. "Well," he said, "you asked me for some old-time songs, songs from when I was young. That's what they used to make us sing in those days."
>
> Trento didn't know me, when I first recorded him...I had thought I was not supposed to "intrude" my own beliefs and identity into the interview, and Trento had responded not to me as a person, but to a stereotype of my class, manner, and speech. I had been playing the "objective" researcher, and was rewarded with biased data.[51]

The lesson that Portelli took from this encounter is that the "two-sided" intersubjective relationship that life story research entails has worked best for him when there is honesty and full disclosure on both sides. Obviously, this doesn't remove all sources of distortion or secrecy, but it at least eliminates the second-guessing produced in situations where the analyst leaves him- or herself open to misinterpretation on the part of the life storyteller. In his words:

> An interview is an exchange between *two* subjects: literally a mutual sighting. One party cannot really *see* the other unless the other can see him or her in turn. The two interacting subjects cannot act together unless some kind of mutuality is established.[52]

Of course, as Portelli recognizes, mutual respect is both an important ethical and methodological aim and also difficult to accomplish in practice. Inequalities in status and power between the analyst and the storyteller complicate the research situation even further, whether the inequalities stem from "interviewing down" (the situation Portelli described), "interviewing up" (as in the case of Pierce interviewing male litigators), or crossing racial or cultural boundaries (as was the case for Mbilinyi). Sociologist Marjorie DeVault provides useful and relevant insights based on her experiences of interviewing across racial differences in her analysis of public health professionals' career stories. What interests DeVault is that references to race were oblique and indirect in her interviews with women of color. Rather than dismiss these indirect references, DeVault argues that everyday talk "is often full of oblique references and resonances that could make race relevant, but listeners have to have the requisite interpretive competences to hear and understand meanings located in social contexts where race and ethnicity (like gender) virtually always matter."[53] For DeVault, who is a white woman, "hearing" race and ethnicity in the stories she was being told required active attention and analysis rather than passive listening. DeVault's narrative analysis entails a close reading of pauses, qualifiers, and oblique references for their potential meaning and significance. In her interpretation of her interview with Janetta Thompson, an African American woman, she writes:

> First, it contains talk that circles around race, though without making it an explicit topic. Thompson speaks of wanting to work "in, a sort of like inner city kind of thing" and goes on to explain that this means working with "people who were like me." Without securing fixed meaning for these words, she provides clues to the significance, for her of the community health setting. She was really excited about that... It is also important to note her hesitations, as she marks time while thinking how to say these things, in this context, and especially to me, a relatively unknown white woman, and a professional, though in a different field. At this point we have spoken no more than five minutes. It is perhaps too early in our conversation for race comfortably to have become an explicit topic.[54]

Near the end of the same interview, DeVault finds that Thompson is willing to talk more explicitly about race than she has before. Here, Thompson talks about her concerns with professionals "from outside" who work in the black community. At the same time, however, DeVault notes:

> the rather tentative character of her speech (her slight hesitations as she characterizes these professionals: "You know who, who may or may not, I mean...") and the qualifications she adds ("they may be really sincere

about it…”) indicate that she speaks with an awareness of the difficulties of talking about race and ethnicity—an awareness of entering what
Susan Chase (1995) labels a realm of unsettled discourse.[55]

For DeVault, this close reading that is sensitive to the relative positions of the
two subjectivities involved in the conversation uncovers Thompson's somewhat
hidden sense of the pervasive influence of race in her career. Such a reading also
provides important methodological lessons for analysts of personal narratives
who may wonder why certain topics are not explicitly discussed in interviews,
life histories, and other forms of personal narratives. Silences, tentative qualifications, and indirect references can all be read for deeper significance and meaning.
At the same time, DeVault also provides a final important caution to analysts who
attempt such speculative interpretations about meaning. She calls for what she
terms "a light-handed approach" to the interpretation of personal narratives:

> I have treated the transcript of my interview with Janetta Thompson as
> a text to be presented gently, even somewhat tentatively. Her words were
> spoken to me in a moment when we came together; I grasped at the
> time, at least some of what she meant, and I have worked at deepening
> that understanding through sustained attention to her interview and
> by investigating the context that has shaped our story and its telling.
> I put forward an argument, but since my argument focuses on how cul-
> tural differences complicate interpretation, it would be self-negating if
> it claimed a final objective truth. Instead, as Collins (1990) suggests the
> acknowledgement of locatedness and partiality in this kind of analysis
> can move it toward a stronger and more credible truth.[56]

We will return to this final point in chapter 5. Our suggestion here, following
DeVault's lead, is that attention to the particularities of any intersubjective communication brings implications for the kinds of arguments, and truths, that can
be established through it.

Because of their interpersonal dimension, the face-to-face interviews in life
history research can also bring about the revelation of long-held secrets. These
revelations can lead to the disclosure of significant truths, to be sure, but also
present particular methodological and ethical difficulties for both life story narrators and analysts. Narrators or people implicated in their stories may feel that
they have revealed too much. For example, Katie Cannon, one of the narrators in
Sara Lawrence-Lightfoot's life history project *I've Known Rivers,* discovered that
her family was appalled by what she had revealed about them in her interview:

> "Did you forget the tape recorder was on?" her mother asked. Katie
> had spoken about the alcoholism in her family… She had also spoken

openly about the tough hierarchies of skin color in her family, about the distancing and rejection by the light-skinned aunt who hated their blackness...The extended family responded to Katie's published revelations with horror. How dare she air dirty laundry in public?[57]

How might the telling or concealment of secrets be influenced by the relationship between narrator and analyst or between narrator and a presumed audience? In cases of oral histories, how can stories best be probed around sensitive topics or events? What are the strategies analysts have used in reading narratives to uncover and interpret what seems to be missing, hidden, or dissembled?

A provocative example that addresses the emergence of sensitive material in life history interviews comes from a joint essay by historians Michelle Mouton and Helena Pohlandt-McCormick. They compared their life-history research on peoples' experiences under politically repressive regimes, specifically Germany during the Third Reich and South Africa under apartheid.[58] They seek to examine the dynamics of historical memory about a troubled political past as recalled in a specific context of later retelling. Mouton and Pohlandt-McCormick's research experiences also serve to underscore the difficulties that narrators and analysts can face when secrets are revealed in telling life stories.

In Mouton's interviews with German women who came of age during the Third Reich, Frau Peters, one of the narrators, tells Mouton about an affair she had with a married man. Like Frau Peters, this man was also critical of the Third Reich; they shared a lengthy correspondence containing anti-Nazi sentiments. If the mail had been censored, according to Frau Peters, then they both "would have hung for it. Oh well...And, after that he was actually drafted and died in Russia."[59] As Mouton discovers, Frau Peters had never told anyone other than her husband about the affair, and the links between this highly personal relationship and Frau Peters' relationship to the Nazi past. Mouton also discovers the strong emotions the memories still evoked. At the conclusion of the interview Frau Peters shows Mouton the letters from her former lover, reads them aloud, and becomes distraught. Mouton, in turn, feels guilty "for having caused Frau Peters to re-live past pain, and like a victim myself, since I had no way of stopping the flow of the story or of easing the anguish it had caused."[60]

Mouton struggles with guilt for having caused Frau Peters pain, even though the revelation was a product of the research encounter and a contribution to the historical knowledge she and Peters together produced. Pohlandt-McCormick reports responding very differently when one of her narrators, Lilli Mokganyetsi, reveals a disturbing incident from her past. In telling her life history, Mokganyetsi describes her political coming-of-age in the context of the 1976 Soweto uprising in South Africa. She reveals that as part of a large group of demonstrators she was

involved in stoning a white man to death. Pohlandt-McCormick is psychologically jarred by the story. She writes:

> I found myself forcefully drawn into the story by my own emotional
> responses. Here was the vivid personal experience of one of the most
> violent episodes of the uprising, one which the State, in its retelling,
> tapped mercilessly to prove the "savagery" of the youth in revolt. I was
> silent…My own disquiet at the sudden fragility of line that separated
> heroes from villains in Lilli's story caused me to ask no further ques-
> tions and the story hastened on.[61]

Pohlandt-McCormick and Mouton's experiences point to the potential vola-
tility of life history interview situations and to the ways in which the analysts' own
responses and responsibilities are implicated in what comes out in interviews.
They suggest the very close relationship between the disclosures that emerge
through personal narratives and the intersubjective context of their recitation.
In one case, the analyst allowed or encouraged the painful revelation to emerge
fully; in the other, the analyst's unease likely worked to suppress fuller disclosure.
In both cases, these moments of hesitation, revelation, and suppression (echoing
DeVault's experiences) signaled the sensitivity of the terrain being entered and its
relevance, even if not fully understandable, for the story being told. As Pohlandt-
McCormick suggests, this jarring moment prompted her to reexamine her own
assumptions about the history she was reconstructing of protests against apartheid and interpret Mokganyetsi's story as well as other life histories in a different
way. Similarly, Mouton learns about the power of norms operating to silence
experiences that, while of historical significance, are generally not retold.

These last examples not only underscore the intersubjective dynamics of
research involving personal narrative evidence but also remind us of the contingency of the conclusions drawn from it, a theme on which we will elaborate
in chapter 5. Here, we have argued that the interpretation and analysis of personal narrative sources are always shaped by the intersubjective relationship
between narrator and analyst. Certainly, narratives told to a specific person in a
face-to-face interview situation magnify the impact of intersubjectivity, but, as
we have also argued, considerations of intersubjective influences are no less relevant to the analysis of preexisting texts such as diaries and autobiographies. The
subjectivity of personal narrative evidence is what makes it distinctly useful for
social analysis; interpretation of such evidence necessarily entails intersubjective
understanding. The mere assertion of their unique value as a form of evidence,
however, is not adequate for a persuasive and effective personal narrative analysis. In conducting personal narrative research and in presenting its results, it is
necessary to be transparent about both how the narratives were constructed or

collected and how they were interpreted. DeVault's self-reflective analysis of how the dynamics of interracial interviewing led to significant pauses, word choices, silences, and qualifications in the narrator's story provides a good illustration of this point. Her close attention to and analysis of the specific intersubjective context in which the stories were told alerts readers to the locatedness and partiality of the analyst's—any analyst's—interpretation and knowledge. It is appropriate to return here to DeVault's call for "a light-handed approach" in interpretation, which also brings us back to the epistemological and methodological concerns with which we started this chapter. By making the narrator-analyst relationship visible throughout the process of collecting and working with personal narratives, analysts can make clearer, stronger, and more credible claims about their interpretation. The next chapter pursues this topic, focusing on making persuasive arguments based on personal narratives evidence.

5

MAKING ARGUMENTS BASED ON
PERSONAL NARRATIVE SOURCES

Personal narrative analysis produces a different type of knowledge than do many other approaches to social science and history. In an essay she wrote about several works (by now familiar) that employ personal narratives to address debates about historical memory, political scientist Darrah McCracken hit the nail on the head. Many analyses of personal narratives, she noted:

> implicitly and explicitly raise questions relating to the project of generating knowledge in the social sciences. While philosophy of science questions are relevant to all research, such issues may be particularly important to studies of personal narratives, which seem to be at odds with social science commitments to generalization and researcher objectivity. Many...emphasize their particularity and their distinction from the monolithic "official story." In writing about narratives of escape from the working class, Carolyn Steedman suggests that "the first task is to particularize this profoundly a-historical landscape." Similarly, the boundary crossings described by Michelle Mouton and Helene Pohlandt-McCormick are "atypical ruptures" that challenge conventional stories. Dorothee Wierling states that "there is no way, it seems, to come up in conclusion with a coherent and collectively shared story of the past." All of this leads to the question, "Is generalization still possible?" Does the accumulation of personal narratives constitute the improvement of our historical knowledge? What happens when we are ready to move beyond challenges to the official story to reconstruction?[1]

As a reader of personal narrative analyses, McCracken voices key questions about the epistemology, methodology, and rhetoric of social science that personal narrative analyses provoke. Any response to these questions necessarily involves two perspectives: that of the writer and that of the reader of personal narrative analyses. We keep both of these perspectives in mind in this final chapter focusing on methodological and rhetorical strategies for making arguments based on personal narrative analysis.

In many respects, our suggestions here follow from our discussion and characterization of personal narrative evidence. It is by nature subjective and highly personal. We have argued that every life story is unique but also that life stories, whatever their form, can only be understood in light of their social, cultural, and historical context. Moreover, although it is invaluable for many analytic purposes, personal narrative evidence is always to some extent incomplete, open-ended, and contingent, which presents a challenge in the face of the expectations of many readers in audiences schooled in the social sciences.

Much published research in the social sciences, especially in the disciplines of sociology, economics, and geography, is based on the analyses of data about entire populations or specified subcategories, or else of samples meant to represent an aggregate or an average of that population. In these types of analyses, there is little logical space for the personal or the subjective, although evidence about individuals, often qualified as "anecdotal," can serve to bring home or exemplify an argument that is nevertheless made according to another logic. Such analytic logics are comfortable with claims made on the basis of probability, but less so with contingency; they are equipped to handle the average but not the individual case. The corresponding rhetorical strategies reflect these presumptions and methods.

Personal narrative analysis, in contrast, builds from the individual and the subjective. It gleans its truths from subjective perceptions about social phenomena, and more particularly through the narrative logics that structure experiencing, recalling, and understanding social action. Subjectivity and narrativity are at the core of the alternative epistemological presumptions associated with personal narrative analysis. Personal narrative analysis can provide powerful insights into social action and human agency, but given its epistemological presumptions that are so different from those of positivist social science, it needs to employ its own specific methods and rhetorics of persuasion.[2]

As research on communities of discourse reminds us, only part of the story of persuasion depends on the analysts; the other involves readers and their expectations, perceptions about appropriate rules of evidence and interpretation, and ways of distinguishing between legitimate and illegitimate conclusions drawn from the evidence. Writing analyses of personal narratives that are persuasive *as social science* requires using epistemological, methodological, and rhetorical techniques that are appropriate to these kinds of sources and legible to audiences. As has been true in the case of previous methodological innovations, this can involve teaching audiences new techniques for reading and evaluating analytic writing.[3] It is more than usually necessary for analysts to be transparent about their concepts, methods, and logic of argument. Considering the following sorts of questions helps to move toward that transparency:

- What kinds of claims are most appropriately based on personal narrative analysis?
- What sorts of generalizations are possible and appropriate to draw from life stories?
- Whose stories best answer a particular research question or illuminate a theoretical claim, and why?
- How is narrative evidence best presented to make an argument?

As noted in the opening observation by McCracken, working with personal narrative evidence presents particular challenges to the historian or social scientist, but, the same can be said of every form of evidence. And, like other types of analysis, personal narrative analysis can be more or less systematic and more or less persuasive depending on how it is done. This chapter draws on personal narrative research, much of it introduced in previous chapters, to address questions about what makes personal narrative analysis sound, persuasive, and logical to readers.

Beyond the Individual Story: Generalizing from Personal Narratives

If personal narrative analyses are to be of interest as social science or history—whether they rest on one narrative or many, and whatever their analytic goal—they must go beyond the individual and they must grapple with issues of generalization. However individual the evidence base, most personal narrative analysts who are social scientists or historians aim to generalize in some sense by claiming that an individual story either speaks to a broader social experience or positionality or illuminates a symbolic framework or a historical event or process.

In thinking about different ways of generalizing from life stories, it is useful to differentiate among various types of arguments common in the social sciences and history. However, it is also important to remember that there are elements in common across the various disciplines and that forms of persuasive argument share some of these elements. In his discussion of analyses of events, sociologist Philip Abrams argues that for both historians and sociologists, "knowledge is achieved by abstraction. In both cases, detail is what is selected as evidence not what is given by the world."[4] Our focus here is on the specific kinds of generalizations (or, in Abrams's terms, abstractions) within these broader rhetorics of persuasion that can be constructed on the basis of personal narrative evidence.

Some personal narrative analyses build toward what we call *sociological generalizations*. Sociological generalizations based on personal narrative evidence are claims that a given personal narrative illuminates a particular social position or social-structural location in a society or institution or social process and that it illustrates how agency can operate at this locus. Although we use a disciplinary-based term here, the focus is meant to be on the type of logic employed, *not* on the disciplinary location of the analyst. For example, a historian or an anthropologist might well employ sociological generalization. Moreover, it is important to distinguish between the sorts of sociological generalizations we are discussing here from statistical generalizations (often) based on quantitative analysis of evidence about populations or samples of populations. These quantitatively based generalizations often rest on correlations among discrete measures; they are meant to be predictive, whereas personal narrative analyses are interpretive. Nevertheless, there are generalizations beyond the individual case that can be drawn from personal narrative evidence, and it is these we have in mind here.

Sociological generalizations can be employed in studies that focus on many narratives from a particular social type as, for example, in the cases of Daniel Bertaux and Isabel Bertaux-Wiame's "Life Stories in the Bakers' Trade," Jake Ryan and Charles Sackrey's *Strangers in Paradise: Academics from the Working Classes*, or Norbert Ortmayr's *Knechte* (farmhands).[5] Analysts often suggest that their general portraits, however much and however necessarily they are based on the stories of particular individuals, would have revealed similar truths about the society in question had they drawn on the stories of other, similarly situated, individuals (although some do interest themselves with the "exceptions"). Sociological generalizations often rest on a number of stories, but they can also be based on just a few or even just one particular story. Thus, for example, Ruth Behar is employing sociological generalization, although not exclusively so, in telling and analyzing Esperanza's story, which in Behar's own terms is a portrait of a social "type"—an analysis that is meant to enrich our understanding of the situation of "a woman from the margins of the other America" and substitute for existing stereotypes of Mexican women another more complicated portrait of someone in that sociohistorical location.[6]

Another type of generalization, which might be termed *ethnographic generalization*, uses personal narratives to open up a culture and reveal the operation of otherwise obscured transactions, social conventions, mythologies, meanings, and motivations. The stories gathered in ethnographic studies are not meant to be merely personal or idiosyncratic, but somehow symptomatic of cultural constructions at play in the wider culture from which they are drawn. Faye Ginsburg's study of activist women in Fargo, North Dakota (discussed in chapter 4), is an example of this sort of approach. In her interviews with women on both sides of the abortion controversy, Ginsburg found two divergent but linked narratives structuring their life stories. All the women tell stories that connect them to the abortion controversy in terms of what Ginsburg calls "procreation stories" centered on issues such as sexual activity, reproduction, and motherhood. However, the plots that each side constructed reveal different interpretations of the place of motherhood in women's lives and their roles in society.

Ginsburg compares two groups. Pro-choice activists, who typically came of age in the context of women's movement activism in the 1960s and 1970s, stressed the right for women to work but did so within a context of female values of nurturing. Pro-life activists, who were mostly younger and, in contrast to stereotypes, having strong feminist sympathies, had changed their views as they were confronted with what they saw as new moral challenges. They were, according to Ginsburg, "astute, alert to social and political development, and on many issues...not anti-feminists." For them, the "unborn child" was the "root metaphor" that structured most of their storytelling. Ginsburg's analysis involves finding the meanings each group attributes to abortion, meanings that provide "each position with opposed but interrelated paradigms that reconstitute and claim a possible vision of being female."[7] Ginsburg links the life stories of these women involved in a regional moral and political controversy to broader cultural currents surrounding the value of motherhood and paid work for women in the United States.[8]

Another kind of generalization, *historical generalization,* is concerned with temporality, with the ways in which separate and individual pathways and intersections occur over time, in which events lead to other events in sequence. In these kinds of analyses, personal narratives help to explain historical processes or events from the perspectives of people defined through a particular relationship to that event. Martin Duberman's *Stonewall* (discussed in chapter 2) serves as a good illustration of historical generalization. Duberman is explicit in justifying his research in terms of the need for the stories he collects never to be forgotten and for individual lives never to be lost. Countering trends he opposes in social history that tend to flatten out differences in human experience, Duberman intentionally seeks to place Stonewall in its concrete historical context as seen from the perspectives of individual actors. He chose people "whose stories themselves were absorbing odysseys, yet at the same time speak to other gays and lesbians...Their stories were different enough to suggest the diversity of gay and lesbian lives, yet interconnected enough to allow me to interweave their stories when, in the second half of the book, the historical canvas broadens out into the Stonewall riots, gay politics and the first Christopher Street Liberation Day March."[9]

In a way, Duberman's study moves from a kind of sociological generalization ("whose stories…speak to other gays and lesbians") into historical generalization (the mode that allows Duberman to "to interweave their stories when, in the second half of the book, the historical canvas broadens out into the Stonewall riots, gay politics and the first Christopher Street Liberation Day March.") Clearly, despite his interest in individual stories, some forms of generalization are acceptable to Duberman, and they take a narrative, historical form as well as at times a social categorical one. Among the stories elicited and told, there emerge variations along the lines of race, gender, and class. Certainly this is not accidental—the stories are supposed to tell us something about the tremendous diversity among the gay community and it's "coming together," at least temporarily, at Stonewall. *Stonewall* provides a powerful historical narrative that is the focus of the analysis and provides the overarching frame for choosing which stories to discuss. Duberman's choice of stories and his way of generalizing from them reflects his theoretical claims about how coalitions can be built, how competing identities can at least momentarily coalesce around a focused political identity, and about the potential for people with diverse sociological experiences to nevertheless coalesce politically. For Duberman's purposes, perhaps the best way to illustrate this claim is precisely through diverse stories that converge into a common historical plot. As analyst, Duberman constructs the plot based on historical events, but he relies heavily on talkative subjects to help him construct the individual paths that led to the convergence and hence the event itself. The reader comes away having learned a tremendous amount about how Stonewall happened as well as about why particular individuals participated in it. There is also much to be learned about identity construction and the logic of social movements (which may have been of more interest to someone interested in sociological generalization), but this type of knowledge is mostly left up to the reader to interpret because of Duberman's reluctance to make these other kinds of generalizations.[10]

Beyond the Individual Story: Categorizing Personal Narratives

Up until now we have been discussing various logics of generalization, claims that particular life stories reveal truths that go beyond the narrators' individual lives or apply beyond their particular context. Some analysts instead emphasize generalizations about life *stories* themselves rather than about their narrators as social or historical individuals. In this quite different logic, the truth claim takes the form that there are a set number of relevant plots or stories "out there" in any given culture that are of interest for a particular theoretical or research problem. The research strategy often focuses on uncovering these stories and revealing their operation in individual cases and finding out how the stories reveal the constraints and opportunities imaginable at a certain point in time or particular social location and how they influence motivation. It also considers the possibilities and variants from one individual to another in the same social location—to see the influence of individual psychology, cultural influences, generational experiences, or historical contingencies within a social-structural category.

Sometimes, the aim is to explore the storied dimensions of social life, and to investigate how narratives play a role in individuals' sense-making operations and in their construction of themselves as social actors. This narrative dimension is not simply given by a social position or historical experience, but rather is a creative process shaped by culturally available models of self-construction that are brought to bear on encounters with the social world. These narrative logics incorporate available plots and also reflect the psychological makeup and lifelong learning experiences that predispose an individual to see him- or herself as fitting into a particular narrative, as the hero of one story and not another. Such shared plots again underscore the ways in which subjectivities are embedded in social, historical, and cultural relations and illustrate the permeability of the line between the individual and the social. Some of these plots are specific to a particular time and place—for example, the "coming-out stories" explored by Kath Weston in *Render Me, Gender Me* and Arlene Stein in *Sex and Sensibility*, the "political coming of age stories" and "activist stories" Temma Kaplan discusses in *Crazy for Democracy*, or the "militant stories" and "success stories" Maynes analyzes in *Taking the Hard Road*.[11]

Sociologist Wendy Luttrell's *Schoolsmart and Motherwise* offers a good illustration of the way this sort of analysis works. Luttrell collected black and white working-class women's stories about schooling and its consequences in their lives. She uses their stories to discuss questions of identity, connections between identity construction and social mobility, and the intersections of race, class, and gender identities as they crystallize around personal stories told about refusing (or being refused) the role of "the teacher's pet." Luttrell's notion of "storied selves" emphasizes the role that storytelling itself plays in the construction of selfhood and identity and how these accounts also draw on previous kinds of stories told in many other situations.[12]

Sociologist Ken Plummer's *Telling Sexual Stories* offers another interesting example of the way this kind of analysis works by focusing on what he terms "sexual stories" or personal narratives focused on the "intimate" and "erotic" in late-twentieth-century Britain and the United States. His study focuses on three types of narratives—rape survivors' stories, "coming out" stories, and "recovery" stories—and his central interest lies in exploring the role that these kinds of stories play at different levels of analysis—"the personal, the situational, the organizational, and the cultural/historical."[13]

For Plummer, sexual stories are always created through "*the interactions which emerge around story telling*" (emphasis in original). The women's movement, the lesbian and gay movement, and the recovery movement all serve as the important communities that have encouraged the telling of such stories. In the 1970s many women learned to forge new identities through consciousness-raising groups, political work, and texts spawned by the feminist movement, all of which provided the cultural tools through which a different kind of identity for victims of rape could be forged. As Plummer's study reveals, this new identity broke with the previous cultural interpretations of rape that had driven many women to keep experiences of rape secret. With the rise of the women's movement, a "new culture of survival" provided "the means by which women come to identify what has happened to them, communicate with sympathetic others and to construct narratives to make sense of their experience in much more positive ways." Furthermore, Plummer shows how these types of stories, initially given voice by the women's movement, begin to circulate in wider communities and cultural arenas, creating self-narratives that are both new and linked with the first model. Just as feminists came to speak publicly about the problem of rape and their identity as survivors, gays and lesbians began to break their silence about their sexual identities and claim new positive identities. As Plummer argues, the common cultural trope in all three kinds of sexual stories lies in their modernist logic of the triumphant individual—one who has "suffered, survived, and surpassed." For both Luttrell and Plummer, then, the stories themselves are a central focus of research; their structure and operation *as stories* reveals social dynamics.[14]

Whose Stories? And How Many?

Whatever type of general argument a personal narrative analysis puts forward, the persuasiveness of that argument for an audience of social scientists and historians will depend on not just the richness of the life story evidence but also its aptness for the research questions at hand. Obviously, the identity of the ideal personal narrator (or narrators) depends on the problems to be explored. Many of the studies we have been discussing focus on life stories "from the margins" and on ways of reading these stories as evidence about how individuals are embedded in personal, social, and political relations that allow them to engage in meaningful social action within the constraints of their particular cultural and historical contexts. However, even though it presents its own challenges (the dynamics of "interviewing up," for example) personal narrative evidence about elites also holds an important place in understanding social action and human agency.[15] A thorough understanding of relations of dominance and subordination along the lines of hierarchies—of class, race, ethnicity, gender, sexuality, familial role, and so forth—stems from comprehending multiple positionalities; the main point here is that the number and array of life stories analyzed needs to fit the analytic aims of the research. Sound strategies for using personal narrative evidence require it to be collected and analyzed with an eye toward the positions into which it taps, those it silences, and where it fits in hierarchies of power, as well, of course, toward its relevance to the question at hand.

A clear example of an analyst's explication of choice in story collecting can be found in R. W. Connell's *Masculinities,* a book to which we have returned several times. Connell describes how she decided what sorts of men to interview:

> Life-history, as well as being one of the richest methods in social science, is also one of the most time-consuming. Using it to study large-scale social changes requires a trade-off between depth and scope. A life-history study of masculinity, for instance, cannot sample a broad population of men while gaining any depth of understanding of particular situations. Rather than spread the research thin, I decided to concentrate on a few situations where the theoretical yield should be high...I tried to identify groups of men for whom the construction or integration of masculinity was under pressure.[16]

As we mentioned earlier, Martin Duberman also explicitly discusses his choice of life story narrators for *Stonewall,* though in somewhat different terms. He decries the "sociologizing" tendencies that "seal off and silence familiar human sounds," but still defends his choice on theoretical as well as historical grounds:

> The six people I ultimately decided to profile seemed to "fit" well together. Their stories were different enough to suggest the diversity of gay and lesbian lives, yet interconnected enough to allow me to interweave their stories when...the historical canvas broadens out into the Stonewall riots, gay politics, and the first Christopher Street Liberation Day March.
>
> This is not to say that these six lives represent all possible variations on gay and lesbian experience in the Stonewall period...No group of six could possibly represent the many pathways of gay and lesbian existence.

But they can suggest some of the significant childhood experiences, adult coping strategies, social and political activities, values, perceptions and concerns that centrally characterized the Stonewall generation.[17]

The choice here was driven by the Duberman's requirement that the narrators have been involved in a particular historical event. The theoretical relevance of the perspective from which each story was told also mattered to Duberman, but it was not the most necessary element. In each of these two studies, although the specific grounds for choice were somewhat different, the explicit discussion and clarity of thinking about the kinds of stories that were included in or excluded from the analysis helps the reader better to assess the analysts' findings.

In *TANU Women,* Susan Geiger chose yet another strategy of research and writing: She interwove one main, lengthy, and detailed life history—that of Tanzanian nationalist leader Bibi Titi Mohammed—with several dozen shorter life stories of other women activists in the Tanzanian nationalist movement. This strategy allowed Geiger to delve into the complexities of gender and culture in the nationalist movement through extensive interviews with and supplemental research about the best-known and relatively well documented leader. At the same time, doing a series of shorter life history interviews, many of them with women in hinterland areas of Tanzania often neglected in studies of nationalism, enabled Geiger to broaden her understanding of female agency in Tanzanian nationalism and to better grasp its variant forms. As Geiger puts it: "in writing this book, I have tried to reflect the view of Bibi Titi and other women activists interviewed that the task of creating and performing nationalism during the 1950s was not one woman's work, it was *women's* work".[18] Geiger can make this claim precisely because she analyzed several stories illustrating both the range of experiences and the commonalities shared by many of the Tanzanian women nationalists. The rationale, a sort of combination of those employed by Connell and Duberman, is simultaneously historical and theoretical.

Where the narratives that are the focus of analysis are already in existence, rather than deliberately elicited by the researcher, the question of "whose stories?" is of course even more complicated. For example, Mary Jo Maynes described a theoretically driven process of choosing from among published French- and German-language working class autobiographies, a process that took into account the contingencies surrounding the writing, publication, and preservation of such texts: "The set of autobiographies [studied] was structured not randomly but rather to include examples of the different sorts of texts, and hence life trajectories, that isolate particular phenomena." Obviously, the skewed nature of these sources, and their "improbability" in terms of the historical record, had to become part of the analysis: "The peculiar characteristics of authors of personal narratives do not invalidate their testimony. But the selectivity that affected *whose* memories were recorded in the autobiographies needs to be an intrinsic part of the history told from them."[19]

Whatever the logic of choice that determined whose stories were collected or analyzed, it is important that the criteria be made clear to readers and also that, like other forms of social-scientific or historical evidence, the stories not be preselected to produce anticipated results. This may not be done intentionally, but it can sometimes come about as a result of the process of interviewing or collecting stories. For example, in Lillian Rubin's *The Transcendent Child,* a book about how abused children survive to become successful adults, Rubin is not entirely clear about how she chose the eight life stories on which the analysis is based. Many of the people she interviewed were apparently either patients in her counseling practice or people sent to her by acquaintances who felt that their stories illustrated some of Rubin's ideas about transcendence. This process of selection—which seems to have privileged cases based on prior knowledge that they seem to fit a pattern that the study is meant to demonstrate—leads to circular reasoning. This is not to say that there is nothing to be learned from such stories, but it is hard to accept them as evidence in support of the book's main argument. While drawing on personal networks in the search for personal narratives, such as Rubin did, is common and even necessary where the researcher is asking for considerable time and self-revelation, it is important to ensure that these networks don't produce *only* the stories the analyst wants or expects to hear. In *Strangers in Paradise: Academics from the Working Class,* Jake Ryan and Charles Sackrey fall into a similar methodological dilemma as a result of the process they used to gather stories. Like Rubin, they began their study by asking people they knew personally, who, like themselves, were academics from working-class backgrounds, to participate in their study by writing autobiographical essays. They also followed through on recommendations made by their narrators of other academics who came from similar backgrounds. It seems likely that their method of recruiting stories pulled in narrators whose stories resembled one another to a greater degree than would have been the case of stories drawn more widely. The stories are quite provocative and the analysis interesting, but the authors do acknowledge that their sample of stories cannot be taken as somehow representative of the experiences of all working-class academics in general (they note, for example, that of the 140 submissions, there were only two by women and none by African Americans); they necessarily limit their claims accordingly.[20]

The number of stories analyzed varies widely depending on the goals of the analyst. Some highly effective analyses of social action and human agency focus on just one story, richly detailed, whereas others draw on a large number of stories. Each approach has its advantages and limitations. Biographies focus typically, though not necessarily, on a single life. Moreover, they tend to be focused on well-known and well-documented figures. Life histories based on oral data have become popular because they allow for the telling of single life stories of people for whom the documentary record is insubstantial. In both cases, the focus on the single life holds the fullest potential of bringing to light the complex and multidimensional character of human social action and of illustrating how the acting individual is embedded in the social.

Barbara Laslett's biographical research on the influential American sociologist William Fielding Ogburn is simultaneously a study of the history of sociology in the United States. Laslett explores the turn that the discipline took after World War I from an emphasis on social problems and social reform to an emphasis on empirical research, particularly quantitative, and a professional culture of objectivism. Her analytic method depends on biographical detail that deploys personal narrative materials among others. Laslett's account of Ogburn's life veers between personal dimensions (e.g., his growing up in the South, the death of his father when he was four and the accompanying decline in his family's class and status positions, and his ambitions and accomplishments in adulthood) and institutional and collective historical dimensions (e.g., changes in class and status hierarchies and gender relations that were occurring in the United States in the late nineteenth and early twentieth centuries, the rise of the research university, and the expansion of a scientific culture in academia and government).

Focus on one life in context allows Laslett to explore individual and collective dimensions of masculinity. She argues that masculinity had become a problematic for middle-class professional men like William Fielding Ogburn. An appropriate notion of masculinity had to be defined in response to the changing historical and social context; for Ogburn, the professional and scientific differentiation between emotion and objectivity was part of this redefinition of masculinity that had both personal and societal resonances.[21] Laslett uses Ogburn's biography to demonstrate the intersection of the social and the individual; the biographical research delves into the realm of highly personal, even psychodynamic, processes to demonstrate the intersection of personal and public life. Nevertheless, new definitions of masculinity and efforts to institutionalize it in social science were not constructed by Ogburn alone; his individual experience is telling in terms of men of his generation and class. The biography suggests how a study of an individual personal life can provide these clues to understanding broader intellectual, political, and institutional developments.

This example of biographical analysis focuses on a man of prominence and power, but like other forms of personal narrative analysis, biographies and life histories that focus on a single individual can also serve to bring more marginal stories to light. For example, Bonnie Smith used the life story of her Parisian concierge, Madame Lucie, as a basis for a fresh perspective on the broad "history of twentieth-century France." By delving into, recording, and analyzing various aspects of Madame Lucie's life—from her youth and migration from Brittany to Paris in the early twentieth century, through her un–self-conscious revelation of her Vichy sympathies, through her ingenious manipulation of and then diminishing effectiveness in her role as a *concierge*—Smith both elicits and ponders a personal narrative that, for all of the modesty of its narrator's social position and for all her particularities, does indeed produce a strikingly original take on French history. Madame Lucie has a way of particularizing or relegating to the background the expected historical metanarratives—about the two world wars, fascism, class conflict, the urban growth of Paris—to create of story with herself as the improbable and resourceful heroine. Life history analyses such as this one, most common in anthropology but also increasingly used by historians and sociologists, typically rely on a close reading of a single life. In contrast with biographies of powerful individuals who are often simply presumed to be masters of their own fate and that of others, life histories such as Smith's use the analysis of the life history of an "ordinary" person to question power, agency, epistemology, and historical metanarratives.[22]

Studies that draw on multiple life stories tend to do so for more specific analytic purposes; they cannot deal in as much detail about each life but instead make claims based on comparisons across a set of stories. Sometimes the stories are those of a small group of individuals interconnected, for example, through a family relationship, involvement in a common organization, or participation in the same historical events. Historians such as Sara Evans, Martin Duberman, Susan Geiger, Annalise Orleck, as well as anthropologists and sociologists such as Faye Ginsburg, Barbara Laslett and Barrie Thorne, for example, all collected life histories of groups of social movement participants (participants in the early phase of the U.S. women's liberation movement, in the Stonewall riots, in the Tanzanian national liberation struggle, in the U.S. women's labor movement, in pro-choice and pro-life movements, and feminist sociology, respectively). To return to one example of this approach, Faye Ginsburg's *Contested Lives* draws on stories from "both sides" of the abortion rights controversy in order to examine dimensions of women's life histories that may have led them first to a strongly held position on and then to political activism around the question of abortion. Since her aim was to explore the similarities as well as the differences among various generations of women involved in abortion activism, it was important for her to gather a sufficiently large number of stories to make convincing comparisons among them, but not so many that she could not delve into their life stories in adequate detail.[23]

The complex dynamics of family business have been the subject of life story research involving different members of the same family. Bertaux and Bertaux-Wiame, mentioned earlier, studied the intersection of family and business relations in the families of Parisian artisanal bakeries (and they note that the "family operation" through which they did the research—Daniel Bertaux interviewed male bakers, and Isabelle Bertaux-Wiame interviewed their wives— brought aspects of family dynamics to light that might otherwise have escaped notice).[24] Anthropologist Sylvia Yanagisako's study of Italian family firms in the silk industry provides another intriguing example. She collected life histories of three generations of individuals involved in family firms in the Italian silk industry. Her study, like that of Bertaux and Bertaux-Wiame, uncovers "invisible" but crucial dynamics involved in the maintenance of such firms over the generations. This is not just the work of fathers and sons, but "of mothers and daughters, husbands and wives, brothers and sisters, and uncles and nephews." In the gendered division of labor of the family firm, the husband's goal was to keep the firm together for adult sons, while the wife's role was to keep the family together. However, after the children had become adults, these goals and desires often came into conflict with the success of the firm: while fathers hoped to ensure the patrimony of the firm, mothers often wanted to distribute this patrimony equally among the adult children. Dynamics among various family members changed not just life-historically but also in response to external factors; for example, family relations became even more complicated as Italy's inheritance laws changed in the 1970s and daughters too could reasonably expect to inherit an interest in the family firm. Yanagisako's findings about the operation of family firms was made possible by her pointed collecting of life stories from the various relevant gender and generational perspectives.[25]

Often analyses are based on a small number of personal narratives that have been collected or selected by the analyst not because their narrators were already personally interconnected with each other but because they bring particular, theoretically relevant perspectives to a research question or because pointed comparisons among the stories serve particular methodological purposes. R. W. Connell's work, mentioned above, demonstrates this approach, for example. So does Wendy Luttrell's study of women's educational histories, ambitions, and subsequent lives. Luttrell made a point of eliciting life histories of two different groups of working-class women: white Northerners and Southern women of color. Since her research questions centered on the place of schooling and stories about schooling and mobility in working-class women's lives, her choice of drawing on a large numbers of stories from two groups who differed along the crucial fault line of race allows for a more specific documentation of the circulation of story plots and a fuller interpretation of her findings about the circulation of certain types of stories among these different subgroups.[26]

More rarely, analysts draw on very large numbers of personal narratives. The methodological cost of this choice is relatively high in that it is harder to go into depth about each of the narrators or to grasp their subjectivity and their contexts fully and convincingly without enormous investment in time. But the value of studies of this sort is that large numbers are useful for getting at the widest range of "possible" stories, for reaching a point of theoretical saturation.[27] Often, this approach has been used to analyze preexisting sets of narratives such as published autobiographies, unpublished sets of memoirs, or interviews. Even in these "large *n*" studies, appropriate analysis still ought not to focus on personal narrative sources merely or primarily as residues of straightforward empirical data, but instead on seeing their potential for understanding the subjective and "storied" dimensions of human motivation, agency, and action. When the large set of narratives is pre-existent, questions about the origins and aims of the original selections or production process do still need to be addressed. Where such sets are read selectively, of course, it is also important to clarify the logic of the sampling strategy, keeping in mind that it is a subset of stories that is drawn from a larger "population."

For example, historian Birgitte Søland found three very large (totaling thousands) sets of short memoirs collected and archived at various points in the late twentieth century in Denmark. In a study assessing women's changing expectations about work and leisure, Søland describes the value of these sets of memoirs:

> the specific memoirs from these three archival collections share a number of characteristics that make them particularly intriguing as historical sources. First, with very few exceptions, they were written by women who grew up in poverty…these women generally lived their entire lives as part of the least privileged groups in Danish society, a fact that set their stories apart from most published memoirs and other sources about girlhood. Secondly, unlike most autobiographers whose recollections have been published, these women did not make the self-confident decision to write down their life stories unsolicited. On the contrary, they only chose to put pen to paper in response to a request from archivists. Not surprisingly, many of their memoirs thus include self-deprecating apologies for "not having much to tell" or "not being somebody important." Others insisted on anonymity or expressed their delight in the promised twenty-five year moratorium on public access to the documents. These narrators may therefore best be described as "accidental autobiographers," as individuals who came to write their

life stories without having given much thought to such a project prior to being asked to do so. This does not mean that their memoirs are less "constructed" or more "authentic" than other personal narratives, but it does mean that their stories offer insights into the ways in which a particular group of historical subjects (whose voices might otherwise easily have been lost) recalled, explained, and made sense of their past.[28]

In total, Søland read 1,100 of these short memoirs, of the several thousand texts collected between 1955 and 1980, all written by women born between 1880 and 1930. Her initial analysis of this large number of texts focuses on generational changes in the kinds of stories being told about expectations of what youth should have been like. In her analysis, she points to central tendencies in the kinds of stories told, and in their tone, as well as to unusual or aberrant stories. The logic of her strategy is thus deliberately to examine both "normative" understandings and expectations as recorded in the stories, and also their hints about the limits of what was imaginable, questionable, or negotiable. For example, in her discussion of women's accounts of their entry into the workforce, Søland argues that:

> Even narrators who recall having been successful in school generally expected to support themselves from their early adolescence, and as a result they quickly settled into the new realities of their lives. Kirstine Hansen, for example, briefly recalled her childhood dream of becoming a teacher before she matter-of-factly proceeded: "But then I left school and then I got a job in a cardboard box factory and then I took a liking to that [job]."
>
> Like Hansen, a large number of narrators from this generation repeatedly use the phrase "and then," recalling their lives as if consisting of a series of consecutive, discrete events, about which they do not find personal reflections necessary or appropriate. However, there is one notable exception to this general rule: When speaking of work many narrators were uncharacteristically forthcoming, carefully recalling the options they had, the choices they made, and the motivations that informed their decisions. Surely, those options were severely limited and wages were always minimal, but, as these narrators point out, each job had its own advantages and disadvantages, which were carefully considered.[29]

This study, like some others based on large numbers of texts,[30] required the development of methods for simultaneously analyzing individual texts and describing or categorizing stories or subsets of stories, for reading both for the logic of each account and the tendencies of large numbers of accounts. (The associated method of categorizing stories was discussed above.) Though very different in their research design and logic from close readings of single personal narratives, many of these studies share key epistemological and theoretical presumptions of other approaches to personal narrative analysis: They are interested in subjectivity; they are self-reflective in their approach to genres of storytelling and their relationship to self-construction; they recognize the interplay between individual self-construction and social-historical context; and they are transparent about the interpretive process.

The Rhetorics of Personal Narrative Analysis

In our discussion of the methods of personal narrative analysis, we have emphasized several points. First, effective analysis of personal narratives should start from and build on the particular kinds of knowledge that personal narratives can yield. The epistemology and methodology departs at key points from the positivism that underlies many other approaches to social science and history, but this does not mean that arguments based on personal narratives need to remain outside of conversations with proponents of other methods. Arguments based on personal narratives can be made transparently, systematically, and persuasively even to audiences that might include skeptical readers. What makes personal narrative analyses more or less persuasive? Up until now we have focused on methods for eliciting or selecting and interpreting personal narratives in a transparent and systematic fashion, appropriate to the theoretical questions at hand. Clarity about these issues in publications based on personal narrative research goes a long way toward convincing readers. Here we will focus on specific questions about strategies for incorporating personal narrative evidence into analytic texts so as to make persuasive arguments—that is, on the rhetorics of arguments based on the analysis of personal narratives. Developing effective rhetorical strategies requires attention to such issues as how to present the original narrative evidence, how to summarize or paraphrase narrators, when or how much to quote them, and how much evidence is required to make a persuasive case.

It is useful to begin with a reminder that there is a rhetorical dimension to all types of arguments, including those based on positivist assumptions that deploy quantitative evidence. Deirdre McCloskey's classic analysis of the rhetoric of economics and economic history reminds us that even in this most scientific of the social sciences, what readers find persuasive is the result of an evolving historical relationship between authors and their audiences.[31] McCloskey tracks a historical process through which new models and arguments, and the evidence supporting them, were introduced. She argues that this process involves audience education and persuasion rather than simply the "weight of facts." Only through a gradual process of education did audiences learn how to read, understand, and accept certain kinds of economic arguments. The personal narrative analyst faces a similar task of persuasion, complicated by their greater familiarity with and receptivity toward positivistic approaches among some segments of their audience. Drawing on McCloskey's insights about the rhetoric of economics, personal narrative analysts should keep in mind that part of their task is to educate their readers about the logic of their methods, even while they are building a specific argument.

In *Masculinities,* R. W. Connell takes up this challenge explicitly. Compared with most personal narrative analysts, Connell is extraordinary in her facility at incorporating into her analyses information about her own rules and logic in eliciting and interpreting stories. She is one of the few, for example, who tells readers how she tries to systematize her reading:

> In the first phase of analysis I listened to tapes, read transcripts, indexed, and wrote up each interview as a case study. In each case study the interview as a whole was examined from three points of view: (a) the narrative sequence of events; (b) a structural analysis, using a grid provided by the three structures of gender relations; (c) a dynamic analysis, tracing the making and unmaking of masculinity, trying to grasp the gender project involved. Writing up each case study was both an attempt at a portrait of a person, and a reflection on the portrait's meaning as evidence about social change.
>
> In the second phase, I analysed the case studies in groups. Here the goal was to explore the similarities and difference in the trajectories of men in certain social locations and to understand their collective location in large-scale change. Again I used a grid derived from gender theory to make comparisons. I abstracted and reindexed the cases so that, as each topic came to be analysed, the whole group was in view, while the narrative shape of each life was preserved. I wrote this analysis for each group separately, making each report an attempt at a collective portrait of men caught up in a certain process of change.[32]

In addition, in her presentation of the stories upon which the analysis is based, there is always a judicious mix of stories and interpretation so as to keep the reader's interest alive while also persuading him or her that Connell's interpretation is plausible. Her prose goes back and forth between the stories and the analysis in a conversational fashion. She draws heavily on excerpts from the stories to illustrate her points and to question her analytic categories. The reader can observe both Connell's interpretive framework and its evolution in response to interviews. While Connell definitely has her own "take" and clearly draws on theoretical language that is not used by the interviewees, she keeps a conversation going and thus uses the stories to interrogate the analytic categories and remind readers of how in real lives the categories are fluid and negotiable. In her analytic writing, this back-and-forth makes Connell's method and presumptions transparent, "teaches" the reader how she operates, and persuades the reader that Connell is an honest interpreter.

Moreover—and this is a significant point in our observations about techniques of presentation across a wide range of studies—Connell returns often enough to the same named individuals, and she works with a small enough number in each case, that the narrators become familiar as individuals to readers. This relates directly to another important aspect of the rhetorics of personal narrative analysis; namely, the question of how much of the story is enough. According to sociologist Amy Kaler:

> The most interesting uses of personal narratives occur when the narratives form the basis for the scholar's work, and are supplemented by other forms of representation. This usually means that the narratives are presented verbatim (or close to verbatim) and in good-sized chunks. The size and presentation of these chunks will vary according to the format of the text (article, monograph, experimental vs. traditional writing). However, I think the narratives should be long enough and central enough to convey to the reader some of the atmosphere of the times and places of the narrative, and to let the reader see how processes like cause and effect, action/reaction, or gradual coming to fruition work themselves out in the narrator's life.[33]

Like Connell, Kaler emphasizes the need to present narrators' stories in sufficient detail so that readers get to know narrators as individuals. Since, as we have argued, intersubjective understanding is intrinsic to the analytic process in working with personal narratives, so is it important to the persuasiveness of the argument. The added advantage is that readers have enough of the evidence to make their own judgments about whether the analyst's reading is the best possible one or whether other interpretations might be offered. The reader can, so to speak, "check" the analyst's interpretation, in a way that is analogous to the presentation of a summary table in support of an argument based on quantitative data. In both cases, the reader views some of the data that has already been forcibly shaped by the analyst. The rhetorical power of seeing some version of the "raw data" and having the opportunity to follow that analyst's logic makes the whole project more compelling.

In practice, of course, extremely lengthy excerpts from memoirs, letters, or life history interviews are not practical from the point of view of publishers' word limits or readers' patience. Wherever the particular choice of words, nuance, or a causal dynamic and its complexities are at issue, it is generally most persuasive to rest the argument on narrators' actual words, but summary, paraphrase, and categorization of narrators' stories (the personal narrative analyst's equivalent of data tables) are all necessary, even when there is only one story involved and all the more when many stories are under scrutiny. Moreover, it is also important to remember that, no matter how eloquent the narrators are, their stories never "speak for themselves." Or, rather, they do speak for themselves but they almost never speak for the analyst—that is, they cannot be expected to make the analytic argument. Excerpts from narrators' stories always need to be framed, contextualized, and interpreted by the analyst. As a rule of thumb, the most effective rhetorical strategies combine enough of the personal narrative to make the narrator's world and logic accessible, enough of the analyst's prose to make the analyst's logic apparent, and enough clarity, transparency, and honesty to make it possible for the reader to keep the two perspectives separate. The image of a "conversation" between narrator(s) and analyst is a good rhetorical model.

The balance that Connell accomplishes in this respect eludes many other analysts. And some deliberately choose different strategies. Susan Geiger's heavy reliance on extensive quotations pushes the reader's limits (more on this below), whereas James Amelang's study of artisan memoir in early modern Europe suffers from the opposite tendency. Readers who might be expecting to get a flavor of the artisan writing and viewpoints are disappointed by *The Flight of Icarus* in that, with the exception of one narrator, there is not much elaborated textual evidence presented in the artisan authors' own words. Instead, the argument rests on Amelang's wide reading of a range of texts supported by brief quotations or paraphrases. Similarly, Gunilla-Friederike Budde's readers never get a sense of the German and English middle-class autobiographers she studies as individuals with stories to tell, nor of their texts as either exemplary or atypical of the genre. In this case, the very size of the database (over 400 texts) makes it difficult for the analyst to get beyond paraphrase and summary. In contrast with other studies, the memoirists rarely emerge as identifiable individuals. Similarly, Joan Brumberg's study of American girls' diaries (discussed in chapter 3) is less persuasive than it might otherwise be because of Brumberg's tendency to cite short snippets of evidence for a wide range of texts; relatively few individual profiles emerge in enough detail to bring home Brumberg's claims. The few more complete sketches interspersed throughout the analysis are rich and compelling. This would suggest that even in studies that are based on readings of a large number of stories, it is important to tell at least some of those stories, in an exemplary fashion, fully enough to both relay the sense of the whole individual and persuade readers that the analyst's reading of the sources is credible.[34]

It is necessary to acknowledge as well that part of the persuasiveness of personal narrative analyses rests on the appeal of the narratives themselves, and their ability to lure in readers by dint of a tale well told. This presents interesting challenges where authors want to analyze personal narratives that do not or cannot be expected to evoke empathy on the part of readers. This can be either because the narrator's position or stake in an issue is one that is alien to the analyst or audience or because the cultural chasm between the narrator and the audience is wide. For example, Vincent Crapanzano obviously feels little empathy for many of the individuals whose life stories he collected for his book *Waiting: The Whites of South Africa* (discussed in chapter 2). He does convey that it is important to understand their position, however, and to relay that understanding to his readers. He manages through collecting and analyzing their stories to project the narrators' complex subjectivities located in local and international discourses and in contemporary and historical moments.[35]

Cross-cultural studies present particular problems of positionality in the research process (as discussed in chapter 4), and they also present unique challenges in the realm of rhetorical strategy. Susan Geiger's *TANU Women* provides an especially instructive example in this regard. Geiger relies on unusually long excerpts from the life stories she collected, very likely in part because she knows that their lives will be unfamiliar to her audience, which includes many Western readers. In making her argument about the "counter narrative" of nationalism, Geiger often begins directly with the words of the Tanzanian women activists. Without preface, these narratives come across to readers unfamiliar with Tanzanian culture and history as dense and complex. Much is gained by Geiger's use of extensive quotations, but this is demanding for the reader and much of the analytic material has been relegated to footnotes that in a more intrusive style of presentation might have been written directly into the analytic text. Moreover, the retelling in the book reflects the original telling in that the life stories emerge in a scattered and seemingly incoherent manner that follows to some extent the form in which Geiger was able to elicit the stories.[36] She focuses on the narrator's role in the nationalist movement (which was the narrators' desire and to a large extent also Geiger's aim), which means that other aspects of life and earlier periods of the life stories get truncated in ways that limit the appeal of the stories.[37]

Consistent with her interest in eliciting historical analysis from the interviews rather than imposing it on them, Geiger makes little effort to reorganize the personal narrative accounts into any "standard" life history form. On the surface, it also seems as if there is insufficient attention to subjective dimensions of motivation, the pursuit of which, we have suggested, is among the more interesting payoffs for doing life history analysis. However, in keeping close to the original form of narration, as structured by the questioner's focus on the nationalist movement, these excerpts hint at some of the culturally and historically specific narrative traditions and motives that lay behind the stories Geiger was told. To the largely Western readers of the book, the narrators remain enigmatic as individuals—the subjective dimension, though present and analytically significant, takes forms that are elusive and depart from familiar Western tropes. Readers do not get "whole" life stories, in part because Geiger does not ask for them, but in part because those do not seem to be the kind of stories the nationalist activist women wanted to tell her. So the emotional content is as muted in the reception as it seems to have been in the telling. This makes these stories and their narrators less effective as storytellers for contemporary Western readers. In other words, the narrative traditions and expectations of Geiger's narrators and her audience are at odds with one another. What makes for a "good story" is not shared.

Of course, Geiger could have translated these life stories not only from Kiswahili into English but also from the narrative traditions of "storied selves" meaningful in Tanzania to those more expected in the West so that her audience could better relate to them. However, she chose not to do so. Her refusal to "normalize" these stories for the convenience of her Western audience recalls the discussion in chapter 4 of the important epistemological, methodological, ethical, and geopolitical questions involved in translating stories across boundaries. Geiger's analysis reminds us of the profound ways in which notions of subjectivity and related ideas about life stories vary cross-culturally and historically. The point here is to underscore the power of life stories as forms making sense of the world, and the specificity of narrative models and traditions of telling stories. Further, this example shows how cultural differences can affect how persuasive an analysis based on stories is, and for which audiences.[38]

The Truth of Personal Narrative Analysis

It goes without saying that people who write or tell their life stories are deeply interested in having a particular version of that story come to light. They are selective in what they recall and relate, self-serving in their emphases, and sometimes downright deceptive. For social scientists and historians who work with personal narrative sources, these characteristics have to be acknowledged in the particular epistemological, methodological, and rhetorical practices that govern their work. This issue has been highlighted dramatically in recent controversies involving distortions and deceptions in popular published memoirs, but of course skepticism about memoirs has existed as long as the genre has. The German socialist activist Wilhelm Kaisen, who was born in 1887, prefaced his memoir with a wry note to his readers. "'Somebody once said to me,' he wrote, 'that he really loved reading memoirs because people tell such wonderful lies in them. What I'm now about to relate, he would certainly reckon among these.'"[39] More seriously, the controversy surrounding the memoirs of Guatemalan indigenous rights activist and Nobel Prize winner Rigoberta Menchú when David Stoll published a book challenging the veracity of key details of her 1984 memoir, *I, Rigoberta Menchú*, demonstrated how high the stakes can be for narrators who tell their stories and analysts who rely on them.[40] Some scholars finesse such critiques by pointing out that all understandings of truth are the result of discursive conventions and that there is, of course, not one truth but many. As Ruth Behar, for example, says of life story narrator Esperanza: "the intimation that she has been telling me lies, not the true story of her life in any sense, emphasizes the fictional or storied nature of the blended text we have been producing together over the years. There is no *true* version of a life, after all. There are only stories told about and around a life."[41] Nevertheless the question remains about what kinds of truth claims can be made on the basis of personal narrative evidence, truth claims that will pass muster among a wide range of historians and social scientists even while respecting the perspectives and personhood of narrators of dubious or inconsistent stories.

It is certainly necessary to recognize that personal narratives do not in any simple sense reveal the past as "it actually was"—no philosophy of history or social science would demand or expect that of any type of evidence. The value of personal narratives is related precisely to their tendency to go beyond the simple facts: They tap into the realms of meaning, subjectivity, imagination, and emotion. Donald Spence makes a similar point in distinguishing between "historical truth" and "narrative truth" in psychoanalytic dialogues. While the former regards stories as something through which a historical truth can be discovered, *narrative truth* highlights the role stories play in the creation of meaning about self and other. Personal narratives in comparison with other sources can reveal both kinds of truth, but in Spence's view the latter is more valuable because it enables us to understand how individuals construct meaning in their lives.[42]

Developing effective strategies for making persuasive arguments based on life stories means not taking them simply at face value, but rather providing the necessary context for understanding and interpreting their possible meanings and significance and for appreciating their storied quality. Effective analyses of personal narratives must take into consideration that *any rendition of the past has to be seen in the context of its motives in the present (i.e., at the time of the telling), its symbolic power, and its contextual framing.*[43] As Luisa Passerini has written "all autobiographical memory is true: it is up to the interpreter to discover in which sense, where, and for what purpose."[44] An implicit pledge of veracity begins with what autobiographical theorist Philippe Lejeune has termed the "autobiographical pact" between the narrator and listeners or readers that the story being told is essentially true. But the burden of proof, so to speak, rests on the analyst. R. W. Connell suggests (here paralleling Lejeune's emphasis on the implicit promise of truth telling) that analysts need to take seriously the efforts and intentions of life story narrators "to speak the truth," even if they cannot presume that they will succeed.[45] For many analytic purposes, this commits life story researchers to the hard work of assessment, doubt and checking, puzzling over anomalies, and finally acknowledging unresolved contradictions or suspicions. According to Connell:

> There is a tendency, in recent discussions of method, to treat any story as a fiction; to "read" it for the figures of speech, motivated silences and narrative devices by which the teller as author constructs a meaningful tale. Any serious researcher using life-histories must be aware of these features of stories. But if the language is all we can see, then, we are missing the point of a life-history—and spurning the effort the respondents themselves make to speak the truth…This evidence is not necessarily easy to use; it takes time and effort to examine the story from different angles and compare it with other evidence.[46]

In comparing narrators' accounts against other sources of evidence, analysts are likely to uncover discrepancies. While such discoveries are crucial to analysis, we are not proposing that analysts simply assess the "truth" of a narrator's words in terms of their factual accuracy, the reliability of memory, or the correspondence with some other form of evidence. Important insights can also be gleaned from mistakes, distortions, and lies.

A fascinating example of work with an unreliable narrator's life story comes from historian Daniel Roche's edition of the manuscript autobiography of an obscure eighteenth-century French window maker, Jacques-Louis Ménétra.[47] In the life story, *Journal of My Life,* Ménétra recounts his travels through France as a series of wild escapades; he seduces women, wins fights, rescues drowning children, puts out fires, and dupes yokels. Roche does a meticulous job of tracing events or acts referred to in the text to external referents. In this case, the autobiographer's memory proved startlingly sound and accurate on many points including, for example, the precise details about the amount of his wages in different regions of France. However, there is also much in *Journal of My Life* that was inaccurate or demonstrably fictive. For instance, Ménétra recounts meeting folk-hero-bandit Louis Mandrin in 1762, but, as Roche points out, this was not possible because Mandrin was executed in 1755. Other tall tales that Ménétra tells as his own appear to be drawn from other stories. As Robert Darnton points out in the Foreword to the English-language edition,

> [Ménétra] took a great deal of his material from the popular literature of the time, which featured the sort of thing that he passed off as

everyday occurrences on his travels: hideous crimes, encounters with ghosts, black magic, dramatic rescues, practical jokes (the funniest at the expense of priests), and orgies (the juiciest in nunneries). Ménétra's favorite genre was the sexual yarn. It gave him a chance to assert his own prowess, because he always cast himself as the seducer; yet it often seems to come straight out of Boccacio or from the oral equivalents of the *Decamerone* that circulated among the story tellers of the Old Regime.[48]

For Ménétra, the funniest pranks are often about cuckolding the "bourgeois," the term that French workers called their bosses. In one tale, Ménétra transmits a venereal disease to the boss's wife who, in turn, passes it on to her husband. The unsuspecting husband, in turn, takes his problem to Ménétra whose skills in folk medicine allow him to cure his boss. Ménétra gleefully reports leaving town blessed with the gratitude of the very man whom he had cuckolded. While the veracity of such tales cannot be verified, this theme reveals important class and gender hierarchies that informed Ménétra's worldview.

Importantly, for Roche, the value of the narrative does not lie solely in its factual accuracy: "misrepresentation, exaggeration, and error [also] take on meaning, as do omissions and fantasies."[49] The high-blown rhetoric of Ménétra's account and his relentless focus on his sexual prowess reveal some sense of the norms and values of the world of artisans in eighteenth-century France if not their actual behavior. As Darnton reminds us, even in its artistry and fantasy, *Journal of My Life* has value, for "Ménétra gives us a chance to see what eighteenth-century dreams were made of."[50] In this way, Roche's work provides important methodological strategies for analysts of personal narratives. *Persuasive interpretation requires an enormous range of contextualization and fact checking;* exaggerations and fictionalizations are sometimes obvious and sometimes more subtle. It is only through the comparisons with other forms of documentation—whether the sociohistorical staples such as wage rates or cultural historical evidence such as plots commonly circulating in popular culture—that the groundwork for interpreting Ménétra's story is laid.

Alessandro Portelli's investigation of a false collective memory in *The Death of Luigi Trastulli* is a pertinent example of the significance of misremembering among a network of narrators of oral life histories who share a local history. Portelli begins precisely with an error of misdating that commonly occurred in the life stories he collected in the town of Terni, Italy. Luigi Trastulli was killed in a clash with police in 1949; about this the documentary evidence is consistent and uncomplicated. In story after story, however, workers who talked to Portelli in the 1970s placed the death four years later in the context of demonstrations that took place on the occasion of a plant closing involving massive layoffs. Rather than simply dismissing or "correcting" the inaccurate stories, Portelli begins to dig into them, on the theory that " 'wrong tales,' like the many versions of Trastulli's death, are so very valuable. They allow us to recognize the interests of the tellers, and the dreams and desires beneath them."[51] In this case, Portelli's unpacking of the errors he was told by narrators, his comparison of the various versions of the event of Trastulli's death, allowed him access into the symbolic universe through which workers in Terni made sense of their world and their history and their need to connect the death of Trastulli with the historical moment in which it made the most symbolic sense.

A final example of analytic insights derived from misrepresentations is provided in Beth Roy's *Bitters in the Honey: Tales of Hope and Disappointment across Divides of Race and Time,* which draws on life histories with black and white community members who lived through the court-ordered desegregation of Central High School in Little Rock, Arkansas, in 1957. Of particular interest to Roy are the discrepancies she uncovers in the life histories of whites who attended Central High. In contrast to black students' accounts of daily harassment, ridicule, and threats of violence, most white students insisted that student behavior was peaceful that year and that no one was harassed.[52]

Whites still recall with contempt and hostility Minnijean Brown, one of the nine black students who enrolled that year, whom they regard as a "trouble maker," the one black student who behaved badly. When Brown's way was intentionally blocked in the cafeteria several times by white boys, she apparently retaliated by dumping chili on the head of one of the provocateurs, and she was later suspended from school. This is one reason she is considered a trouble maker; white students criticize her on other grounds as well. Sally, for instance, says:

> I remember, uh, what was that girl's name? Big girl, Minnijean. She had an attitude, it was like, OK, white folks, here I am...I can't recall words that happened, it was just a haughty, snotty, look-down-your nose at me attitude that she had.[53]

Similarly, Jane, another narrator, says:

> I would describe her as unlike all the rest of the blacks. I'd put it in class terms. First of all she was overweight, so that made her more, what?—easy to tease. She was a stereotype of a mammy, a young mammy by white standards. Remember how there used to be the mammy with [sketches big belly with her hands]. OK? Because she was big and overweight, and she was more challenging, more asserting, she was more set. Whereas the others were very almost docile.[54]

For Jane and Sally, like many of the other white students, if Minnijean had "stayed in her place," there never would have been any trouble at Central High.

The emotionally intense focus on Minnijean Brown puzzled Roy. She and the eight other black students faced the threat of violence in attempting to enroll at Central High. Because the state of Arkansas refused to comply with the court order, President Eisenhower sent in the 101st Airborne to accompany the nine black students to school. Whatever Minnijean had done, daily life at Central High could not have been easy for her or any of the other black students. Why, forty years later, do their accounts of Brown in particular carry so much disdain? A serendipitous event combined with a careful reading of the context of the narrators' lives provided Roy with some clues. At the end of her interview, Jane notices an old newspaper clipping that Roy had in her files. "It was a picture of the Nine, and Minnijean stood to one side, tall and stately—not overweight. On her face was a self-conscious smile; she seemed shy, chin tucked down, perhaps unsure of herself in front to the camera." Jane is shocked and upset when she realizes that Minnijean looked "nothing like a mammy." "How could I remember her that way?" she asks.[55]

Roy draws on this mistake to illustrate how over time strong emotions, political motivations, and culture converge to reconstruct memory. From the perspective of the white students at Central High, the school desegregation crisis disrupted—even ruined—the normal course of events in their school year. They resented the presence of the guards in the hallways, the media attention, and the canceling of various school activities. As Roy's analysis reveals because integration was forced on them, many described feeling powerless and resentful, and these powerful feelings, in turn, helped to construct a scapegoat. Because Minnijean had retaliated, she stood out in their minds as a trouble maker. Further, calling upon racist cultural representations of the mammy served to recast in their minds what Minnijean actually looked like. Depicting her as big and overweight also created the means to discredit her: Big women are often considered figures of fun, and in this way, she was "easy to tease." Jane's memory colored by resentment, segregationist politics, and cultural representations helped to create an image and reputation for Minnijean—one that Jane and the other white students actively collaborated in constructing. As Roy suggests, "all that talk among the girls about Minnijean had in fact constituted a political act of protest against Minnijean's disturbance of normalcy, against the threat implied by their place in a promised class order."[56]

Roy's thoughtful analysis reveals the ways in which suspect accounts can be telling. As in Portelli's analysis, here too the present-day context at the moment of storytelling is important in understanding why particular stories are remembered and what is meaningful about them. Jane's story portrays Minnijean as powerful and larger than life, while at the same time rendering herself—a white woman—as a victim of integration. Her reversal of the Civil Rights narrative of white discrimination against African Americans is not unintentional. Jane and many others white former students complained vociferously to Roy about a documentary that was made about integration at Central High as well as a book written by one of the black students—both focusing on the harassment of black students by whites. The subsequent circulation of these critical public narratives offers a powerful motive for constructing a narrative to counter the story of black victimization. Roy's attentiveness to the present context of motives, broader cultural representations, politics, and emotions reveals the many layers of meaning that narrators draw on to make sense of their experiences even when they are not factually true.

As we have been insisting, transparency about the logic and process of interpreting personal narrative evidence contributes forcefully to the persuasiveness of arguments based on it. This transparency also includes acknowledging the limits of what can be known and the tentativeness of proffered interpretations when necessary. Portelli's and Roy's studies and Marjorie DeVault's close reading of the interracial dynamics of the interview situation discussed in chapter 4 provide good examples. DeVault's call for a "light-handed approach" to interpreting personal narratives, one that recognizes that some of the truths that emerge from it are tentative rather than "a final objective truth" is worth attending to.[57] Liz Stanley makes a similar point about the contingency of knowledge based on personal narratives in her astute discussion of her work with collections of letters, which are always "emergent"—that is, ongoing, incomplete, tentative.[58]

Even transgressive methods such as the use of imaginary data or fictionalized evidence can be effective in making an analysis persuasive as long as the methods are transparent, self-reflexive, and not arbitrary. We have discussed examples of analyses that employ such techniques, for example Amitav Ghosh's *In an Antique Land,* in previous chapters.[59] We will elaborate on a final example here to illustrate the use of fictionalizing life history evidence in a manner that avoids confusing, deceiving, or angering readers and instead evokes empathy—an act of intersubjective imagination that is so crucial to the power of personal narrative analysis.

American Studies scholar Tiya Miles in *Ties That Bind: The Story of an Afro-Cherokee Family in Slavery and in Freedom* constructs an imaginary but possible subjective framework in a case where actual documentation is insufficient. Her book reconstructs a life story of Shoe Boots, a Cherokee war hero and farmer, and Doll, an African slave he acquired in the late 1790s. Over the next thirty years, Shoe Boots and Doll lived together not only as master and slave but also as life-long partners who, with their children and grandchildren, experienced key events in U.S. history—including slavery, the founding of the Cherokee Nation, the subsequent removal of Native Americans along the Trail of Tears, and the Civil War. The central challenge Miles faces in writing the story of this family is that Doll's life is known primarily through the records of actions and events inflicted on her—her purchase, her marriage, and the loss of her children. The evidence of her life—like that of countless other slaves and subaltern people—cannot be made to speak directly to her subjective experience. As Miles writes:

> This place of the unrepresentable, the unknowable, and in the language of Toni Morrison, "the unspeakable," is where the slave lives. It is where a slave woman named Doll Shoeboots lived until her old age. Unlike [the slave autobiographer] Harriet Jacobs, though, who told her unknowable story in her own words, Doll did not write. A record of Doll's interior life, her ruminations and fleeting thoughts, might reveal something of her world to us. But like millions of other slave women, Doll left nothing behind that attests to her character, her strategies and ideologies, the quality of her days and years. The available sources on Doll's life are a reflection of that life itself—limited, ambiguous and fragmented.[60]

Nevertheless, Miles remains committed to trying to capture not just a glimpse of the daily texture of this one woman's life but also what it might have seemed like to her. She asks:

> To what body of evidence do we turn in our effort to remain responsible to historical methods while at the same time drawing as near as we can to the subjective experience of those who have gone before us? It is my belief that imaginative reconstructions of the past, tightly welded to historical knowledge, can aid us in our quest. While historical fiction cannot supplant the disciplined accounts that historical work produces...I believe that fiction as its own form of truth, can bridge the gaps in our evidence and allow us access to the marrow of human feeling.[61]

To give the reader a sense of the contours of Doll's life, Miles provides the historical background of black and Cherokee history during this time period and meticulously documents every "scrap of paper" that speaks to Doll's life; at certain points, she introduces insights from novelists and literary scholars such as Toni Morrison, Hortense Spillers, and Saidiya Hartmann into the narrative. She makes it apparent to readers that she is engaged in a process whereby "historical narratives are shaped, not found." In doing so, she makes it clear when she is relying on extant historiography and archival records and when she is speculating about Doll's feelings when no record is available. In her chapter on motherhood, for instance, she notes that the only record of the birth of Doll's first child is a descriptive account of the birth from a nephew. Other than this two-sentence description of the birth of her daughter, we know nothing about how Doll experienced her pregnancy or how Doll felt after the baby was born. Miles writes:

> As an African woman in a Cherokee woman's world, Doll *may have felt* adrift during her pregnancy. She *may have missed* the ways of women from her own culture; she *may have longed* for her mother. She *may have felt* her exclusion most at this time of ceremonial and spiritual importance, when the centrality of clan membership rose to the fore.[62]

Significantly, Miles makes it evident that her speculations are derived from the historiography on cultural practices surrounding motherhood among Cherokee women at this particular historical moment and from the fact that Doll, as a black woman, would be regarded as an outsider in this setting. She does not tell readers what these experiences meant to Doll, but asks them instead, given the historical context, to imagine the possibilities.

Doll's status as a subject and agent of history is further complicated by the historical facts of slavery. Before the Civil War, children of enslaved mothers, regardless of paternity, inherited the status of bondage; as Miles's careful historical overview reveals, the Cherokee were complicit in the legal definition of slaves as "property." Consequently, Doll's experience of pregnancy and childbirth not only raises questions about the personal meanings of her status as an outsider but also her feelings about the future of her child. Again, there is no historical record revealing Doll's feelings about having a child marked by bondage. Turning to the documentary records of the time period, Miles finds that some slave women practiced infanticide because they knew their children would be sold away, and first-person accounts such as Harriet Jacobs's *Life of a Slave Girl* reveal the ambivalence of an enslaved mother who loves her newborn, but wishes her dead because death was better than slavery. Miles takes her readers one step further toward imagining how Doll might have experienced this event by reminding us of Sethe, the central character in Toni Morrison's novel *Beloved,* who is haunted by the death of her child whom she killed to prevent her from becoming enslaved. Miles pointedly asks in the conclusion of the chapter: "What is the psychic, spiritual, emotional and ontological condition of the enslaved black 'mother,' whose relationship to her child will be defined not by the call of kinship but by the prerogative of property?" In Doll's case, we don't know the answer: not only her child's status as an individual, but Doll's status, too, as a mother and more broadly as an historical subject, was formulated in the context of the institutions of slavery. To imagine Doll's subjectivity requires a huge imaginative leap on the part of the analyst and readers of the book, even as it calls into question their usual categories for understanding historical agency and historical narratives. Miles, "in writing this ineffable tale," necessarily cast her net wide "hoping to provide a glimpse of untold lives with honesty, complexity, and compassion."[63]

Like DeVault's "light handed approach to interpretation," what makes Miles's account compelling is that she makes transparent the logic and the contingency of her interpretations. Because the evidence is incomplete, she provides additional information to suggest possible alternative readings of Doll's life. In giving readers a glimpse into Doll's possible subjectivity, her aim is not to establish a fixed and certain truth, but rather to broaden the perspectives on which knowledge is built, to build perspectivity itself into analysis, and to make more visible the subjectivity and individuality of relatively marginal and underdocumented historical agents.

Fictionalizing goes well beyond what many historians and social scientists regard as acceptable rhetorical modes. And of course, this example digresses also in the sense that the analysis is not based on personal narrative evidence as we have been defining it in *Telling Stories*. Still, it is worth discussing Miles's quite atypical approach because, at the method's limit, it confronts many of the issues and challenges associated even with the more conventional forms of personal narrative analysis that have been our focus: (1) the relationship between historically specific ideas about selfhood and cultural variants in forms of life storytelling; (2) the storied character of lives and of analytic narratives of all sorts; (3) the importance of understanding the intersections between the individual and the social and the methodological complexity of viewing these intersections from the perspectives of the marginal and powerless as well as of the hegemonic and powerful; and (4) the particular nature of the truths revealed through the analysis of life stories, and the acts of empathy or imagination this entails for both analysts and their audiences.

The most persuasive analyses, we have argued, acknowledge and take advantage of the particular characteristics of personal narratives as evidence. Such analyses construct appropriate kinds of generalizations. They focus on stories that are well chosen and well justified in terms of the particular problems or questions the research addresses. They are transparent in describing the research process and the relationships and positionalities that structured it. They retell the life stories on which they are based in enough detail that the intersubjective leaps of understanding that were central to the analysis are also possible for the analyst's audiences. They acknowledge that for all of its richness, personal narrative research brings its own uncertainty and incompleteness. The truths that emerge from the analysis of personal narratives can be precious and are often otherwise unknowable, but they are also complex, contingent, and subject to revision.

Notes

INTRODUCTION: THE USE OF PERSONAL NARRATIVES IN THE SOCIAL SCIENCES AND HISTORY

1. Bridging this dualism has long been an important theoretical project among social theorists. See Anthony Giddens, *Central Problems in Social Theory* (Berkeley and Los Angeles: University of California Press, 1979); Philip Abrams, *Historical Sociology* (Ithaca, NY: Cornell University Press, 1982); Pierre Bourdieu, *Outline of a Theory of Practice* (Cambridge: Cambridge University Press, 1977) and *The Logic of Practice* (Stanford: Stanford University Press, 1980), both translated by Richard Nice; Pierre Bourdieu and Loic Wacquant, *An Invitation to Reflexive Sociology* (Chicago: University of Chicago Press, 1992); George Steinmetz, "Bourdieu's Disavowal of Lacan: Psychoanalytic Theory and the Concepts of "Habitus" and "Symbolic Capital," *Constellations* 13, no. 4 (2006): 445–464; James Coleman, "Social Theory, Social Research and a Theory of Action," *American Journal of Sociology* 91, no. 6 (1986): 1309–1335 and *Foundations of Social Theory* (Cambridge, MA: Harvard University Press, 1990); Jurgen Habermas, *The Theory of Communicative Action*, vol. 2, *Lifeworld and System: A Critique of Functionalist Reason* (Boston: Beacon Press, 1985).

2. There is a considerable literature on the underpinnings of narrative and narrativity as well as empirical studies that adopt a narrative approach to social-scientific analysis. Works that are particularly helpful in terms of the approach we develop here include: Paul Ricoeur, *Time and Narrative*, 2 vols., translated by Kathleen McLaughlin and David Pellauer (Chicago: University of Chicago Press, 1984–86); Charles Taylor, *Sources of the Self* (Cambridge, MA: Harvard University Press, 1989); Personal Narratives Group, *Interpreting Women's Lives: Feminist Theory and Personal Narratives* (Bloomington: University of Indiana Press, 1989); Margaret Somers, "Narrativity, Narrative Identity, and Social Action: Rethinking English Working-Class Formation," *Social Science History* 16, no. 4 (1992): 591–630; Patrick Ewick and Susan S. Silbey, "Subversive Stories and Hegemonic Tales: Toward a Sociology of Narrative," *Law and Society Review* 29 (1995): 197–226; Francesca Polletta, "Contending Stories: Narrative in Social Movements," *Qualitative Sociology* 21, no. 2 (1998): 419–446; Jaber F. Gubrium and James A. Holstein, "At the Border of Narrative and Ethnography," *Journal of Contemporary Ethnography* 28 (1999): 561–573; Richard Price, *The Political Use of Racial Narratives: School Desegregation in Mobile, Alabama, 1954–97* (Urbana: University of Illinois Press, 2002); Joseph Davis, ed., *Stories of Change: Narrative and Social Movements* (Albany: State University of New York Press, 2002); Ronald J. Berger and Richard Quinney, eds., *Storytelling Sociology: Narrative as Social Inquiry* (Boulder, CO: Lynne Riemer, 2005).

3. For examples of works demonstrating a wide range of approaches to narrative analysis in the social sciences beyond the subset we call analyses of personal narratives, see Jerome Bruner, *Actual Minds, Possible Worlds* (Cambridge, MA: Harvard University Press, 1986); Kenneth J. Gergen and Mary M. Gergen, "Narratives of the Self," in *Studies in Social Identity*, ed. Theodore R. Sarbin and Karle E. Schelbe, 254–273 (New York: Praeger, 1983); Susan Chase, *Ambiguous Empowerment: Work Narratives of School Superintendents* (Amherst: University of Massachusetts Press, 1995); Elliot Mishler, *Research Interviewing: Context and Narrative* (Cambridge, MA: Harvard University Press, 1986);

Richard Delgado, "Legal Storytelling for Oppositionists and Others: A Plea for Narrative," *Michigan Law Review* 87 (1989): 2411–2441; Cheryl Mattingly, *Healing Dramas and Clinical Plots: The Narrative Structure of Experience* (Cambridge: Cambridge University Press, 1998); Francesca Polletta, *It Was Like a Fever: Storytelling in Protest and Politics* (Chicago: University of Chicago Press, 2006). English-language journals that have explored narrative analysis in the social sciences and history include, for example, *Narrative Inquiry, Qualitative Sociology, Journal of Narrative and Life History, History Workshop Journal, Oral History Review,* and *Auto/biography.*

4. For a useful discussion, see E. G. Mishler, *Storylines: Craftartists' Narratives of Identity* (Cambridge, MA: Harvard University Press, 1999), which includes a helpful account of the methods used in his research and its grounding in sociolinguistic research traditions. Susan E. Bell, "Intensive Performances of Mothers: A Sociological Perspective," *Qualitative Research* 4 (2004): 45–75, provides an interesting discussion of the author's use of artwork to trace a narrative of the meanings of intensive motherhood over the first year of an infant's life. See also Paul Atkinson and Sara Delamont, "Rescuing Narrative from Qualitative Research," *Narrative Inquiry* 16 (2006): 164–172; Mike Bury, "Illness Narratives: Fact or Fiction," *Sociology of Health & Illness,* 23 (2001): 263–285; Cheryl Mattingly, "Pocahontas Goes to the Clinic: Popular Culture as Lingua Franca in a Cultural Borderland," *American Anthropologist* 108 (2006): 494–501; E. G. Mishler, *Research Interviewing: Context and Narrative* (Cambridge, MA: Harvard University Press, 1986); Lee Quinney, "Narrative in Social Work," *Qualitative Social Work* 4 (2005): 391–412; Catherine Kohler Reissman, "Beyond Reductionism: Narrative Genre in Divorce Accounts," *Journal of Narrative and Life History* 1 (1991): 41–68 and *Narrative Methods for the Human Sciences* (Thousand Oaks, CA: Sage, 2007).

5. Jake Ryan and Charles Sackrey, *Strangers in Paradise: Academics from the Working Class* (New York: South End Press, 1984); William I. Thomas and Florian Znaniecki, *The Polish Peasant in Europe and America: A Classic Work in Immigration History* (Urbana: University of Illinois Press, 1996), ed. Eli Zaretsky (first published in five volumes in 1918–1920); Daniel Bertaux and Isabelle Bertaux-Wiame, "Life Stories in the Bakers' Trade," in *Biography and Society,* ed. Daniel Bertaux (London: Sage Publications, 1981), pp. 169–190; Mary Jo Maynes, *Taking the Hard Road: Life Course in French and German Workers' Autobiographies in the Era of Industrialization* (Chapel Hill: University of North Carolina Press, 1995); Gunilla-Friederike Budde, *Auf dem Weg ins Bürgerleben: Kindheit und Erziehung in deutschen und englischen Bürgerfamilien 1840–1914* (On the path to bourgeois life: childhood and education in German and English bourgeois families, 1840–1914) (Göttingen: Vandenhoeck & Ruprecht, 1994); Arlene Stein, *Sex and Sensibility: Stories of a Lesbian Generation* (Berkeley: University of California Press, 1997); Joan Brumberg, *The Body Project: An Intimate History of American Girls* (New York: Random House, 1997); Sylvia Yanagisako, *Producing Culture and Capital: Family Firms in Italy* (Princeton, NJ: Princeton University Press, 2002).

6. Bertaux and Bertaux-Wiame, "Life Stories."

7. Personal Narratives Group, *Interpreting Women's Lives,* pp. 7–8.

8. See, e.g., Dorothy Smith, *The Everyday World as Problematic: A Feminist Sociology* (Boston: Northeastern University Press, 1987); Joan Scott, "Gender: A Useful Category of Historical Analysis," in *Gender and the Politics of History* (New York: Columbia University Press, 1988); Donna Haraway, "Situated Knowledges: The Science Question in Feminism as a Site of Discourse on the Privilege of Partial Perspective," *Feminist Studies* 14, no. 3 (1988): 575–599; Gayatri Spivak, "Can the Subaltern Speak?" in *Marxism and the Interpretation of Culture,* ed. Cary Nelson and Lawrence Grossberg (Urbana: University of Illinois Press, 1988); Patricia Hill Collins, *Black Feminist Thought* (New York: Allen and Unwin,

1990); Sandra Harding, *Whose Science? Whose Knowledge? Thinking from Women's Lives* (Ithaca, NY: Cornell University Press, 1991).

9. We discuss examples in chapters 2 and 5. These include R. W. Connell, *Masculinities* (Berkeley and Los Angeles: University of California Press, 1995); Kath Weston, *Render Me, Gender Me: Lesbians Talk Sex, Class, Color, Nation, Studmuffins* (New York: Columbia University Press, 1996); Arlene Stein, *Sex and Sensibility;* Ken Plummer, *Telling Sexual Stories: Power, Change, and Social Worlds* (London: Routledge, 1995).

10. We discuss many examples of work in this vein in subsequent chapters. These include, for example, Sara Lawrence-Lightfoot, *I've Known Rivers: Lives of Loss and Liberation* (New York, Penguin Books, 1994) and *Respect: An Exploration* (Cambridge, MA: Perseus Books, 2000); Mamie Garvin Fields with Karen Fields, *Lemon Swamp and Other Places: A Carolina Memoir* (New York: The Free Press, 1983).

11. See, e.g., Marjorie Shostak, *Nisa: The Life and Words of a !Kung Woman* (Cambridge, MA: Harvard University Press, 2000); Jan Vansina, *Oral Tradition As History* (Madison: University of Wisconsin Press, 1985); Allen Isaacman, *Cotton Is the Mother of Poverty: Peasants, Work, and Rural Struggle in Colonial Mozambique, 1938–1961* (London: Heinemann, 1995); Marcia Wright, *Strategies of Slaves and Women: Life-Stories from East/Central Africa* (London: Currey, 1993); Shula Marks, *Not Either an Experimental Doll: The Separate Worlds of Three South African Women* (Bloomington: Indiana University Press, 1988); Heidi Gengenbach, *Naming the Past in a "Scattered" Land: Memory and the Powers of Women's Naming Practices in Southern Mozambique* (Boston: African Studies Center, 2000).

12. Again, there are many examples, and we discuss a number of them in greater detail in subsequent chapters. See, e.g., Norbert Ortmayr, *Knechte: Autobiographische Dokumente und sozialhistorische Skizzen* (Vienna: Böhlau Verlag, 1992); James Amelang, *The Flight of Icarus: Artisan Autobiographies in Early Modern Europe* (Stanford: Stanford University Press, 1998); Elizabeth Faue, *Writing the Wrongs: Eva Valesh and the Rise of Labor Journalism* (Ithaca: Cornell University Press, 2005); Frederick Cooper, *Struggle for the City: Migrant Labor, Capital, and the State in Urban Africa* (Beverly Hills: Sage, 1983); Michael Keith Honey, *Black Workers Remember: An Oral History of Segregation, Unionism, and the Freedom Struggle* (Berkeley: University of California Press, 1999).

13. Wally Seccombe, "Starting to Stop: Working-class Fertility Decline in Britain," *Past and Present* 126 (1990): 153–178.

14. Maynes, *Taking the Hard Road*, esp. pp. 83–84. For the larger epistemological critique, see Spivak, "Subaltern"; and Joan Scott, "The Evidence of Experience," *Critical Inquiry* 17 (1991): 773–797.

15. Barbara Laslett, "Unfeeling Knowledge: Emotion and Objectivity in the History of Sociology," *Sociological Forum* 5 (1990): 413–433 and "Biography as Historical Sociology: The Case of William Fielding Ogburn," *Theory and Society* 20 (1991): 511–538.

16. Michelle Mouton and Helena Pohlandt-McCormick, "Boundary Crossings: Oral History of Nazi Germany and Apartheid South Africa—A Comparative Perspective," *History Workshop Journal* 48 (1999): 41–63.

17. See Harding, *Whose Science? Whose Knowledge?;* George Steinmetz, ed., *The Politics of Method in the Human Sciences: Positivism and Its Epistemological Others* (Durham, NC: Duke University Press, 2005).

18. George Steinmetz, "American Sociology before and after World War II: The (Temporary) Settling of a Disciplinary Field," in *Sociology in America: A History,* ed. Craig Calhoun (Chicago: University of Chicago Press, 2007), p. 339.

19. As discussed in the preface, our selection of personal narrative analyses also reflects our areas of interests and expertise in history and sociology.

1. AGENCY, SUBJECTIVITY, AND NARRATIVES OF THE SELF

1. This conceptualization of "inside" and "outside," is itself, of course, historically structured. Joel Pfister and Nancy Schnog, eds., *Inventing the Psychological: Toward a Cultural History of Emotional Life in America* (New Haven, CT: Yale University Press, 1997) provide useful accounts of the emergences of this distinction in the United States. See, especially, the two introductory essays.

2. Alessandro Portelli, *The Death of Luigi Trastulli and Other Stories: Form and Meaning in Oral History* (Albany: State University of New York Press, 1991), p. 130.

3. Paul John Eakin's discussion of Leslie Marmon Silko's *Storyteller* (New York: Arcade Publishing, 1981) provides an interesting analysis of connections between Silko's strategies in her own autobiographical writing and the collective storytelling traditions of Laguna narrative culture. See Paul John Eakin, *How Our Lives Become Stories: Making Selves* (Ithaca: Cornell University Press, 1999), pp. 69–74. For another example, see the discussion of "alternative subjectivities" in James A. Holstein and Jaber F. Gubrium, *The Self We Live By: Narrative Identity in a Postmodern World* (New York: Oxford University Press, 2000), pp. 71–75.

4. See Jan Goldstein, *The Post-Revolutionary Self: Politics and Psyche in France, 1750–1850* (Cambridge, MA: Harvard University Press, 2005). For an older argument linking historical change and selfhood, see Albert O. Hirschman, *The Passion and the Interests: Political Arguments for Capitalism before Its Triumph* (Princeton, NJ: Princeton University Press, 1977).

5. Richard Wolin, "Foucault the Neohumanist?" *The Chronicle of Higher Education*, September 1, 2006. http://chronicle.com/weekly/v53/i02/02b01201.htm.

6. Joan Scott, *Only Paradoxes to Offer: French Feminists and the Rights of Man* (Cambridge, MA: Harvard University Press, 1997), pp. 20–25. For another feminist engagement with the "gender troubles" encountered by post-Revolutionary liberals, see Dagmar Herzog's "Liberalism, Religious Dissent, and Women's Rights: Louise Dittmar's Writing from the 1840's," in *In Search of a Liberal Germany,* ed. Konrad Jarausch and Larry Jones (New York: St. Martin's Press, 1990) as well as her book *Intimacy and Exclusion: Religious Politics in Pre-Revolutionary Baden* (Princeton, NJ: Princeton University Press, 1996). On the historiographic debates that have evolved in the context of "the linguistic turn," see Kathleen Canning's collected essays in *Gender History in Practice: Historical Perspectives on Bodies, Class, and Citizenship* (Ithaca, NY: Cornell University Press, 2006).

7. For some classic examples from this debate, see Judith Butler and Joan W. Scott, eds., *Feminists Theorize the Political* (New York: Routledge, 1992). This project has been of interest to many feminist political philosophers as well. Diana Meyers provides a succinct summary of the context of their discussions:

> Two views of the self have been prominent in contemporary Anglo-American moral and political philosophy—a Kantian ethical subject and homo economicus. Both of these conceptions see the individual as a free and rational chooser and actor—an autonomous agent...Whether the self is identified with pure abstract reason or with the instrumental rationality of the marketplace, though, these conceptions of the self isolate the individual from personal relationships and larger social forces.

Meyers goes on to discuss the efforts of feminist theorists of the late twentieth century to reinterpret agency in social context, pointing out how the Enlightenment philosophers' "decontextualiz[ation of] individualism and their privileging of reason over other capacities trouble many feminist philosophers." Diane Meyers, "Feminist Perspectives on the Self," in *Stanford Encyclopedia of Philosophy,* ed. Edward N. Zalta (fall 1999 ed.), http://plato.stanford.edu/entries/feminism-self/.

8. For feminist critiques of Enlightenment political theory, see Carole Pateman, *The Sexual Contract* (Stanford: Stanford University Press, 1988); Joan Landes, *Women and the Public Sphere in the Age of the French Revolution* (Ithaca, NY: Cornell University Press, 1988); Karin Hausen, "Family and Role Division: The Polarization of Sexual Stereotypes in the Nineteenth Century," in *The German Family*, ed. R. J. Evans and W. R. Lee (London: Routledge, 1981), pp. 51–83. Carole Pateman argues that the "sexual contract" between men and women that complemented the "social contract" among men undoubtedly undermined women's claims to political selfhood. For a summary of Enlightenment conflicts over gender, see Dena Goodman, "Women and the Enlightenment," in *Becoming Visible: Women in European History*, ed. Renate Bridenthal, Susan Stuard, and Merry Wiesner (Boston: Houghton Mifflin, 1998), pp. 233–294. On women's activism during the French Revolution, see Darlene Gay Levy and Harriet B. Applewaite, "A Political Revolution for Women? The Case of Paris," in *Becoming Visible: Women in European History*, ed. Renate Bridenthal et al. (New York: Houghton Mifflin, 1998), pp. 233–294. For an introduction to ongoing feminist debates around these issues, see Butler and Scott, eds., *Feminists Theorize the Political*.

9. Carla Hesse, *The Other Enlightenment: How French Women Became Modern* (Princeton and Oxford: Princeton University Press, 2001), p. xv.

10. Ibid., p. 74.

11. Felicité Kéralio-Robert wrote an innovative biography of Queen Elizabeth of England that thematized the contradictions between women's public and private virtue. Isabelle de Charrière, like many women writers of this era, chose to debate the question of women's moral autonomy in novels. Charrière wrote fiction because it allowed her to disguise her social, political, and philosophical commentary at a time when women were not supposed to engage with such matters, deploying a favored strategy of subaltern writers in other times and places as well. See Carla Hesse, *The Other Enlightenment*.

12. See, e.g., Nancy Armstrong, *Desire and Domestic Fiction* (New York: Oxford University Press, 1990); Wolfgang Emmerich, ed. *Proletarische Lebensläufe. Autobiographische Dokumente zur Entstehung der Zweiten Kultur in Deutschland* (Proletarian lifecourse: autobiographical documents of the emergence of an alternative culture in Germany), 2 vols. (Reinbek bei Hamburg: Rowohlt, 1974), intro., pp. 14–16.

13. See Regenia Gagnier, "The Literary Standard, Working-Class Autobiography, and Gender," in *Revealing Lives: Autobiography, Biography, and Gender*, ed. Susan Groag Bell and Lilian Robinson (Albany: State University of New York Press, 1991), pp. 93–114; Jacques Rancière, *The Nights of Labor: The Workers' Dream in Nineteenth-Century France*, trans. John Drury (Philadelphia: Temple University Press, 1989).

14. Mary Jo Maynes, *Taking the Hard Road: Life Course in French and German Workers' Autobiographies in the Era of Industrialization* (Chapel Hill: University of North Carolina Press, 1995), p. 32.

15. Emmerich, *Proletarische Lebensläufe*, esp. pp. 14–22.

16. Maynes, *Taking the Hard Road*, p. 33.

17. For a discussion of the connection between the personal and institutional life of one influential early twentieth-century American sociologist and the appeal of positivist theoretical frameworks, see Barbara Laslett's biographical study of William Ogburn in "Unfeeling Knowledge: Emotion and Objectivity in the History of Sociology," *Sociological Forum* 5 (March 1990): 413–433.

18. Margaret R. Somers and Gloria Gibson, "Reclaiming the Epistemological 'Other': Narrative and the Social Construction of Identity," in *Social Theory and the Politics of Identity*, ed. Craig Calhoun (Oxford: Blackwell, 1994), p. 49.

19. On Halbwachs, see the introduction to Maurice Halbwachs, *On Collective Memory*, edited, translated, and with an introduction by Lewis A. Coser (Chicago: University of

Chicago Press, 1992), pp. 1–34. See also Susan A. Crane, "Writing the Individual Back into Collective Memory," *American Historical Review* 102, no. 5 (1997): 1372–1385.

20. For an interesting account of this tradition, see Holstein and Gubrium, *The Self We Live By,* esp. pp. 17–37.

21. Anthony Giddens, *The Constitution of Society: Outline of the Theory of Structuration* (Cambridge: Polity Press, 1984) is one of several relevant works. Philip Abrams's work is not as widely known, despite its important contributions. See esp. *Historical Sociology* (Ithaca, NY: Cornell University Press, 1983). The preface to *Historical Sociology,* in which he discusses the ongoing theoretical problem of social structure and human agency, is especially pertinent here. See Raewyn Connell, "Northern Theory: The Political Geography of General Social Theory," *Theory & Society* 35 (2006): 237–264, for a useful discussion of several major theorists: James Coleman, Anthony Giddens, and Pierre Bourdieu.

22. "Agency concerns events of which an individual is the perpetrator, in the sense that the individual could, at any phase in a given sequence of conduct, have acted differently." Further, "to be able to 'act otherwise' means being able to intervene in the world or to refrain from such intervention, with the effect of influencing a specific process or state of affairs." Giddens, *The Constitution of Society,* p. 14.

23. See, e.g., Talcott Parsons, *The Structure of Social Action* (Glencoe, IL: Free Press, 1949); Nicos Poulantzas, *Political Power and Social Classes* (London: New Left Books, 1968); Patricia Hill Collins, *Black Feminist Thought* (New York: Routledge, 1991). For an example of work by Collins that develops a more agent-centered argument, see *Fighting Words: Black Women and the Search for Justice* (Minneapolis: University of Minnesota Press; 1998).

24. Coleman's understanding of the rational actor derives from the individualist assumptions of contract theory in law. See James S. Coleman, "Social Theory, Social Research, and a Theory of Action," *American Journal of Sociology* 91, no. 6 (1986): 1309–1335 and *Foundations of Social Theory* (Cambridge, MA: Harvard University Press, 1990). For other examples of rational choice theory, see Edgar Kiser and Michael Hechter, "General Theory's Role in Comparative Historical Sociology," *American Journal of Sociology* 97 (1991): 1–30; Margaret Marini, "The Role of Models of Purposive Action in Sociology," in *Rational Choice Theory: Advocacy and Critique,* ed. James Coleman and Thomas Fararo (Newbury Park, CA: Sage, 1992). See also, e.g., Gary Becker, *A Treatise on the Family* (Cambridge, MA: Harvard University Press, 1991). According to the book's publisher, Becker sees the family as "a kind of little factory—a multi-person unit producing meals, health, skills, children, and self esteem from market goods and the time, skills, and knowledge of its members." Note, however, that Becker's more recent works have begun to grapple with the economist's "black box"—tastes and personal preferences—which Becker seeks to analyze using modified market choice models. See *Accounting for Tastes* (Cambridge, MA: Harvard University Press, 1996).

25. Michael Burawoy, *Manufacturing Consent* (Chicago: University of Chicago Press, 1979); James Scott, *Weapons of the Weak* (New Haven, CT: Yale University Press, 1985).

26. Avery Gordon, *Ghostly Matters: Haunting and the Sociological Imagination* (Minneapolis: University of Minnesota Press, 1997), p. 4. Gordon, like other poststructuralists, provides a more complicated understanding of these terms by refusing the conceptual apparatus of resistance and consent. Michel Foucault sees social actors as always imbricated within webs of power that can neither be refused nor embraced. See Foucault, *Discipline and Punish* (New York: Vintage, 1997); *Power/Knowledge* (New York: Pantheon, 1980); *The History of Sexuality* (New York: Vintage, 1985).

27. Scholars in sociology and anthropology have subjected emotions to serious scholarly analysis in empirical research over the past thirty years. Arlie Hochschild's

path-breaking book, *The Managed Heart,* for example, was the first study to consider how emotions such as friendliness, concern for others, and even intimidation become part of many service-sector jobs and, further, to examine the consequences such "emotional labor" posed for workers, particularly for women. This scholarship exerted a powerful critique of social science research and theory: Hochschild and other feminist scholars, for instance, uncovered implicit assumptions valorizing the "rational" male actor and, by implication, devaluing emotionality and the feminine. The main limitation we see in this scholarship is its focus on individual-level or interpersonal interactions; there is rarely adequate consideration of the larger cultural and historical frame in which these interpersonal relations play out. See Arlie Hochschild, *The Managed Heart* (Berkeley and Los Angeles: University of California Press, 1983); Catherine Lutz, *Unnatural Emotions* (Chicago: University of Chicago Press, 1988); Candace Clark, *Misery and Sympathy* (Chicago: University of Chicago Press, 1997).

28. For a discussion of this intellectual tradition, see Holstein and Gubrium, *The Self We Live By,* pp. 35–37.

29. Everett C. Hughes, *Men at Work* (Glencoe, IL: Free Press, 1958); Howard Becker, *Outsiders: Studies in the Sociology of Deviance* (London: Free Press, 1963). In *Asylums: Essays on the Social Situation of Mental Patients and Other Inmates* (Garden City, NY: Anchor Books, 1961), Goffman describes the various ways mental patients "manage" the impressions they make on staff so as to "make out" in the best possible way on the ward of a mental institution. See also his *The Presentation of Self in Everyday Life* (Garden City, NY: Doubleday, 1959).

30. Of course, there are some exceptions. See, e.g., Ken Plummer, *Telling Sexual Stories* (London: Routledge, 1995). Plummer describes himself as a symbolic interactionist, but he uses a life history method and carefully historicizes the life stories he uses.

31. Nancy J. Chodorow, *The Power of Feelings: Personal Meaning in Psychoanalysis, Gender, and Culture* (New Haven, CT: Yale University Press, 1999), pp. 4–5.

32. Nancy J. Chodorow, "Gender as a Personal and Cultural Construction," *Signs* 20, no. 3 (1995): 516–544.

33. Chodorow, *Power of Feelings,* p. 17.

34. For an exception, see Nancy J. Chodorow, "Seventies Questions for Thirties Women: Gender and Generation," in her *Feminism and Psychoanalytic Theory* (New Haven, CT: Yale University Press, 1991), pp. 199–218.

35. Maureen A. Mahoney and Barbara Yngvesson, "The Construction of Subjectivity and the Paradox of Resistance: Reintegrating Feminist Anthropology and Psychology," *Signs* 18, no. 1 (1992): 44–73.

36. Mahoney and Yngvesson, p. 45. They refer to Anthony Giddens, whose understandings of agency they complicate.

37. Ibid., p. 46.

38. Ibid., p. 49.

39. Generally, although with some exceptions, life histories/personal narratives do not contain the empirical detail that is available to Chodorow in clinical situations. Mahoney and Yngvesson, psychoanalytically steeped anthropologists, do use empirical examples in developing their theoretical model; the evidence is drawn from personal narratives. However indeterminate analyses of life stories/personal narratives may be, especially interpretations of how their psychological dimensions relate to agency, the significance of psychological dimensions of motivation necessitates their inclusion among social scientists' analytic models.

40. Sara Lawrence-Lightfoot, *I've Known Rivers: Lives of Loss and Liberation* (New York, Penguin Books, 1994) and *Respect: An Exploration* (Cambridge, MA: Perseus Books, 2000).

41. For Charles Ogletree's life story, see Lawrence-Lightfoot, *Rivers,* pp. 109–185.

42. Ibid., p 144.

43. Ibid., p 144.

44. Ibid., pp. 147–148.

45. Ibid., p. 149.

46. Ibid., p. 164.

47. Ibid., pp. 162–163.

48. Ibid., p. 188.

49. Lawrence-Lightfoot, *Respect,* p. 176.

50. Ibid., p. 177.

51. According to Lawrence-Lightfoot, "The ghosts of David's father, and his father's father, and his father's brothers are all around us as we sit talking in David's office… David's mother's side of the family has also had a history of being ambitious, achieving and prominent, but it is his *paternal lineage,* that seems to haunt David the most, that seems to define David's identity and be the source of his greatest strength and anguish… 'I've always had a fear of not being good enough.'" *Respect,* pp. 179–180.

52. Ibid., p. 184.

53. Ibid., p. 161.

54. Eakin, *How Our Lives Become Stories: Making Selves* (Ithaca, NY: Cornell University Press, 1999), pp. ix, 18.

55. Ibid., pp. 21, 64–66. For a discussion of the changing role of narrativity in sociological accounts of identity formation, see Somers and Gibson, "Narrative and Social Identity," pp. 58–80. See also the discussion of interpersonal processes in linguistic theory in Dorothy Holland et al., *Identity and Agency in Cultural Worlds* (Cambridge, MA: Harvard University Press, 1998), pp. 4–46, 169ff. and 227ff. Holland et al. argue that literary critic Mikhail Bakhtin provides theoretical formulations for examining intraindividual processes that are critical to both subjectivity and action without entailing unobservable psychodynamic processes. The authors also draw on L. S. Vygotsky's studies of children's play and processes internal to individuals that language makes possible.

56. See, e.g., the works cited in notes 8 through 12, above and Lieselotte Steinbrugge, *The Moral Sex: Woman's Nature in the French Enlightenment* (New York: Oxford University Press, 1995); Isabel Hull, *Sexuality, State, and Civil Society in Germany, 1700–1815* (Ithaca, NY: Cornell University Press, 1996).

57. In addition to the works cited in notes 7 and 8 above, see Carol Gilligan, *In a Different Voice: Psychological Theory and Women's Development* (Cambridge, MA: Harvard University Press, 1983); Donna Haraway, *Simians, Cyborgs, and Women: The Reinvention of Nature* (New York: Routledge, 1991); and Judith Butler, *Gender Trouble: Feminism and the Subversion of Identity* (London: Routledge, 1990).

58. Kathleen Canning, "The Body as Method? Reflections on the Place of the Body in Gender History," in *Gender History in Practice* (Ithaca, NY: Cornell University Press, 2006), pp. 170–181.

59. See Eakin, *How Our Lives Become Stories,* pp. 37–42. Eakin discusses a wide range of provocative illustrations, especially drawn from the realm of self-narratives of illness and disability. See also Holstein and Gubrium, *The Self,* pp. 197–204.

60. See Pierre Bourdieu, *Outline to a Theory of Practice* (New York: Cambridge University Press, 1977), 72.

61. Joel Pfister, "On Conceptualizing the Cultural History of Emotional and Psychological Life in America," in Pfister and Schnog, *Inventing the Psychological,* pp. 17–59. See also Bourdieu's argument in "L'illusion biographique," *Actes de la recherché en sciences sociales,* no. 62/63 (1986): 69–72, translated by Yves Winkin and Wendy Leeds-Hurwitz in *Working Papers and Proceedings of the Center for Psychosocial Studies,* no. 14, 1987.

62. Here Eakin is referring to Ian Burkitt, *Social Selves: Theories of the Social Formation of Personality* (London: Sage, 1991) and "The Shifting Concept of the Self," *History of the Human Sciences* 7 (1994): 7–28. Cited in Eakin, *How Our Lives Become Stories*, pp. 64–65.

63. Pierre Bourdieu, *The Logic of Practice* (Stanford: Stanford University Press, 1990) and *Homo Academicus* (Stanford: Stanford University Press, 1980).

64. In a 2006 article, George Steinmetz suggests that in the last decade of his life, Bourdieu seemed to recognize "that psychoanalysis was intrinsic to his own project." Reviewing a substantial range of Bourdieu's writings over the course of his career, Steinmetz argues that while Bourdieu resisted biologically based or ahistorical versions of psychoanalytic theory, a historicized view of subjectivity was of more interest to him. In *Masculine Domination*, for example, Bourdieu argues that "what appears, in history, as being eternal is merely the product of a labour of externalization performed by interconnected institutions such as the family, the church, the state, the educational system, and also, in another order of things, sport and journalism (these abstract notions being simple shorthand markers for complex mechanisms which must be analyzed in each case in their historical particularity)." Steinmetz suggests that "psychoanalysis has long been concerned with the same problem that Bourdieu sets out to explain here, namely the ways in which masculine domination is *historically* reproduced as a *dehistoricized* form." In that sense, Bourdieu's analysis of gender relations is consistent with our arguments here about the historicity of subjectivity. Citation and discussion is from George Steinmetz, "Bourdieu's Disavowal of Lacan: Psychoanalytic Theory and the Concepts of 'Habitus' and 'Symbolic Capital,'" *Constellations* 13, no. 4 (2006): 445–464.

65. Carolyn Kay Steedman, *Landscape for a Good Woman* (New Brunswick, NJ: Rutgers University Press, 1991).

66. Ibid., p. 7.

67. Parts of the argument of this section were presented in Mary Jo Maynes, "Age as a Category of Historical Analysis: History, Agency, and Narratives of Childhood," *Journal of the History of Childhood and Youth* 1, no. 1 (forthcoming).

68. Anonymous [Adelheid Popp], *Die Jugendgeschichte einer Arbeiterin. Von ihr selbst erzählt* (Munich: Ernst Reinhardt Verlag, 1909), pp. 9–11. This story is discussed in Maynes, *Taking the Hard Road*, pp. 63 ff.

69. Anna Maier, "Wie Ich Reif Wurde," in *Gedenkbuch. 20 Jahren österreichische Arbeiterinnenbewegung*, ed. Adelheid Popp (Vienna: Kommissionsverlag der Wiener Volksbuchhandlung, 1912) pp. 107–109. Cited in Maynes, *Taking the Hard Road*, p. 81.

70. For a discussion of changing understandings of childhood over a long chronological sweep of Chinese history, see Anne Behnke Kinney, ed., *Chinese Views of Childhood* (Honolulu: University of Hawai'i Press, 1995), esp. pp. 1–78. The debates over the child's nature and the relationship between childhood and adulthood often turn on stories of child prodigies discussed in several of the book's chapters. Prodigies are mentioned in the essay by Kenneth J. DeWoskin on early dynastic biography and prodigious children. Such childhood stories become prominent in later texts as elaborated in Richard B. Mather's essay based on a fourth century b.c. collection of anecdotal life histories. DeWoskin argues that the emphasis on writing "exemplary" lives in early dynastic histories resulted in disconnected and moral bearing stories. Mather, in contrast, argues that the later sources he reads allow more room for individuality on the part of children; precociousness associated with prodigious children could flourish once the restraints of Confucian expectations were loosened. These two different uses of the figure of the child prodigy demonstrate different notions about the nature of childhood and its place in biography.

71. Kath Weston, *Render Me, Gender Me* (New York: Columbia University Press, 1996), p. 45.

72. For example, see Lawrence-Lightfoot, *Rivers*, pp. 82–83.

73. Jennifer L. Pierce, "'Racing for Innocence': Whiteness, Corporate Culture and the Backlash Against Affirmative Action." *Qualitative Sociology* 26, no. 1 (2003): 53–70.

74. Jennifer L. Pierce, Interview with Randall Kingsley, January 1989.

75. Pierce, "'Racing,'" p. 64.

76. Ibid., p. 65.

77. Jennifer L. Pierce, interview with Randall Kingsley, February 1999.

78. For a related point, see Avery Gordon, *Ghostly Matters: Haunting and the Sociological Imagination* (Minneapolis: University of Minnesota Press, 1997), p. 4.

79. Some aspects of memory in personal narrative analysis having to do with narrator-analyst relationships—especially issues around the evocation of painful memories in the interview situation—will be more fully addressed in chapter 4.

80. The following section is based in part on the research of Lisa Blee, "Politics of Historical Memory: Bibliography," unpublished manuscript, Minneapolis, August 2005, pp. 4–5. Discussions of the historical literature on memory, and the intersection between personal and historical memory, have been shaped by discussion that took place during the University of Minnesota History department graduate seminar "The Politics of Historical memory," taught in spring 2006 by M. J. Maynes, Pat McNamara, and Eric Weitz.

81. Halbwachs, *On Collective Memory*, esp. pp. 21–28, 43–45, 52–83.

82. Eakin, *How Our Lives Become Stories*, p. 102.

83. Jan Goldstein uses the term "self talk," which, she argues, was proliferating in French society in various forms beginning in the late eighteenth century. See Goldstein, *Post-Revolutionary Self*, pp. 6–7 and throughout. For an interesting discussion of recent work on family photographs and historical memory, see Peter Fritzsche, "The Case of Modern Memory," *Journal of Modern History* 73 (March 2001): 109–111.

84. Eakin, *How Our Lives Become Stories*, p. 107.

85. See, e.g., Veena Das and Ashis Nandy, "Violence, Victimhood, and the Language of Silence," in *The Word and the World: Fantasy, Symbol and Record*, ed. Veena Das (New Delhi: Sage, 1986); Richard Johnson et al., eds., *Making Histories* (Minneapolis: University of Minnesota Press, 1982); Rigoberta Menchu with Elisabeth Burgos-Debray, *I, Rigoberta Menchu: An Indian Woman in Guatemala* (New York: Verso, 1984).

86. See Alessandro Portelli, *Luigi Trastulli*. Many of the essays reprinted here were originally published in the late 1970s and early 1980s.

87. Portelli, *Luigi Trastulli*, pp. 68–70.

88. There is an enormous literature based on Holocaust memoirs and their analysis. See, e.g., Primo Levi's first account of his time in Auschwitz—*Survival in Auschwitz: The Nazi Assault on Humanity* (New York: Collier Books, 1961) and his much later *The Drowned and the Saved* (New York: Summit Books, 1988). They also include such forms as Art Spiegelman's comic book biographical memoirs *Maus I & II* (New York: Pantheon, 1986 and 1991). Historical analyses of Holocaust memory include Saul Friedlander's work; e.g., *Memory, History, and the Extermination of the Jews of Europe* (Bloomington: Indiana University Press, 1993) and "Trauma, Transference, and 'Working Through' in Writing the History of the Shoah," *History and Memory* 4 (Spring-Summer 1992): 39–59, and Dominic LaCapra, *Representing the Holocaust: History, Theory, Trauma* (Ithaca, NY: Cornell University Press, 1994) and *History and Memory after Auschwitz* (Ithaca, NY: Cornell University Press, 1998). On Japanese atrocities and memory controversies, see Iris Chang, *The Rape of Nanking* (New York: Basic Books, 1997); Charles Maier and Joshua Fogel, eds., *The Nanjing Massacre in History and Historiography* (Berkeley: University of California Press, 2000). For a thoughtful and critical discussion of the evolution of various trends relating historiography and memory, see Kerwin Lee Klein, "On the Emergence of Memory in Historical Discourse," *Representations* 69 (2000): 127–150.

89. See, e.g., Pierre Nora, "Between History and Memory: Les Lieux de Memoire," *Representations* 26 (Spring, 1989): 7–24. For analyses of subsequent discussions and critiques of Nora's work, see Klein, "Emergence of Memory," and Fritzsche, "Modern Memory." Fritzsche contends that what Nora was actually documenting was not so much the disappearance of oral memory cultures as nostalgia for it among French intellectuals:

> As his history demonstrates so well, the notion that authentic memory had disappeared or that genuine national feeling had lapsed permeated nineteenth- and twentieth-century thought. It is not loss per se, but the sensibility of loss and the history of that sensibility, that needs to be examined more closely. Had Nora historicized the category of loss, he would have avoided making such grandiose claims for the authenticity of memory, the dispossession of history, and the comity of the nation. Pierre Nora would not have kept slipping into his own primary sources. (Fritzsche, "Modern Memory," pp. 93–94)

90. Bourdieu, "L'illusion biographique."

91. Joan Scott, "The Evidence of Experience," *Critical Inquiry* 17 (1991): 773–797.

2. INTERSECTING STORIES: PERSONAL NARRATIVES IN HISTORICAL CONTEXT

1. This generalization should be qualified to acknowledge the common practice of narrators to include anecdotes told to them by older family members, especially parents, about their early childhood, for example, or about ancestors. In many cases it is hard to distinguish hearsay from remembered experience; one provocative example is provided by the life stories told to Dorothee Wierling by Germans born in 1949 who "remember" and include in their childhood stories incidents of deprivation that occurred at the end of and just following World War II—that is, before they were born. See Dorothee Wierling, "Conflicting Narratives? The First Postwar Generation in the GDR and the Nazi Past" (paper presented at the meeting of the American Historical Association, Boston, January 5, 2001), and *Geboren im Jahr Eins: Der Jahrgang 1949 in der DDR—Versuch einer Kollektivbiographie* (Born in the year one: the 1949 cohort in the GDR) (Berlin: Links Verlag, 2002).

2. Margaret R. Somers and Gloria Gibson, "Reclaiming the Epistemological 'Other': Narrative and the Social Construction of Identity," in *Social Theory and the Politics of Identity*, ed. Craig Calhoun (Oxford: Blackwell, 1994), p. 62. In this essay, Somers and Gibson have laid out a useful framework for examining the operation of narratives relevant for social identities. They distinguish between four types of narratives: *ontological, public, conceptual,* and *metanarratives* or master narratives. For our purposes, the first two categories are the most relevant. *Ontological narratives* are the types of narratives that predominate in life stories. They "are the stories that social actors use to make sense of—indeed in order to act in—their lives" (p. 61). Ontological narratives are in continual negotiation with public narratives.

3. Michael Keith Honey, *Black Workers Remember: An Oral History of Segregation, Unionism, and the Freedom Struggle* (Berkeley: University of California Press, 1999), p. 8.

4. Somers and Gibson, "Reclaiming," p. 59 (emphasis in the original).

5. Luisa Passerini, *Autobiography of a Generation: Italy, 1968,* translated by Lisa Erdberg and foreword by Joan Wallach Scott (Hanover, NH: Wesleyan University Press, 1996).

6. Ibid., p. 22. The "international book" to which Passerini refers is the book of which she was one of many co-authors, Ronald Fraser et al., *1968: A Student Generation in Revolt* (New York: Pantheon, 1988).

7. Passerini, *Autobiography,* p. 53.

8. Ibid., p. 29.

9. Ibid., p. xii.

10. Ibid., p. 23.

11. James S. Amelang, *The Flight of Icarus: Artisan Autobiography in Early Modern Europe* (Stanford, CA: Stanford University Press, 1998).

12. The book's appendix on Popular Autobiographical Writing offers information on over two hundred such texts by European artisan authors born before 1770.

13. Amelang, *Flight of Icarus*, pp. 1 and 164.

14. Honey, *Black Workers Remember*, pp. 2–3. For a full account of King's assassination in the context of national and local historical events connected to African American labor history and the national Civil Rights movement, see, by the same author, *Going Down Jericho Road: The Memphis Strike, Martin Luther King's Last Campaign* (New York and London: W. W. Norton, 2007).

15. Honey, *Black Workers Remember*, pp. 2–3.

16. Ibid., p. 7.

17. Ibid., pp. 370–371.

18. Ibid., pp. 370–371.

19. Ibid., p. 368.

20. See, e.g., R. W. Connell, *Masculinities* (Berkeley and Los Angeles: University of California Press, 1995); Kath Weston, *Render Me, Gender Me: Lesbians Talk Sex, Class, Color, Nation, Studmuffins* (New York: Columbia University Press, 1996); Arlene Stein, *Sex and Sensibility: Life Stories of a Lesbian Generation* (Berkeley and Los Angeles: University of California Press, 1997); Martin Duberman, *Stonewall* (New York: Dutton, 1993); Susan Krieger, *The Mirror Dance* (Philadelphia: Temple University Press, 1983); George Chauncey, *Gay New York* (New York: Basic Books, 1995); Elizabeth Kennedy and Madeleine Davis, *Boots of Leather, Slippers of Gold* (New York: Routledge, 1993); Elizabeth Kennedy and Madeleine Davis, "Constructing an Ethnohistory of the Buffalo Lesbian Community," in *Out in the Field: Reflections of Lesbian and Gay Anthropology*, ed. Ellen Lewin and William L. Leap (Urbana-Champagne: University of Illinois Press, 1996).

21. Connell, *Masculinities*, p. 90.

22. Ibid., p. 155.

23. Ibid., p. 161.

24. Ibid., p. 157.

25. Arlene Stein makes a similar argument about lesbians in the women's movement in *Sex and Sensibility*.

26. Connell, *Masculinities*, p. 153.

27. See, e.g., the essays in Michael Warner's *Fear of a Queer Planet* (Minneapolis: University of Minnesota Press, 1993); and Kath Weston's *Render Me*, which considers the different renditions of gender lesbians reiterate in butch, femme, top, bottom, and so forth. The Twin Cities GLBT Oral History Project addresses similar issues. See Kevin Murphy, Jennifer L. Pierce, and Larry Knopp, eds., *Queer Twin Cities: Politics, Histories, and Spaces* (Minneapolis: University of Minnesota Press, forthcoming).

28. Candace West and Don Zimmerman, "Doing Gender" *Gender & Society* 1, no. 2 (1987): 125–151.

29. For an exploration of some of these performative differences, see Peter Hennen's doctoral dissertation, "Gendered Sexuality in the Age of AIDS" (Ph.D. diss., University of Minnesota, 2000). See also Kath Weston's *Render Me*.

30. Connell, *Masculinities*, p. 89.

31. See, e.g., Nancy Chodorow, *The Reproduction of Mothering* (Berkeley and Los Angeles: University of California Press, 1978); Jessica Benjamin, *The Bonds of Love* (New York: Pantheon, 1988).

32. Duberman, *Stonewall*, p. 43.

33. Ibid., pp. 41–42

34. Ibid., pp. 41–42.

35. Ibid., p. 221.

36. Ibid., p. 233.

37. Ibid., p. 269.

38. Ruth Behar, *Translated Woman: Crossing the Border with Esperanza's Story* (Boston: Beacon Press, 1993), p. 290.

39. Denise Kandiyoti, "Bargaining with Patriarchy" *Gender & Society* 2, no. 3 (1988): 274–290.

40. Nancy Chodorow and Susan Contratto, "The Fantasy of the Perfect Mother," in *Rethinking the Family*, ed. Marilyn Yalom (New York: Longman, 1982).

41. Ellen Ross, "Fierce Questions and Taunts: Married Life in Working-class London, 1870–1914," *Feminist Studies* 8 (1982): 575–602; and *Love and Toil: Motherhood in Outcast London, 1870–1918* (New York: Oxford University Press, 1993).

42. See the classic formulation and critique in Claude Levi-Strauss, *The Elementary Structures of Kinship*, ed. Rodney Needham (London: Eyre & Spottiswoode, 1969) and Gail Rubin's "The Traffic in Women: Notes on the Political Economy of Sex," in *Toward an Anthropology of Women*, ed. Rayna R. Reiter (New York: Monthly Review Press, 1975), pp. 157–210. Carolyn Kay Steedman, *Landscape for a Good Woman* (New Brunswick, NJ: Rutgers University Press, 1991), p. 69.

43. Steedman, *Landscape*, pp. 30, 21, 33–34.

44. Ibid., p. 20.

45. See Peter Fritzsche, "The Case of Modern Memory," *Journal of Modern History* 73 (March 2001): 87–117. Fritzsche makes this point most directly in his discussion, on p. 96, of James Chandler, *England in 1819: The Politics of Literary Culture and the Case of Romantic Historicism* (Chicago: University of Chicago Press, 1998).

46. Vincent Crapanzano, *Waiting: The Whites of South Africa* (London: Granada Publishing, 1985), p. 291.

47. Ibid., p. 195.

48. Ibid., p. 197.

49. Ibid., pp. 339–340 (emphasis in original).

50. Ibid., p. 43. Fritzsche, "Modern Memory," p. 89.

51. Dorothee Wierling, "Conflicting Narratives?" (paper presented at the meeting of the American Historical Association, Boston, January 5, 2001). For other similar studies that connect personal and historical narratives in twentieth-century Germany, see Robert G. Moeller, "War Stories: The Search for a Usable Past in the Federal Republic of Germany," *American Historical Review* 101, no. 4 (1996): 1008–1048; Joyce Marie Mushaben, "Collective Memory Divided and Reunited: Mothers, Daughters, and the Fascist Experience in Germany," *History and Memory* 11, no. 1 (1999): 7–40.

52. Wierling, "Conflicting Narratives," p. 12.

53. Fritzsche, "Modern Memory," p. 108.

54. Ibid., pp. 104–106. The works under discussion here from which Fritzsche quotes are: Jay Winter, *Sites of Memory, Sites of Mourning: The Great War in European Cultural History* (Cambridge: Cambridge University Press, 1995) and Jay Winter, "Forms of Kinship and Remembrance in the Aftermath of the Great War," in *War and Remembrance in the Twentieth Century*, ed. Jay Winter and Emmanuel Sivan (Cambridge: Cambridge University Press, 1999), pp. 40–60.

55. Ibid., pp. 104, 105–106, 107–108. The work Fritzsche discusses here is Catherine Merridale, "War, Death and Remembrance in Soviet Russia," in *War and Remembrance in the Twentieth Century*, ed. Jay Winter and Emmanuel Sivan (Cambridge: Cambridge University Press, 1999), pp. 61–83.

56. Amitav Ghosh, *In an Antique Land: History in the Guise of a Traveler's Tale* (New York: Vintage Books, 1992), p. 125.

57. Ibid., pp. 236–237.

58. Ibid., pp. 339–340.

59. Norbert Ortmayr, *Knechte: Autobiographische Dokumente und sozialhistorische Skizzen* (Vienna: Böhlau Verlag, 1992).

60. Bonnie Smith, *Confessions of a Concierge: Madame Lucie's History of Twentieth-Century France* (New Haven, CT: Yale University Press, 1987), p. xvii.

3. THE FORMS OF TELLING AND RETELLING LIVES

1. Bill Griffith, "Zippy the Pinhead," *Star Tribune*, Sunday, August 12, 2001.

2. See Hayden White, *Metahistory* (Baltimore: John Hopkins Press, 1979) and *The Content of Form* (Baltimore: John Hopkins Press, 1989); Estelle Jelinek, ed., *Women's Autobiography* (Bloomington: Indiana University Press, 1980); the works of French sociologist Philippe Lejeune including *L'autobiographie en France* (Paris: A. Colin, 1971), *Le pacte autobiographique* (Paris: Editions du Seuil, 1975), *Je est un autre* (Paris: Editions du Seuil, 1980), and *On Autobiography*, ed. Paul John Eakin and trans. Katherine Leary (Minneapolis: University of Minnesota Press, 1989); Carolyn Steedman, *Past Tenses: Essays on Writing, Autobiography, and History* (London: Rivers Oram Press, 1992); Personal Narratives Group, eds., *Interpreting Women's Lives: Feminist Theory and Personal Narratives* (Bloomington: Indiana University Press, 1989); Joan Scott, "The Evidence of Experience," *Critical Inquiry* (1991): 773–797.

3. Alessandro Portelli, *The Death of Luigi Trastulli and Other Stories: Form and Meaning in Oral History* (Albany: State University of New York, 1991), p. 49.

4. The point here is closely related to our argument in chapter 1 of the relationship between development of a self-identity and self-narrative.

5. Luisa Passerini, *Fascism in Popular Memory: The Cultural Experience of the Turin Working Class* (Cambridge: Cambridge University Press, 1987); Portelli, *Luigi Trastulli;* Ruth Behar, *Translated Woman: Crossing the Border with Esperanza's Story* (Boston: Beacon Press, 1993).

6. Passerini, *Fascism in Popular Memory,* p. 19.

7. Ibid., pp. 22–25.

8. Ibid., p. 31.

9. Portelli, *Luigi Trastulli,* p. 130.

10. Ibid., p. 130.

11. Ibid., pp. 131–132.

12. Behar, *Translated Woman,* p. 270.

13. See R. W. Connell, *Masculinities* (Berkeley and Los Angeles: University of California Press, 1995); Kath Weston, *Render Me, Gender Me: Lesbians Talk Sex, Class, Color, Nation, Studmuffins* (New York: Columbia University Press, 1996); Arlene Stein, *Sex and Sensibility: Life Stories of a Lesbian Generation* (Berkeley and Los Angeles: University of California Press, 1997); Martin Duberman, *Stonewall* (New York: Dutton, 1993); Susan Krieger, *The Mirror Dance* (Philadelphia: Temple University Press, 1983); George Chauncey, *Gay New York* (New York: Basic Books, 1995); Elizabeth Kennedy and Madeleine Davis, *Boots of Leather, Slippers of Gold* (New York: Routledge, 1993); Elizabeth Kennedy and Madeleine Davis, "Constructing an Ethnohistory of the Buffalo Lesbian Community," in *Out in the Field: Reflections of Lesbian and Gay Anthropology,* ed. Ellen Lewin and William Leap (Urbana-Champaigne: University of Illinois Press, 1996); Ken Plummer, *Telling Sexual Stories* (New York: Routledge, 1994).

14. Connell, *Masculinities,* pp. 241–242.

15. Weston, *Render Me;* and Stein, *Sex and Sensibility.*

16. Weston, *Render Me,* p. 46.

17. A common narrative in the United States is the story of upward mobility. See, e.g., Jennifer Hochschild, *Facing Up to the American Dream* (Princeton, NJ: Princeton University Press, 1995).

18. We introduced this connection in chapter 1, in our discussion about the Western history of notions of the self. Here we focus more on generic characteristics that need to be taken into account in interpreting autobiographical evidence.

19. See Wolfgang Emmerich, *Proletarische Lebensläufe. Autobiographische Dokumente zur Entstehung der Zweiten Kultur in Deutschland* (Proletarian life course: autobiographical documents of the emergence of an alternative culture in Germany) (Reinbek bei Hamburg: Rowohlt, 1974), vol. 1, pp. 14 ff. The classic autobiographies referred to are Jean-Jacques Rousseau, *Les confessions* (The confessions) 4 vols., originally published between 1781 and 1788; and Johann Wolfgang von Goethe, *Dichtung und Wahrheit: Aus meinem Leben* (Poetry and truth: from my life), originally published between 1811 and 1830. As we noted in chapter 1, however, the search for a sense of self is not restricted to a single class or gender. Feminist and class analysis of the history of autobiography suggests that autobiography should not be associated exclusively with bourgeois individualism. Autobiographies vary depending on the kinds of people who manage to write and publish them, and the history of the genre is enriched by taking these differences into account.

20. Important works on theory and history of autobiography are mentioned in note 2 above. Of particular relevance are a series of works by Philippe Lejeune, who has undertaken studies of various genres of personal narratives. Lejeune began with autobiography, but has more recently published books on diaries including online diaries. See his *"Cher cahier…". Témoignages sur le journal personnel* (Paris: Gallimard, 1990); *Le moi des demoiselles. Enquête de journal de jeune fille* (Paris: Editions du Seuil, 1993); *"Cher écran". Journal personnel, ordinateur, internet* (Paris: Editions de Seuil, 2000).

21. Philippe Lejeune, "From Autobiography to Life-Writing, from Academia to Association: A Scholar's Story" (Plenary Lecture, 58th Annual Kentucky Foreign Language Conference, 22 April, 2005, University of Kentucky, Lexington), trans. Marie-Danielle Leruez. http://www.autopacte.org/From%20Academy%20to%20Association.html.

22. Peter Fritzsche, "The Case of Modern Memory," *Journal of Modern History* 73 (March 2001), commenting on James Olney, *Memory and Narrative: The Weave of Life Writing* (Chicago, 1998), p. 98.

23. Diane Bjorklund, *Interpreting the Self: Two Hundred Years of American Autobiography* (Chicago: University of Chicago Press, 1998). See also Philippe Lejeune, "The Autobiographical Pact," in *On Autobiography*, ed. Paul John Eakin and trans. Katherine Leary.

24. For examples of social-scientific and historical analyses that do use written autobiographies, see Anna Rotkirch, *The Man Question: Loves and Lives in Late Twentieth Century Russia* (University of Helsinki, Department of Social Policy, Research Reports, 2000); Marianne Gullestad, *Everyday Life Philosophers: Modernity, Morality, and Autobiography in Norway* (Oslo, Norway: Scandinavian University Press, 1996); Mary Jo Maynes, *Taking the Hard Road: Life Course in French and German Workers' Autobiographies in the Era of Industrialization* (Chapel Hill: University of North Carolina Press, 1995); Barbara Laslett and Barrie Thorne, *Feminist Sociology: Life Histories of a Movement* (New Brunswick, NJ: Rutgers University Press, 1997); Hokulani Aikau, Karla Erickson, and Jennifer L. Pierce, *Feminist Waves, Feminist Generations: Life Stories from the Academy* (Minneapolis: University of Minnesota Press, 2007).

25. James S. Amelang, *The Flight of Icarus: Artisan Autobiography in Early Modern Europe* (Stanford, CA: Stanford University Press, 1998), p. 194.

26. David Vincent's pioneering book of English workers' autobiographies, *Bread, Knowledge and Freedom* (London: Routledge, 1982) and Jacques Rancière's *The Nights of Labor* (Philadelphia: Temple University Press, 1991) about autobiographies and memoirs by nineteenth-century French artisans point to some of the implications of constraints of genre for self-expression by European workers. For example, autobiographies that were intended for publication (often didactic texts written by politicized artisans) differed from those written with a smaller, more private audience in mind (many of the texts that Vincent unearthed were family documents found in attics).

27. Gunilla-Freiderike Budde, *Auf dem Weg ins Bürgerleben. Kindheit und Erziehung in Deutschen und Englischen Bürgerfamilien, 1840–1914* (Göttingen, 1994).

28. For a more general discussion of these sources and their significance in U.S. history, see William Andrews, *To Tell a Free Story: The First Century of African-American Autobiography* (Urbana: University of Illinois Press, 1986); Marion Wilson Starling, *The Slave Narrative and Its Place in American History* (Washington, DC: Howard University Press, 1988).

29. While some scholars have challenged the veracity of some slave narratives or questioned whether these autobiographical accounts were written by slaves or their northern abolitionist allies, others have authenticated many slave narratives through other sources. For a recent discussion of a significant and now highly contentious slave narrative, *The Interesting Narrative of the Life of Olaudah Equiano, or Gustavus Vassa, the African, Written by Himself*, see Jennifer Howard, "Unraveling the Narrative," in *The Chronicle of Higher Education*, September 9, 2005, http://chronicle.com/weekly/v52/i03/03a01101.htm, which discusses questions about the ex-slave who wrote the definitive first-person account of the Middle Passage but, recent critique contends, may have been born in Virginia, not Africa.

30. Walter Johnson, *Soul by Soul: Life Inside the Antebellum Slave Market* (Cambridge, MA: Harvard University Press, 1999).

31. Ibid., p. 9.

32. Ibid., p. 10.

33. Ibid., p. 11.

34. Liz Stanley, "The Epistolarium: On Theorizing Letters and Correspondences," *Auto/Biography* 12 (2004): 208.

35. Ibid., pp. 202–203.

36. Ibid., pp. 210–235.

37. Ibid., p. 211.

38. William I. Thomas and Florian Znaniecki, *The Polish Peasant in Europe and America: A Classic Work in Immigration History*, ed. Eli Zaretsky (Urbana and Chicago: University of Illinois Press, 1996), first published in five volumes in 1918–1920.

39. Of course, its significance was not immediately acknowledged. Soon after the publication of the first two volumes, W. I. Thomas was arrested by the FBI for violation of the Mann Act, and then fired by the University of Chicago, who stopped publication of the last three volumes. (They were later published by another press.) Although Thomas's arrest detracted from immediate acknowledgment of the book's importance, it has had an influence on generations of scholars in American sociology as well as immigration history. See Eli Zaretsky's "Introduction," in Thomas and Znaniecki, *The Polish Peasant*, p. xiv.

40. Ibid., pp. 25–26.

41. See Michael Burawoy's discussion of *The Polish Peasant*, "Introduction," in Michael Burawoy et al., *Global Ethnography* (Berkeley and Los Angeles: University of California Press, 1990), p. 7.

42. Thomas and Znaniecki, *The Polish Peasant*, p. 31. Brackets in original.

43. Wróblewski's father, for example, writes of the dire economic straits in Poland in one letter, and in later ones requests financial assistance. Eli Zaretsky, "Introduction," in ibid., p. 28

44. See Burawoy, *Global Ethnography*, p. 8.

45. Shula Marks, ed., *Not Either an Experimental Doll: Three Separate Worlds of Three South African Women* (Bloomington: Indiana University Press, 1987); Shula Marks, "The Context of Personal Narrative: Reflections on *Not Either an Experimental Doll: Three Separate Worlds of Three South African Women*," in *Interpreting Women's Lives*, ed. Personal Narratives Group (Bloomington, IN: Indiana University Press, 1989), pp. 39–58.

46. Marks, "The Context of Personal Narrative," pp. 39–40.

47. Johnson, *Soul by Soul*, p. 13.

48. Ibid., p. 24.

49. Mary Jo Maynes. "Marital Decisions and Consenting Selves," paper presented to the Workshop on the Comparative History of Women, Gender, and Sexuality, Department of History, University of Minnesota, Minneapolis, April 27, 2007.

50. Olwen Hufton, *The Prospect Before Her: The History of Women in Western Europe*, vol. 1, *1500–1800* (London: HarperCollins, 1995), p. 107.

51. The source that Hufton cited was Caroline Michaelis, Letter to Louise Gotter, 12 January 1781, published in *La femme au temps de Goethe* (Paris, 1987). The correct letter turned out to be a different one—written to Julie von Studnitz on 17 February 1784.

52. Letter to Louise Gotter, 16 June 1780, in *Caroline. Briefe aus der Frühromantik*, vol. 1, ed. Erich Schmidt (Leipzig: Insel Verlag, 1913), pp. 26–27.

53. Letter to Louise, 12 January 1781, in ibid., pp. 34–35, 47.

54. Letter to Louise, 28 May 1784, in ibid., p. 84.

55. Lejeune, "From Autobiography to Life-Writing," np.

56. Laurel Thatcher Ulrich, *A Midwife's Tale: The Life of Martha Ballard Based on Her Diary, 1785–1812* (New York: Vintage, 1991).

57. Samuel Pepys, *Diary and Correspondence of Samuel Pepys., Esq.* 6 vols. (London: Bickers and Son, 1875–1879).

58. In his book *Le moi des demoiselles* Lejeune provides an interesting introduction to and reading of nineteenth-century diaries of French girls of bourgeois origins. At the time the book was published, his collection of such diaries had reached over one hundred examples, and was still growing.

59. Joan Brumberg, *The Body Project: An Intimate History of American Girls* (New York: Random House, 1997), p. xxvii.

60. Ibid., pp. 100–107.

61. Carolyn Steedman, *Landscape for a Good Woman: A Story of Two Lives* (New Brunswick, NJ: Rutgers University Press, 1987).

62. Amitav Ghosh, *In an Antique Land: History in the Guise of a Traveler's Tale* (New York: Vintage Books, 1992). Ghosh was trained as an anthropologist at Oxford University. He has subsequently written a number of novels. See Amitav Ghosh, *The Shadow Lines* (New York: Oxford University Press, 1995); *The Glass Palace* (New York: Random House, 2001); *The Hungry Tide* (Boston: Houghton Mifflin, 2005).

63. The travel writing genre is another form of autobiographical writing that has been mined in history, anthropology, and other disciplines. For an excellent review and critique of such writing, see Mary Louis Pratt, *Imperial Eyes* (New York: Routledge, 1992).

64. For a discussion of this genre in anthropological analyses, see Deborath Reed-Danahay, ed., *Auto/Ethnography: Rewriting the Self and the Social* (New York: Berg, 1997).

65. See Reed-Danahay, ed., *Auto/Ethnography;* Anne Menely and Donna Young, eds. *Autoethnographies: The Anthropology of Academic Practices* (Peterborough, Ontario: Broadview Press, 2005); Ruth Behar, *The Vulnerable Observer: Anthropology That Will Break Your Heart* (Boston: Beacon Press, 1996); Laurel Richardson, *Fields of Play: Constructing an Academic Life* (New Brunswick, NJ: Rutgers University Press, 1997); Carolyn Ellis, *Final Negotiations* (Philadelphia: Temple University Press, 1995); Carolyn Ellis, *The Ethnographic I: A Methodological Novel About Autoethnography* (Walnut Creek, CA: Alta Mira Press, 2004); Susan Krieger, *The Family Silver* (Berkeley and Los Angeles: University of California Press, 1996).

66. Carolyn Ellis, *Final Negotiations: A Story of Love, Loss, and Chronic Illness* (Philadelphia: Temple University Press, 1995), p. 3.

67. Behar, *The Vulnerable Observer*.

68. Deirdre McCloskey, *Crossing: A Memoir* (Chicago: University of Chicago Press, 1999).

69. McCloskey, *Crossing*, p. 117.

4. PERSONAL NARRATIVE RESEARCH AS INTERSUBJECTIVE ENCOUNTER

1. Lila Abu-Lughod, "Writing Against Culture," in *Recapturing Anthropology: Working in the Present,* ed. Richard Fox (Santa Fe, NM: School of American Research, University of Washington Press, 1991), p. 141. For other discussions of this critical epistemological point, see Donna Haraway, "Situated Knowledges: The Science Question in Feminism as a Site of Discourse on the Privilege of Partial Perspective," *Feminist Studies* 14, no. 3 (1988): 575–599; Barbara Laslett, "Unfeeling Knowledge: Emotion and Objectivity in the History of Sociology," *Sociological Forum* 5 (1990): 413–433; Helen Longino, *Science as Social Knowledge: Values and Objectivity in Scientific Inquiry* (Princeton, NJ: Princeton University Press, 1990); Susan Krieger, *Social Science and the Self: Personal Essays on an Art Form* (New Brunswick, NJ: Rutgers University Press, 1991); Naomi Scheman, *Engenderings: Constructions of Knowledge, Authority, and Privilege* (New York: Routledge, 1993); Sandra Harding, *Whose Science? Whose Knowledge?* (Ithaca, NY: Cornell University Press, 1991).

2. Susan Geiger, *TANU Women: Gender and Culture in the Making of Tanganyikan Nationalism, 1955–1965* (Portsmouth, NH: Heinemann Press, 1997). Examples of works of epistemological and methodological critique include Personal Narratives Group, *Interpreting Women's Lives: Feminist Theory and Personal Narratives* (Bloomington: Indiana University Press, 1989); Sherna Gluck and Daphne Patai, eds., *Women's Words: The Feminist Practice of Oral History* (New York: Routledge, 1991); Diane Wolfe, ed., *Feminist Dilemmas in Field Work* (Boulder, CO: Westview Press, 1996). Additional case studies include, e.g., Daniel Bertaux and Isabelle Bertaux-Wiame, "Artisanal Bakery in France: How It Works and Why It Survives," in *The Petite Bourgeoisie, Comparative Studies of the Uneasy Stratum,* ed. Frank Bechhofer and Brian Elliott (New York: MacMillan 1981); James Barrett, "Revolution and Personal Crisis: William Z. Foster and the American Communist Personal Narrative," *Labor History* 43, no. 4 (2002): 465–482.

3. Here we take up a set of issues introduced by the Personal Narratives Group, *Interpreting Women's Lives* (Bloomington: Indiana University Press, 1989), and discuss them in light of work by that group and subsequent scholarship.

4. Luisa Passerini, *Autobiography of a Generation: Italy, 1968,* trans. Lisa Erdberg (Hanover, NH: University Press of New England, 1996), p. x.

5. Marjorie Shostak, "What the Wind Won't Take Away: The Genesis of *Nisa—The Life and Words of a !Kung Woman,*" in Personal Narratives Group, *Interpreting Women's Lives,* p. 232. See also Roger Sanjek, ed., *Fieldnotes: The Making of Anthropology* (Ithaca, NY: Cornell University Press, 1990).

6. Faye Ginsburg, *Contested Lives: The Abortion Debate in an American Community* (Berkeley and Los Angeles: University of California Press, 1989), p. 5.

7. Jennifer L. Pierce, *Gender Trials: Emotional Lives in Contemporary Law Firms* (Berkeley and Los Angeles: University of California Press, 1995).

8. Ibid., p. 206.

9. Richa Nagar, "Exploring Methodological Borderlands through Oral Narratives," in *Thresholds in Feminist Geography: Difference, Methodology, Representation,* ed. John Paul Jones III, Heidi J. Nast, and Susan M. Roberts (Lanham, MD: Rowman & Littlefield, 1997), pp. 203, 208.

10. Ibid., pp. 209–210.

11. Ibid., p. 216.

12. Ibid., p. 217.

13. Ibid., pp. 220–221.

14. Ibid., p. 213.

15. Barbara Laslett, "On Finding a Feminist Voice: Emotion in a Sociological Life Story," in *Feminist Sociology: Life Histories of a Movement,* ed. Barbara Laslett and Barrie Thorne (Rutgers, NJ: Rutgers University Press, 1997). See also Barbara Laslett, "Biography as Historical Sociology: The Case of William Fielding Ogburn," *Theory and Society* 20 (1991): 511–538; "Unfeeling Knowledge: Emotion and Objectivity in the History of Sociology," *Sociological Forum* 5 (1990): 413–433; "Gender in/and Social Science History," *Social Science History* 16 (1992): 303–315; "Gender and the Rhetoric of Social Science: William Fielding Ogburn and Early Twentieth Century Sociology in the United States," in *Contesting the Master Narrative: Essays in Social History,* ed. Jeff Cox and Sheldon Stromquist (Iowa City, IA: University of Iowa Press, 1998).

16. For further elaboration of Ogburn's career and changing intellectual interests, see Laslett, "Unfeeling Knowledge."

17. *Caste and Class in a Southern Town* was originally published by Yale University Press in 1937 and came out in at least two subsequent editions. The Appendix to the volume "Life Histories of Middle-Class Negroes" is also of interest in terms of a historical contextualization of psychological ideas in the United States at the time.

18. Laslett, "Unfeeling Knowledge," p. 422 and Laslett, "Biography," p. 523.

19. See Laslett, "Biography," p. 515. This quotation comes from a page of an undated typescript given to Laslett by Ogburn's son during her interview with him; there was no author's name on it and it was not part of the collection of his papers at the University of Chicago. This might lead a skeptical reader to believe that its content was too good to be true, and maybe it was. The typeface and imprint of this document were similar to those found in many of Ogburn's documents that Laslett read in the course of her research. Ogburn's feelings about emotion and objectivity are, however, supported by many other aspects of his life story and the historical context in which he lived, even if not so directly as in his allusion to the impact of his mother on his work.

20. For further elaboration, see Laslett, "Unfeeling Knowledge," and note 2 in Laslett, "Biography."

21. See, e.g., Barbara Laslett, "Feminist Voice."

22. Mary Jo Maynes, *Taking the Hard Road: Life Course in French and German Workers' Autobiographies in the Era of Industrialization* (Chapel Hill, NC: University of North Carolina Press, 1995), pp. 204–205.

23. Julia Swindell, "Liberating the Subject? Autobiography and 'Women's History': A Reading of *The Diaries of Hannah Cullwick*," in Personal Narratives Group, *Interpreting Women's Lives*, pp. 24–38.

24. Marjorie Mbilinyi, "'I'd Have Been a Man': Politics and the Labor Process in Producing Personal Narratives," in Personal Narratives Group, *Interpreting Women's Lives*, p. 216.

25. Ibid., p. 219.

26. Ibid., p. 220.

27. Ruth Behar, *Translated Woman: Crossing the Border with Esperanza's Story* (Boston: Beacon Press, 1993), pp. 12–13.

28. Ibid., p. 16.

29. Mamie Garvin Fields with Karen Fields, *Lemon Swamp and Other Places: A Carolina Memoir* (New York: The Free Press, 1983), p. xii.

30. Ibid., pp. xii–xiii.

31. Judith Stacey, *Brave New Families: Stories of Domestic Upheaval in Late-Twentieth-Century America* (Berkeley and Los Angeles: University of California Press, 1998), pp. 273, 274, 278.

32. For relevant discussions, see the works cited in notes 1 and 2.

33. Michael Honey, *Black Workers Remember: An Oral History of Segregation, Unionism, and the Freedom Struggle* (Berkeley: University of California Press, 2000), p. 9.

34. Ibid., p. 1.

35. Shostak, "What the Wind Won't Take Away," p. 228.

36. Ibid., p. 233.

37. Mbilinyi, " 'I'd Have Been a Man,' " pp. 210–212.

38. Ibid., p. 221.

39. Richa Nagar, "Footloose Researchers, Traveling Theories and the Politics of Transnational Feminist Praxis," *Gender, Place and Culture* 9, no. 2 (2002): 181. See also Richa Nagar, " 'I'd Rather be Rude than Ruled': Gender, Place, and Communal Politics among South Asian Communities in Dar es Salaam," *Women's Studies International Forum* 23, no. 5 (2000): 571–585; Sangtin Writers, *Playing with Fire: Feminist Thought and Activism Through Seven Lives in India* (Minneapolis: University of Minnesota Press and New Delhi: Zubaan, 2006). Other feminist works that address the question of global inequalities and researcher positionality include, e.g., Diane L. Wolf, ed. *Feminist Dilemmas in Fieldwork* (Westview Press, 1996); Chandra Talpade Mohanty, *Feminism Without Borders: Decolonizing Theory, Practicing Solidarity* (Durham, NC: Duke University Press, 2004); Jacqui Alexander, *Pedagogies of Crossing: Meditations on Feminism, Sexual Politics, Memory, and the Sacred* (Durham, NC: Duke University Press, 1996); Cindi Katz, "On the Grounds of Globalization: A Topography for Feminist Political Engagement," *SIGNS: Journal of Women in Culture and Society* 26, no. 4 (2001): 1213–1234.

40. Richa Nagar and Susan Geiger, "Reflexivity, Positionality, and Identity in Feminist Fieldwork: Beyond the Impasse," in *Politics and Practice in Economic Geography,* ed. Adam Tickell et al. (London: Sage, 2007), as quoted in Nagar, "Footloose Researchers," p. 183.

41. Fields and Fields, *Lemon Swamp,* p. xix.

42. Nancy Chodorow, *Feminism and Psychoanalytic Theory* (New Haven, CT: Yale University Press, 1989), p. 204.

43. Ibid., p. 200.

44. Nagar, "Footloose Researchers," p. 179.

45. Geiger, *TANU Women,* p. 6.

46. Ibid., p. 91.

47. Ibid., p. 91.

48. R. W. Connell, *Masculinities* (Berkeley and Los Angeles: University of California, Press, 1995), pp. 130, 132, 141.

49. Ibid., p. 157.

50. Alessandro Portelli, *The Death of Luigi Trastulli and Other Stories: Form and Meaning in Oral History* (Albany: State University of New York, 1991), p. 61.

51. Ibid., pp. 30–31.

52. Ibid., p. 31.

53. Marjorie DeVault, "Ethnicity and Expertise: Racial-Ethnic Knowledge in Sociological Research," in *Liberating Method: Feminism and Social Research* (Philadelphia: Temple University Press, 1999), p. 85.

54. Ibid., pp. 90–91.

55. Ibid., p. 96.

56. Ibid., p. 103. The reference to Collins is Patricia Hill Collins, *Black Feminist Thought: Knowledge, Consciousness, and the Politics of Empowerment* (Boston: Unwin Hyman, 1990).

57. Sara Lawrence-Lightfoot, *I've Known Rivers: Lives of Loss and Liberation* (New York: Penguin Books, 1994), pp. 22–23.

58. Michelle Mouton and Helena Pohlandt-McCormick, "Boundary Crossings: Oral History of Nazi Germany and Apartheid South Africa—A Comparative Perspective," *History Workshop Journal* 48 (1999): 41–63.

59. Ibid., p. 52.
60. Ibid., p. 53.
61. Ibid., p. 56.

5. MAKING ARGUMENTS BASED ON PERSONAL NARRATIVE SOURCES

1. Darah McCracken, paper posted in the online class discussion for History 8025, "The Politics of Historical Memory" (February 1, 2006). Her comments refer to Carolyn Kay Steedman, *Landscape for a Good Woman* (New Brunswick, NJ: Rutgers University Press, 1991), p. 16; Michelle Mouton and Helena Pohlandt-McCormick, "Boundary Crossings: Oral History of Nazi Germany and Apartheid South Africa—A Comparative Perspective," *History Workshop Journal* 48 (1999): 41–63; Dorothee Wierling, "Conflicting Narratives? The First Postwar Generation in the GDR and the Nazi Past" (paper presented at the meeting of the American Historical Association, Boston, January 5, 2001), p. 12.

2. Of course, other approaches to social science have also developed particular methods and forms of analytic writing including, for example, symbolic interactionism, conversational analysis, and many varieties of cultural anthropology. Journals such as *Narrative Inquiry, Auto/biography, Symbolic Interaction,* and *History Workshop Journal,* to name a few, have been devoted to explication of these approaches.

3. Deirdre McCloskey, *The Rhetoric of Economics* (Madison, WI: University of Wisconsin Press, 1998).

4. Philip Abrams, *Historical Sociology* (Ithaca, NY: Cornell University Press, 1982), p. 194. Abrams is talking about historians and sociologists, but the discussion applies as much to political scientists, geographers, and economists as it does to sociologists.

5. Daniel Bertaux and Isabelle Bertaux-Wiame, "Artisanal Bakery in France: How It Works and Why It Survives," in *The Petite Bourgeoisie, Comparative Studies of the Uneasy Stratum,* ed. Frank Bechhofer and Brian Elliott (London: MacMillan, 1981) and "Life Stories in the Bakers' Trade," in *Biography and Society,* ed. Daniel Bertaux (London: Sage, 1981), pp. 169–190; Jake Ryan and Charles Sackrey, *Strangers in Paradise: Academics from the Working Classes* (New York: Southend Press, 1984); Norbert Ortmayr, *Knechte: Autobiographische Dokumente und sozialhistorische Skizzen* (Vienna: Böhlau Verlag, 1992).

6. Ruth Behar, *Translated Woman* (Boston: Beacon Press, 1993).

7. Faye Ginsburg, *Contested Lives: The Abortion Debate in an American Community* (Berkeley and Los Angeles: University of California Press, 1989), pp. 193, 197.

8. Other examples of ethnographic generalization include Alessandro Portelli, *The Death of Luigi Trastulli and Other Stories: Form and Meaning in Oral History* (Albany: State University of New York Press, 1991); Kath Weston, *Render Me, Gender Me: Lesbians Talk Sex, Class, Color, Nation, Studmuffins* (New York: Columbia University Press, 1996); Jennifer L. Pierce, *Gender Trials: Emotional Lives in Contemporary Law Firms* (Berkeley and Los Angeles: University of California Press, 1995).

9. Martin Duberman, *Stonewall* (New York: Dutton, 1993), pp. xviii and xix.

10. Examples of other works that use personal narrative evidence to make historical generalizations are Susan Geiger, *TANU Women: Gender and Culture in the Making of Tanganyikan Nationalism, 1955–1965* (Portsmouth, NH: Heinemann Press, 1997); Sara Evans, *Personal Politics: The Roots of Women's Liberation in the Civil Rights Movement and the New Left* (New York: Vintage, 1980); Luisa Passerini, *Fascism in Popular Memory: The Cultural Experience of the Turin Working Class* (Cambridge: Cambridge University Press, 1987).

11. Weston, *Render Me, Gender Me;* Arlene Stein, *Sex and Sensibility: Life Stories of a Lesbian Generation* (Berkeley and Los Angeles: University of California Press, 1997); Temma Kaplan, *Crazy for Democracy: Women in Grass Roots Movements* (London: Routledge, 1997); Mary Jo Maynes, *Life Course in Taking the Hard Road: French and German Workers' Autobiographies in the Era of Industrialization* (Chapel Hill, NC: University of North Carolina Press, 1995).

12. Wendy Luttrell, *Schoolsmart and Motherwise: Working Class Women's Identity and Schooling* (New York: Routledge, 1997), p. 4.

13. Ken Plummer, *Telling Sexual Stories: Power, Change, and Social Worlds* (London: Routledge, 1995), p. 34.

14. Ibid., pp. 20, 76.

15. See Jennifer L. Pierce, "Reflections on Fieldwork in a Complex Organization," in *Studying Elites Using Qualitative Methods,* ed. Rosanna Hertz and Jonathan Imber (Thousand Oaks, CA: Sage, 1995), pp. 94–110; Susan Ostrander, *Women of the Upper Class* (Philadelphia: Temple University Press, 1984); Sylvia Yanagisako, *Producing Culture and Capital: Family Firms in Italy* (Princeton, NJ: Princeton University Press, 2002).

16. R. W. Connell, *Masculinities* (Berkeley and Los Angeles: University of California Press, 1995), pp. 89–90.

17. Duberman, *Stonewall,* pp. xviii, xviii–xix.

18. Geiger, *TANU Women,* p. 19 (emphasis in original).

19. Maynes, *Taking the Hard Road,* pp. 8, 4–5 (emphasis in original).

20. Lillian Rubin, *The Transcendent Child: Tales of Triumph Over the Past* (New York: Harper Perennial, 1996); Jake Ryan and Charles Sackrey, *Strangers in Paradise: Academics from the Working Class* (New York: Southend Press, 1984).

21. See Barbara Laslett, "On Finding a Feminist Voice: Emotion in a Sociological Life Story," in *Feminist Sociology: Life Histories of a Movement,* ed. Barbara Laslett and Barrie Thorne (New Brunswick, NJ: Rutgers University Press, 1997).

22. Bonnie Smith, *Confessions of a Concierge: Madame Lucie's History of Twentieth-Century France* (New Haven, CT: Yale University Press, 1987). See also Jo Burr Margadant, *The New Biography: Performing Femininity in Nineteenth-Century France* (Berkeley and Los Angeles: University of California Press, 2000); Marjorie Shostak, "What the Wind Won't Take Away": The Genesis of "*Nisa—The Life and Words of a !Kung Woman,*" in Personal Narratives Group, *Interpreting Women's Lives: Feminist Theory and Personal Narratives* (Bloomington: Indiana University Press, 1989), pp. 228–240; Mamie Garvin Fields with Karen Fields, *Lemon Swamp and Other Places: A Carolina Memoir* (New York: The Free Press, 1983).

23. Ginsburg, *Contested Lives;* Evans, *Personal Politics;* Duberman *Stonewall;* Geiger, *TANU Women;* Anneliese Orleck, *Common Sense and a Little Fire: Women and Working-Class Politics in the United States, 1900–1965* (Chapel Hill: University of North Carolina Press, 1995); Laslett and Thorne, *Feminist Sociology.*

24. Bertaux and Bertaux-Wiame, "Artisanal Bakery in France" and "Life Stories in the Bakers' Trade."

25. Yanagisako, *Producing Culture and Capital,* p. 109.

26. Luttrell, *Schoolsmart and Motherwise,* pp. 1–5.

27. See Daniel Bertaux, ed., *Biography and Society;* Barney Glaser and Anselm Strauss, *The Discovery of Grounded Theory: Strategies for Qualitative Research* (New York: Aldine, 1967).

28. Birgitte Søland, "Employment and Enjoyment: Female Coming-of-Age Experiences in Denmark, 1880s–1930s," in *Secret Gardens, Satanic Mills: Placing Girls in European History, 1750–1950,* ed. Mary Jo Maynes, Birgitte Søland, and Christina Benninghaus (Bloomington, IN: Indiana University Press, 2005), p. 255.

29. Ibid., p. 258. This pattern of telling life stories is not unique to these narrators. As literary scholars of female autobiography have pointed out, women's life stories are typically written in ways that diverge from textual models established by their male counterparts. In comparison with men, women often tend to describe their lives as fragmented. See Carolyn Heilbrun, *Writing a Woman's Life* (New York: Norton, 1988); Shari Benstock, ed., *The Private Self: Theory and Practice of Women's Autobiographical Writings* (Chapel Hill, NC: University of North Carolina Press, 1988); Martine Watson Brownley and Allison B. Kimmick, eds., *Women and Autobiography* (Wilmington, DE: SR Books, 1999).

30. Examples include Philippe Lejeune, *Un journal à soi* (Paris: Éditions Textuel, 2003); Gunilla-Freiderike Budde, *Auf dem Weg ins Bürgerleben: Kindheit und Erziehung in Deutschen und Englischen Bürgerfamilien, 1840–1914* (Göttingen, 1994); Gudrun Wedel, *Lehren zwischen Arbeit und Beruf: Einblicke in das Leben von Autobiographinnen aus dem 19. Jahrhundert* (Vienna: L'Homme Schriften, 2000).

31. McCloskey, *Rhetoric of Economics.*

32. Connell, *Masculinities*, pp. 91–92.

33. Amy Kaler, *Running After Pills: Politics, Gender, and Contraception in Colonial Zimbabwe* (Portsmouth, NH: Heinemann, 2003).

34. James Amelang, *The Flight of Icarus: Artisan Autobiographies in Early Modern Europe* (Stanford: Stanford University Press, 1998); Budde, *Bürgerleben;* Joan Brumberg, *The Body Project: An Intimate History of American Girls* (New York: Random House, 1997).

35. Vincent Crapanzano, *Waiting: The Whites of South Africa* (London: Granada, 1985).

36. On this point, Geiger uses the same practice of following narrators' conventions in telling their life stories as Ruth Behar, as discussed in chapter 4.

37. Geiger, *TANU Women.*

38. On this point, see also Personal Narratives Group, *Interpreting Women's Lives;* Sherna Gluck and Daphne Patai, eds., *Women's Words: The Feminist Practice of Oral History* (New York: Routledge, 1991); Behar, *Translated Woman;* Richa Nagar and Susan Geiger, "Reflexivity, Positionality, and Identity in Feminist Fieldwork: Beyond the Impasse," in *Politics and Practice in Economic Geography,* ed. Adam Tickell et al. (London: Sage, 2007); Leslie Marmon Silko, *Storyteller* (New York: Grove Press, 1981).

39. Wilhelm Kaisen, *Meine Arbeit. Mein Leben* (My work, my life) (Munich: List, 1967), p. 32, cited in Maynes, *Taking the Hard Road,* p. 5.

40. Rigoberta Menchú, *I, Rigoberta Menchú: An Indian Woman in Guatemala,* ed. and intro. by Elisabeth Burgos-Debray (London: Verso, 1984); David Stoll, *Rigoberta Menchú and the Story of All Poor Guatemalans* (Boulder: Westview Press, 1999).

41. Behar, *Translated Woman,* p. 235 (emphasis in original).

42. Donald Spence, *Narrative Truth and Historical Truth: Naming and Interpretation in Psychoanalysis* (New York: Norton, 1982).

43. Mary Jo Maynes, "Autobiography and Class Formation in Nineteenth-Century Europe: Methodological Considerations," *Social Science History* 16, no. 3 (1992): 523.

44. Luisa Passerini, "Women's Personal Narratives: Myths, Experiences, and Emotions," in Personal Narratives Group, *Interpreting Women's Lives,* p. 197. See also Paul Atkinson and Sara Delamont, "Rescuing Narrative from Qualitative Research" *Narrative Inquiry* 16, no. 1 (2006): 164–172.

45. See Philippe Lejeune, *Le pacte autobiographique* (Paris: Éditions du Seuil, 1996); Connell, *Masculinities.*

46. Connell, *Masculinities,* p. 91.

47. Daniel Roche, ed., *Journal of My Life: Jacques-Louis Ménétra,* trans. Arthur Goldhammer (New York: Columbia University Press. 1986).

48. Robert Darnton, "Foreword," in ibid., pp. ix–xx.

49. Ibid., p. 13.

50. Ibid., p. ix.

51. Portelli, *Luigi Trastulli*, p. 2.

52. Beth Roy, *Bitters in the Honey: Tales of Hope and Disappointment across the Divides of Race and Time* (Fayetteville, AR: University of Arkansas Press, 1999).

53. Ibid., p. 176.

54. Ibid., pp. 176–177.

55. Ibid., p. 380.

56. Ibid., p. 380.

57. Marjorie DeVault, *Liberating Method: Feminism and Social Research* (Philadelphia: Temple University Press, 1999), p. 103.

58. Liz Stanley, "The Epistolarium: On Theorizing Letters and Correspondences," *Auto/Biography* 12 (2004): 203.

59. Amitav Ghosh, *In an Antique Land: History in the Guise of a Traveler's Tale* (New York: Vintage Books 1992). Other examples include Barbara Hanawalt, *Growing Up in Medieval London: The Experience of Childhood in History* (New York: Oxford University Press, 1996); Richard Price, *First-Time: The Historical Vision of an African American People* (Chicago: University of Chicago Press, 2002).

60. Tiya Miles, *Ties That Bind: The Story of an Afro-Cherokee Family in Slavery and in Freedom* (Berkeley and Los Angeles: University of California Press, 2005), p. 26. The autobiography to which Miles refers is Harriet A. Jacobs, *Life of a Slave Girl* (Cambridge, MA: Harvard University Press, 1987), which has been published in a variety of editions.

61. Miles, *Ties That Bind*, p. 60.

62. Ibid., pp. 6, 59 (emphasis added).

63. Ibid., pp. 63, 6.

Index

Abrams, Philip, 21, 128–29, 162n21, 177n4
African American studies, 7, 80–81, 172n29.
  See also Fields, Karen; Honey, Michael;
  Johnson, Walter; Lawrence-Lightfoot, Sara;
  Miles, Tiya
African studies, 7–8, 40. *See also* Crapanzano,
  Vincent; Geiger, Susan; Marks, Shula;
  Mbilinyi, Marjorie; Nagar, Richa; Shostak,
  Marjorie
agency: and autobiographies, 77, 79;
  conceptualization of, 22–26; and diaries,
  91; embodiment of, 33; Enlightenment
  notions of, 17–19, 21; and genre, 82; and
  historical context, 45, 48–49, 57, 58, 60,
  68; and identity of narrator, 135; and
  individual/social relationship, 15, 16, 18–19,
  24–25, 26, 44, 96; and letters, 86, 90; and
  memoirs, 95–96; of narrators, 116, 120;
  and personal narrative analysis, 2, 3, 12,
  30, 32, 35, 44, 127; and personal narrative
  evidence, 1, 111; and psychoanalytic
  approaches, 21, 24–25, 26, 45–47, 93; and
  sociological generalizations, 129; sociology's
  oversimplified understanding of, 11; and
  temporalities, 34, 35
Amelang, James S., 47–48, 51, 78–79, 80, 145
analysts: and historical contexts, 45, 53; and
  hybrid forms of personal narrative analysis,
  71–72, 92, 94, 96; influence of genre on,
  71, 75, 76, 96, 97; motivations of, 99,
  113–14; role of, 44; subjectivities of, 2; and
  truth claims, 149. *See also* intersubjective
  processes
Andrews, Alan, 53
audience: and autobiographies, 79, 171n26;
  and genre, 71, 97; and intersubjective
  processes, 99, 109, 119, 123; and
  intersubjective understanding, 156; and oral
  histories, 109, 119; and rhetorical strategy,
  127–28, 142–47; and situated knowledges,
  98; subjectivities of, 2
autobiographical pact, 77–78, 148–49
autobiographies: and agency, 77, 79; and
  audience, 79, 171n26; and genre, 17,

31, 35, 47, 71, 76–82, 96, 171nn19, 20;
  and historical context, 47–48, 51, 78;
  and hybrid forms of personal narrative
  analysis, 71–72, 92, 93; and identity of
  narrator, 135–36; and individualism, 20;
  and intersubjective processes, 99, 100,
  106, 124; and number of stories analyzed,
  140, 145; and self-narration, 30–33; and
  subjectivities, 41, 77; and temporalities,
  34–35, 39, 79, 96; and truth claims,
  148–49
auto/ethnography, 94, 100

Behar, Ruth: and historical context, 56–57,
  58; and rhetorical strategies, 179n36;
  and sociological generalizations, 129;
  and storytelling conventions, 72, 74–75;
  and translation, 94, 108–9; and truth
  claims, 148
Ben Yiju, Abraham, 65–67, 93
Bertaux, Daniel, 6, 129, 139
Bertaux-Wiame, Isabelle, 6, 129, 139
biographies: Chinese biographies, 35, 165n70;
  focus on single life, 136–38; historical
  context of, 58–60; and intersubjective
  processes, 104–6; and motivations, 92–93;
  and selfhood, 94; and subjectivity, 41;
  and working-class history, 33. *See also*
  autobiographies
Bjorklund, Diane, 78, 96
Bourdieu, Pierre, 21, 31–32, 33, 41, 165n64
Brown, Minnijean, 151–52
Brumberg, Joan, 91–92, 145
Bruner, Jerome, 31
Budde, Gunilla-Friederike, 79–80, 91, 145
Burkitt, Ian, 31, 32

Cannon, Katie, 122–23
Charrière, Isabelle de, 19, 161n11
childhood, role of, 34–36, 165n70
Chinese biographies, 35, 165n70
Chodorow, Nancy, 24–25, 57, 115–16, 118,
  163n39
Civil Rights movement, 7, 49, 153